PORTUGAL:
a companion history

This book is part of a series ASPECTS OF PORTUGAL
Currently available: CAMÕES: *Epic and Lyric* translated by Keith
Bosley; illustrated by Lima de Freitas ☐ MAURICE COLLIS: *The
Grand Peregination* ☐ ROSE MACAULAY: *They Went to Portugal Too*
☐ C.R. BOXER. The following: *The Portuguese Seaborne Empire
1415–1825* ☐ *The Christian Century in Japan 1549–1650* ☐ *The Golden
Age of Brazil 1695–1750* ☐ FERNANDO PESSOA: *The Book of
Disquietude* translated by Richard Zenith ☐ *A Centenary Pessoa* edited
by Eugénio Lisboa with L.C. Taylor ☐ EÇA DE QUEIRÓS: The
following: *Cousin Bazilio* translated by Roy Campbell, *The Illustrious
House of Ramires* translated by Ann Stevens, *The Maias* translated by
Patricia McGowan Pinheiro and Ann Stevens, *The Yellow Sofa* and
Three Portraits translated by John Vetch and others, *The Sin of Father
Amaro* translated by Nan Flanagan, *The City and The Mountains* trans-
lated by Roy Campbell ☐ *To the Capital* translated by John Vetch ☐
113 Galician-Portuguese Troubadour Poems translated by Richard
Zenith ☐ SILVIO A. BEDINI: *The Pope's Elephant*

José Hermano Saraiva

Portugal: *a companion history*

Edited and expanded by
IAN ROBERTSON and L.C. TAYLOR

CARCANET

in association with
Calouste Gulbenkian Foundation
Instituto Camões
Instituto da Biblioteca Nacional e do Livro

INSTITUTO
CAMÕES

First published in 1997 by Carcanet Press Limited
4th Floor, Alliance House, 30 Cross Street,
Manchester M2 7AQ

This book belongs to the series *Aspects of Portugal*,
published in Great Britain by Carcanet Press in
association with the Calouste Gulbenkian Foundation and
with the collaboration of Portugal 600
Series editors: Eugénio Lisboa, Michael Schmidt, L.C. Taylor

A CIP catalogue record for this book
is available from the British Library
ISBN 1 85754 201 0 (cased)
ISBN 1 85754 211 8 (paper)

The publisher acknowledges financial assistance
from the Arts Council of England

Set in Meridien by XL Publishing Services, Lurley, Tiverton
Printed and bound in England by SRP Ltd, Exeter

Contents

Illustrations

Plates 1–32 appear after page 48. They illustrate the history of Portugal to the end of the 16th century.
Plates 33–64, after page 80, continue that history to Portugal's entry into the Common Market.

MAPS

Acknowledgements

The editors would like to thank:

Donors of financial support for this publication: the Trustees of the Calouste Gulbenkian Foundation; the Instituto Camões, Lisbon; the Instituto da Biblioteca Nacional e do Livro, Lisbon.

Michael Collins, director of Portugal 600, for negotiations for support in London, Lisbon and with the publishers.

The individuals, institutions and publishers of copyright items referred to in the Map and Plates Acknowledgements.

Dr Manuel da Costa Cabral, director, and staff, at the Art Archive of the Calouste Gulbenkian Foundation in Lisbon.

Bob Drake, who, presented with rough sketches and research notes, improved the raw material and, though limited to black and white, achieved handsome and illuminating maps.

Kim Taylor for the design of a striking cover.

Eugénio Lisboa and Michael Eltenton who have acted as intermediaries in several transactions in Lisbon.

Ursula Fonss, whose verbatim translation of the original Portuguese text provided the valuable base for subsequent editing.

Janet Allan, who has designed this complex book, and supervised the production.

Lynne Cope for intelligently typing a difficult text.

Luís Rebelo, Emeritus Reader in Portuguese at King's College, London and Pedro de Oliveira at the Calouste Gulbenkian Foundation U.K. Branch for reading the maps, map commentaries and illustration captions and suggesting useful amendments. Any remaining deficiencies are the fault of the editors.

The Trustees, Director and Staff of the Calouste Gulbenkian Foundation's UK branch office in London for indispensable administrative and general support. Frequent detailed help has cheerfully been provided by Brian Neville, Jayne Eustiace, Joy Eaton and Ursula Fonss.

Sources of Plates and Maps

Arquivo Nacional da Torre do Tombo, Lisbon 17, 19a. Arquivos Fotográficos, Diário de Notícias, Lisbon 60. Biblioteca Nacional, Lisbon 14, 19b, 20, 21, 27, 31. Bibliothèque Nationale, Paris 22. British Library, London 40, 56, 58. British Museum, London 10,

11, 53, 55. Calouste Gulbenkian Foundation, Lisbon 61 (also for Robert C. Smith collection, see below). Comissão Nacional para as Comemorações dos Descobrimentos Portugueses, Lisbon 39. Government Art Collection, London 54. Instituto Português do Património Cultural 13. Ministério da Cultura e Parque Arqueológico do Vale do Côa 1. Museu Arqueológico do Carmo, Lisbon 7. Museu de Arte Antiga, Lisbon 12, 24, 28. Museu de Arte Contemporânea, Lisbon 62. Museu do Caramulo 25. Museu da Cidade da Lisboa, Lisbon 48, 49. Museu de Évora, Évora 41. Musées Royaux des Beaux-Arts de Belgique, Brussels 43. National Army Museum, London 52. National Maritime Museum, London 36, 42. Pierpont Morgan Library, New York 18a, 18b. Secretaria de Estado do Comércio e Turismo, Lisbon 2, 3, 4, 5, 9. Secretaria de Estado da Comunicação Social, Lisbon 64. Robert C. Smith/Calouste Gulbenkian Foundation, Lisbon 6a, 6b, 15, 29, 30, 47, 50. Michael Teague 16, 23, 26.

The maps have been specially drawn by Bob Drake from research sketches and notes supplied by the editors. Basic reference books used have been: *The Atlas of the World* 2nd ed. George Philip 1992, *The Times Concise Atlas of the World*, Times Books 1986, and *Atlas da Língua Portuguesa na História e do Mundo*, Imprensa Nacional-Casa da Moeda, Lisbon. In addition, for particular maps, the following have been valuable: Map 1, *História de Portugal*, Alfa, Lisbon 1984; and J. de Alarcão *Roman Portugal*, Aris and Phillips 1988. Map 2 and Map 9, *Atlas Histórico*, Círculo de Leitores, Lisbon 1990. Map 3, Joaquim Veríssimo Serrão: *História de Portugal* vol II, Verbo, Lisbon 1978, Map 4, Colin McEvedy: *The New Penguin Atlas of Mediaeval History*, Penguin Books, London, 1992. Maps 5 and 8, *Descobrimentos Portugueses*, Alfa, Lisbon. Map 6, Edgar Prestage: *The Portuguese Pioneers*, A&C Black, London 1933, H.V. Livermore: *A New History of Portugal*, Cambridge University Press 1966 and Kenneth Gordon McIntyre: *The Secret Discovery of Australia*, Souvenir Press, Australia 1977. Map 7, H.V. Livermore, *op. cit.* Map 10, Jaime Cortesão: *História da Colonização Portuguesa do Brazil*; Vicente Tapojõs: *Breve História do Brazil*, Porto Editora, Porto and Luís de Albuquerque: *Portugal no Mundo*, Alfa, Lisbon 1989. Map 11, Richard Aldington: *Wellington*, William Heinemann, London 1946. Map 12, A.H. Oliviera Marques: *History of Portugal*, Imprensa Nacional-Casa da Moeda, Lisbon 1991. Map 13, *Portugal Língua e Cultura*, Comissariado de Portugal para a Exposição Universal de Sevilha, Lisbon 1992.

Preface

During seventeen years as Cultural Counsellor at the Portuguese Embassy in London, I was frequently asked for a good short history of Portugal for English readers. Professor Harold Livermore had filled the needs of serious students, but when his estimable books went out of print in the late seventies no history of Portugal in English remained. Then, in the early nineties a brief history did appear, to my delight – until I read it. It was oddly unhistorical, marred by many serious errors, displaying current political correctness but little understanding of the norms of past times. I found I could not recommend it, and the gap remained unfilled.

For which reason I greet the more warmly Professor José Hermano Saraiva's *Portugal: A Companion History*. He had several substantial academic works to his credit when, in 1978, he produced his *História Concisa de Portugal*. Without the benefit of a catchy title or a lurid dustwrapper it became the most unlikely of bestsellers, and an enduring one, now in its eighteenth edition. Professor Saraiva was asked to do a television series, then another and another and another... To those who have read his books, watched his programmes, enjoyed his conversation, the reason is clear: he can sketch the significant shape of a period, outline themes of continuing importance, and then select vivid details as illustration. The knack of seeing the wood for the trees and yet being able to show what sort of trees comprise the wood is rare anywhere, and particularly rare among distinguished academics.

This capacity, and a happy turn of phrase, suggested Professor Saraiva would prove an ideal exponent of Portuguese history for foreigners. To this end a friend and I approached him, expecting permission to translate his

História Concisa. Instead he offered to write an entirely new work with foreign readers specifically in mind. And it would be brief. We were pleased, for – as users of dictionaries know – the voluminous dimensions of 'concise' may reflect some full work magisterially conceived. This new history is elegant and illuminating at long-essay length – a remarkable achievement.

Professor Saraiva's text has been carefully edited to ensure that assumptions a Portuguese historian might make about what a (Portuguese) reader probably knows already have not been extended to foreign readers starting from scratch. In addition the two editors – one the experienced author of four editions of the *Blue Guide* to Portugal, the other once editor of a series of books about Portugal – have added several items complementary to the main text – fifteen specially drawn maps with explanatory commentaries, chronologies, genealogies, a bibliography, short biographies, glossary, historical gazetteer, and numerous illustrations. The resulting *Companion History* has become a handy work of reference besides being a good read. It should prove as companionable to readers who stay at home as to those who visit Portugal; and as useful for those whose ambitions end with an enjoyable outline as for those who want a brief conspectus before more detailed study.

Alas, it had to be *after* I ceased to be Cultural Counsellor that a short history appeared which I could recommend to enquirers; but at least, dear reader, I can here recommend it to you.

EUGÉNIO LISBOA
Lisbon May 1997

Introduction

JOSÉ HERMANO SARAIVA

The history of Portugal presents some abiding mysteries:

How has so small a nation maintained its independence – traceable in origin to 1140 – against that drive among its Iberian neighbours to combine, which resulted in a unified, centralized Spain? Its long struggle for independence drew Portugal and another Atlantic nation, England, into a profound alliance, embodied in the oldest of all European treaties, one still recognized as relevant in international chancelleries.

How was it that the bastard son of the royal house in Portugal, Dom João, became, in the fourteenth century, the leader of a popular revolution? He married a daughter of John of Gaunt, Duke of Lancaster, a union which produced 'the illustrious generation of high princes' which has left an indelible mark on the memory of the nation.

What then inspired one of those princes, Dom Henrique ('Henry, the Navigator') to embark upon the exploration of the unknown Atlantic and the African coast? The Madeira and Azores archipelagos, autonomous regions with a language and culture entirely Portuguese, still bear testimony to that first, portentous determination to extend European trade, religion and techniques to distant places.

And how could a Portuguese king – at the time João III, 'the Perfect Prince' – negotiate with the King of Castile the division between them of the whole world yet unchristianized? The famous Treaty of Tordesillas (its quincentenary was celebrated in 1994) was not mere play by cosmographers but an agreement which has imprinted history. By means of it Portugal obtained exclusive rights to landfalls made by the route its navigators had discovered round the 'Cabo da Boa

Esperanca', of Good Hope. The consequence was a lively interaction between East and West by way of Lisbon. Goa became for two centuries the 'Rome of the East', and the Portuguese built on Asian shores great edifices which still amaze. A last token of that explosive diaspora of the Portuguese throughout the Orient remains (for two years more) in Macao. It was created not by conquest, nor from purchase but out of mutual convenience. It is the proud boast of Macao never to have been involved in war, to have remained during four centuries a peaceful bridge between Asia and Europe. It was through that same Treaty of Tordesillas that Brazil, now a half of South America, became Portuguese and today gives to both Portuguese language and culture their most eloquent and original forms.

Portugal's 'First Empire' was a trading empire in the Orient, built upon control of the sea-lanes; little territorial occupation was involved, merely a few strategic ports and forts. That empire was dismantled by European rivals in the seventeenth century. The 'Second Empire' was chiefly Brazilian; it was built upon the occupation and settlements of vast areas of land. That empire reached a brief apogee in 1815 at the Treaty of Vienna, when an ephemeral joint kingdom of Portugal-Brazil was recognized. In 1822, however, Brazil became an independent republic and Portugal contracted into Europe's south-western extremity, its launching pad where – in Camões' phrase – 'the land ends and the sea begins'. Unexpectedly, a belated 'Third Empire' emerged: the attempt was made to create a new Brazil out of Angola and Mozambique – the idea of the Sesambrists of 1836, the ideal of the Republic of 1910, the constitutional insistence of the 'Estado Novo' of 1933. But imperial ambitions ceased to convince even the great powers, and in Portugal led finally to revolution in 1974, and the end of the dictatorial regime. The bonds of its last empire released,

Portugal became once more a nation state which, joining the Common Market in 1985, sees its future in European terms.

It is the adventure of Portugal, part national, part international, on every continent, that this book sets out to relate, along a straight narrative path, expressed in simple words – and briefly. Brevity means keeping essentially to political events, for it is these which act like the hands of a clock, enabling us to see and to mark the changes continuously, imperceptively, wrought by time.

Lisbon, May 1997

I *The Ancient Roots*

1. Origins

The earth of Portugal is rich in prehistoric remains. Relics of
its remote past are frequently brought to the surface when
core samples of the soil are taken or when foundations for
buildings are dug. Excavated artefacts disclose gradually
changing techniques, and provide evidence of the unbroken
settlement of the land from the early Stone Age to the Iron
Age, with a succession of tribes establishing themselves in
the Iberian Peninsula. Here, unlike the rest of continental
Europe where they could roam at will over vast areas, these
wandering tribes found themselves hemmed into a cul-de-
sac bound by the sea. Those communities that had already
settled had to put up with unwelcome new arrivals and co-
exist with them in what was a comparatively limited space.
In some areas these tribes remained separate from each
other, retaining an individuality of which traces still persist;
elsewhere, tribes merged, producing hybrids of race and
culture.

Iberia had substantial mineral resources and, during the
Bronze Age, its copper and tin deposits were searched out
and worked by immigrant colonists. Rivers provided natural
means of communication: the Tagus flowed close to the tin
deposits of the Beiras and those of the Trás-os-Montes
further north; the Sado – then navigable for much of its

course – provided a route into the heart of the Alentejo, where ran rich and readily accessible seams of copper, as they still do. The region between these two rivers retains evidence of settlement by tribes from Asia Minor: the *castros* of Zambujal (at Torres Vedras), Pedra de Ouro (near Alenquer) and Vila Nova de São Pedro (on the Azambuja, south-west of Santarém), each have their arsenals and bronze foundries, which compare closely with fortified settlements in their areas of tribal origin.

In about 1000 BC a new wave of colonists, the Celts, entered the Peninsula. They were skilled ironworkers and goldsmiths and they cremated their dead. Since they became integrated with the indigenous inhabitants, already known as Iberians, early writers have referred to them as Celtiberians. Their way of life has been reconstructed by archaeologists who have excavated their fortified hill-top settlements, or *castros*, among them those of Castro de Avelas, Castro Daire, Castro Marim, and Castro Verde. In addition, the Phoenicians, and later the Greeks, were active in trading along the Algarve coast and in exploiting the metal deposits further inland.

When referring to the area between the Douro and the Tagus, sixteenth-century Portuguese humanists preferred to use Latinisms: Lusitania for the place, and Lusitanians for the inhabitants, rather than the simpler Portugal and Portuguese. So Camões, the national poet of Portugal, chose to write: 'Behold, at the summit... of all Europe: the Kingdom of Lusitania...' Many others adopted this practice, which led to the widespread belief, only partly true, that today's inhabitants are descended directly from Roman stock. The belief has taken a nebulous form: it has not prevented an ancestor named Viriatus, assassinated in 139BC, who had fought *against* the Romans, being regarded as a national hero to this day.

2. Roman colonization

Roman legions first marched into the Iberian Peninsula in 218 BC. At that time Rome fought with Carthage for supremacy in the western end of the Mediterranean, just as it had formerly fought with the Greek city states for the control of its eastern end. By 139BC the Roman occupation had incited serious resistance from the native Lusitanians; none the less, by the beginning of the Christian era, the whole of the Peninsula had come under Roman domination, except the mountainous area in the north inhabited by the Basques.

The Romans invaded Iberia chiefly for economic reasons; they were not interested in imposing their culture on the conquered tribes, although this was to happen eventually. For Roman tolerance – by which the natives retained their customs, their ancient gods, their languages, their local laws administered by Roman magistrates – allowed easy co-existence, and this itself in the long run fostered Romanization. Recent research has revealed that local practices persisted far into the period of Roman occupation. In several regions Latin was modified, and two principal forms of Romance developed: one, Castilian, had as a substratum the language still spoken today in the Basque provinces; the other, Gallego-Portuguese, reveals many Celtic influences – it became dominant between the Cantabrian sea and the line of the Douro.

In the region known as 'Lusitania', the main economic activities (some introduced by the Romans, others stimulated by them), were: mining and metal-working; fishing and fish-preserving; raising cattle and tanning hides; pottery and weaving; producing rush or esparto articles (shoes, cord, paper, etc); and, above all, agriculture. Native wheatfields, olive-groves, and vineyards were developed by their new landlords with a view to exporting the produce to Italy. Grain was abundant in many areas, notably on the Alentejan plains, whereas in the mountainous north, bread was made with crushed acorns. The olive-oil of Iberia was held in high repute, and its wines competed successfully with those of Italy. Indeed, commercial pressures were such that the land was increasingly worked to produce such cash-crops, to the point of threatening the basic cereal requirements of the indigenous population.

The century following the reign of Augustus was described by the Romans as the 'Pax Romana', implying that it was one of peace and prosperity throughout the empire; but this was not entirely true of Iberia. In the mountainous north, dotted with fortified 'castros', there was armed resistance to the Roman occupation, which included the presence of soldier-settlers or *limitanei*, given land on condition that they asserted Roman authority. The majority of them, as far as one can tell from the belt-buckles found in their graves, were Germanic in origin, largely from the Rhine basin. Despite periodic local resistance to the Pax Romana, during the first two centuries of the Christian era Iberia reached a high degree of civilization. However by 212AD decline had set in. That was the date of Caracala's edict which granted the *jus romana*, previously restricted to a minority, to all free citizens of the empire; it allowed them the right to vote and to hold office (*jus suffragii*) and to become magistrates (*jus honorum*). The edict was an attempt to broaden the base of institutions already disintegrating, but the decline continued. The reason for the gradual decadence of Lusitanian society, which also applied elsewhere in the Peninsula, may be found in the ethnic division of society between Roman and native, and the judicial division between freemen and slaves, divisions that were not co-terminus. Some of the indigenous population (the *liberati*, who had been freed, and their offspring) obtained most of the rights of Roman freemen and even rose to prominence: but the rest, together with slaves who had been imported, remained members of a slave class. Even the indigenous 'freemen' fell into two classes, gradually polarizing as *honestiores* and *humiliores*, rich and poor, the condition of the latter being hardly distinguishable from that of the slaves. Once it was realized that being a freeman was no security against poverty, few aspired to that status; as Salvianus of Marseille observed at the time: 'No longer did the people wish to become Roman.'

For purposes of taxation, Roman society was subject to a census; and census lists confirm that, in general, economic strength and social status went together. Society was made up of four levels: the *senatores* (the senatorial class) stood at the summit of the pyramid; its members monopolized the main offices, both civic and religious, including that of consul, and owned the great estates. Below them came the *equites* (the equestrian order, or knights), likewise of Roman stock from time immemorial, who were destined for military or political careers, and whose wealth was based on property either in the form of land or acquired by trade. Next in the hierarchy came the *decuriones*, an 'order' which included the indigenous aristocracy, now romanized, who – important in the Iberian Peninsula – had inherited many of the castros, which had subsequently developed into Roman towns. These decurions provided a 'middle class', drawing their wealth from land, from trade, and from owning slaves. Last (among the freemen) were the *plebs*, citizens with rights, but without economic assets or employment. In principle, 'work' could only be done by slaves. If a freeman worked, he lost his status – unless he became a soldier, for if, after serving in the legions, he returned to civil life as a veteran, he could acquire land and move up a step, becoming a decurion. Although in Rome the plebs were very numerous, in conquered territory they were less so, and at first there were comparatively few in Iberia, although with economic prosperity the class grew.

In law, slaves had a common status: all were the property of their masters, even if their condition varied considerably in practice. Some, owned by the State, proved capable of carrying out bureaucratic duties and holding office. Among privately owned slaves there was a distinction between those who had been purchased, and those (the *verna*) born in the household. Occasionally these are tenderly described in tomb inscriptions as *in loco filii habitus* – children of the house – but such happy few were exceptions to the rule. The great majority of slaves – Galicians, Asturians, Cantabrians, and Basques – were the spoils of war, caught in the Iberian highlands and either assigned to the State or sold in the slave markets to private owners. The bronze plaques of Aljustrel in the Alentejo, confirm that slaves provided every sort of labour. Sometimes, free plebians, driven by need, were obliged to perform similar tasks, but punishment for derelictions of duty was more severe for slaves than for plebs; and the most exacting activities, such as rowing the galleys trafficking with Rome or North Africa or working in the mines, were reserved for slaves. A slave's life was usually hard and short. The number of Iberians enslaved is not known, but the range of their recorded tasks suggests that slaves far outnumbered their free compatriots.

3. Barbarian invasions

The first hordes of Barbarians – Alans, Vandals, and Suevi – penetrated the Peninsula in 409. Roman resistance was overcome with ease, for the invasions coincided with a series of disturbances (or *bagaudas*, from the Celtic *bagud* or band of agitators) throughout the country. Braga, for example, was virtually destroyed in such a commotion. The contemporary

Salvianus suggested that these subversive groups collaborated with the invaders, as the natives preferred the prospect of an easy life with few constraints, even if they would technically be conquered and vassals, to the continuance of what amounted to slavery, even if legally they were free. On the other hand, Orósio dismissed the 'bagaudas' as the work of ruthless cut-throats. The connection between the 'bagaudas' and the Barbarian invasions is complex; both played an important part in the collapse of Hispano-Roman society.

As we are concentrating on the history of what was to become Portugal, we need to focus on the events then taking place in the north-west of the Peninsula. The Suevi had already occupied the former Roman province of Gallaecia (Galicia) by 411, and had made several sorties as far south as the Tagus. In 516 it was the turn of the Visigoths. Confederate with Rome, the Visigoths were commissioned to expel the other Barbarians. They soon overpowered both the Alans and Vandals, but the suppression of the Suevi proved no easy matter, and it was not until 585 that this was accomplished. The Visigoths then dominated the region, but only for a little more than a century, until 711. Then the Muslims arrived.

The actual number of Germanic warriors entering the Peninsula cannot have been great, a fact confirmed by the rarity of those archaeological or other remains which would have marked their passage. They had few technical or cultural accomplishments with which to impress the Hispano-Romans, who were in most respects their superior. While the Barbarians may have retained their own institutions, it was not long before they were absorbed culturally into the people on whose land they had settled.

The presence of the Barbarians did nothing to stem the decline of Hispano-Roman civilization. Bagaudista activity intensified, and trade diminished. The Christian Church – an important component of the Visigothic monarchy – regarded trade as exploitation, and therefore sinful. Commerce was fit only for – and was principally conducted by – the sizeable Jewish community, who were subject to discrimination both in law and in society. Cultural life, such as it was, remained largely the preserve of the clergy. Although there were Christians among both the Hispano-Romans and the Visigoths, they did not mix: the Visigoths, christianized before entering the Peninsula, had embraced Arianism (adhering to the tenets of Arius, a fourth-century bishop, who denied the divinity of Christ), and were thus regarded by the Hispano-Romans as heretics.

The Hispano-Romanic nobility, although firmly established as a distinct hereditary social class and, as landowners, richer than those who worked for them, had been of the same race as the general population, had spoken the same language and, broadly speaking, had shared the same culture and tastes. Things were different after the Barbarian invasions. The new landowning nobility were warriors, not cultivators of the land; they were dissociated from those who worked the land. Social superiority came to be defined largely by race rather than by disparities in wealth or power.

Certain features characteristic of Portuguese society were gradually assumed during the Germanic occupation and remained evident well into the medieval period; they may be summarized thus: a military nobility owning the land; a rural population tied to it and dominated by a rich and powerful clergy; a Jewish minority controlling trade, its members often prosperous but living in ghettos, envied yet despised.

4. The Islamic invasion
In 711 an expeditionary force of Arabs (or 'Moors'), embarking in vessels supplied by the Christian governor of

Ceuta, crossed the narrow western straits of the Mediterranean and landed on the Iberian Peninsula. The majority were Berbers, including their leader, Taric, who gave his name to the rock of Gibraltar (Yaabal or Gebel Taric, the mountain of Taric). The Visigothic king, who was at that moment suppressing a Basque insurrection, hurried south to repel the invaders but he was routed and vanished in the mêlée. Taric, unopposed, thrust north and occupied both Cordoba and Toledo, the Visigothic capital [see Map 1].

The control of the Moors over what is now known as Portugal lasted in the Minho, to the north, for a few decades only, but continued in the Alentejo and Algarve, further south, for some five centuries. Cultural impact reflected the length of occupation: weak in the north, where only a few place-names record a brief stay; strong in the south, where Arab influence on agricultural methods was fundamental, and where the philosophy of life was affected.

It was the Visigothic nobles, a military class obliged to support their king in battle, who suffered in attempting to repulse the Moors: indeed, they were virtually eradicated. The indigenous Hispano-Romans were spared and remained comparatively unaffected. No longer directed by their Visigothic masters, they continued to work the land. Decisions still had to be taken in each village over recurrent rural matters: the distribution of plots and utilization of water; whether to raise cattle or grow crops; how to ensure a proper rotation; how to share the use of implements. In addition, there were now problems related to defence and justice that had to be discussed. To fill the vacuum created by the lack of landlords, village *conselhos* (from the Latin *consilium*, a meeting) were held, in which collective decisions were made. In towns, a similar form of local government had different origins: not only had Christian and Jewish craftsmen and merchants to organize their common affairs, but they now needed to defend their joint interests when confronting representatives of new rulers of dissimilar faith and culture.

Under Muslim law, all those who embraced Islam, whatever their origins, were treated as equals; those who preferred to follow their former religious practices were allowed to do so, on payment of a tax. So Christian churches and Jewish synagogues co-existed with Muslim mosques. The 'nation' to which a person belonged was determined not by his race, language or culture, but by his faith. This may explain why, in later centuries, when the Portuguese 'nation' grew, at first in Iberia and then overseas, the process of expansion was thought of more as spreading the influence of Christendom than merely as acquiring national territory.

Arab influence varied in profundity: some Christians who lived under the Moors continued to speak their own language and to follow their old ways, only slightly affected by Arab customs; others, while still remaining Christian, became so deeply assimilated into the Arab way of life that later, during the period of the Reconquest, they were referred to by the term *mozarab*, or 'arabized'; and there were those who converted to Islam and were known as *muwallad* or *muladi*.

With the Moors came some technical advances. For example, among the many hydraulic techniques introduced or reintroduced by them were those which improved the irrigation of orchards, and made use of water-power to drive milling machinery, thereby reducing the need for manual labour. This was an encouragement to the independent small-holder, whereas under the Romans, the emphasis on the production of wine and grain had led to the farming of large tracts dependent for cultivation on many slaves.

5. The Reconquest

Classical historians have used the term 'Reconquest' to describe the re-establishment of Christianity in the Peninsula, beginning with the legendary 'battle' of Covadonga in 718 – little more, in fact, than the successful ambush by guerrillas of a small band of Moors sent to smoke them out of their Asturian fastness – and ending with the capture of Granada by the Catholic kings in 1492.

Galicia, in the north-west of the Peninsula, including what today is northern Portugal, had been ravaged by Arab raids, which left settlements such as Braga and Oporto deserted. The subsequent 'Re-populating' of the region, as historians have termed it, should not be taken to imply that its former inhabitants had been wiped out; rather that they had been dispersed, so that the kings of León and the counts in their service had to reorganize the traditional society thus disrupted. This they did by establishing urban centres, the control of which remained in noble hands or in those of bishops, from which colonists resettled areas further south and the valleys of the interior. Of particular importance was the resettling, as an episcopal river-port on the right bank of the Douro, of what had been a Roman castro named Cale commanding a river-crossing: it was to become known as 'Portucalae' and, in its non-Latin form, Portugal. The Roman fort here had grown during the Suevic period, even becoming the seat of a Christian diocese. Although it changed hands more than once during the Arab occupation, the invaders were evicted definitively in 868, after which it remained Christian. The whole area was described by the same name of Portucalae, and by the early tenth century comprised territory extending north to the river Lima, east to the ranges of Beira Alta, and south to the river Douro.

The counts of Portucalae were vassals of the kings of León, perhaps more so in theory than in fact, for the region was relatively distinct, both linguistically and culturally, from León itself, where 'mozarabism' was much more wide-spread. These counts had a comparatively free hand with which to wage war and negotiate peace with the Moors, and to dictate laws.

Another centre with an important role in the creation of modern Portugal was Coimbra, first re-conquered in 878 and held by hereditary Christian counts, only to be recaptured by the Moors, who were not finally expelled until 1064. It was then governed by Sesnando, a complicated character, who well illustrates the amalgam of cultures, for he was a mozarab of neighbouring Tentúgal, probably of Jewish parentage, who had studied among the Moors, and had been employed at the Islamic court in Seville. It was he who suggested to Fernando 'the Great' of León that Coimbra should be re-conquered, and who then dominated the district until his death, extending his rule over the Mondego valley, and yet still remaining at peace with the Moors.

Perhaps it was the growing tendency towards autonomy in these outlying districts of his kingdom that led Alfonso VI of León to decide in 1095 to bring them under the more direct control of his family. To Urraca, his legitimate daughter, he assigned Galicia, as far south as the Lima. She had married Raymond, son of the Count of Burgundy, thereby establishing a link with the kings of France. The Condado Portucalense, by then extending south to the banks of the Mondego, he gave to his illegitimate daughter, Dona Teresa, married to Henrique, also from the House of Burgundy. From her patrimony and dynasty the future of Portuguese monarchy directly descended.

II *The Founding of Portugal*

6. From Reconquest to independence

On the death of her husband, Count Henrique, Dona Teresa attempted to rule the *condado* or countship of Portucalense herself, assuming the title of queen. She had her eye on Galicia also and, to that end, married a Galician nobleman, Count Fernão Peres de Trava. However, the Portucalense nobility feared they might become subject to the Galicians; many of the leading nobles took up arms against Dona Teresa, led by her son, Dom Afonso Henriques.

In 1128 the two parties met on the field of São Mamede, not far from the castle of Guimarães, with the intention of settling matters. The site was referred to as that of a 'tournament', which may indicate that the dispute was to be resolved by a trial of arms rather than by battle. Whatever the nature of the engagement, the Portucalense were the victors. Dom Afonso Henriques expelled his mother and her consort, and took over the reins of government.

Chroniclers writing shortly after the event have expressed surprise that he should have done so after only one martial encounter. He always regarded the victory of São Mamede as the decisive event of his extraordinary career; soon after it, in a proclamation dated 6 April 1129 (when making a gift to Monio Rodrigues), he confidently referred to himself as 'I, the Infante Afonso, son of Count Henriques, now free from all constraints and with God's providence, and in the peaceful possession of Coimbra and all other towns of Portugal...'.

By 1140 – possibly in the previous year if a dubious date is accepted – he was applying the title of 'king' to himself (rather than *infante* or *principe* or *infans, portugalensium princeps*), emphasizing his royal lineage; in fact, he was only the grandson of Alfonso VI, even if his mother, as a king's daughter, had signed herself *rainha* on occasions. However, from 1135 Alfonso VII had taken to styling himself 'Emperor of Spain', whereupon subordinate provincial princes called themselves 'kings', a title which lent lustre to their master and did not imply independence from him.

In October 1143 Cardinal Guido de Vico, a papal legate, visited the Peninsula to sort out several matters of ecclesiastical administration. He had arranged to meet the 'Emperor Alfonso' and Dom Afonso Henriques at the Leonese town of Zamora. It has been conjectured that the envoy wanted to reconcile the two cousins, whose differences were undermining the cause of Christendom and playing into Moorish hands. Although reference is made to a 'Treaty of Zamora', there is no proof of its existence nor is it known what was agreed. What has survived is a letter sent to the pope that December by Dom Afonso Henriques, in which he declares himself and his successors as being 'censual' to the Church of Rome, and 'man and knight of the Pope and St Peter, on condition that the Holy See will protect him against all other powers, civil or ecclesiastical'. (The word 'censual' refers to the payment of a *censo* or tribute to Rome, which in the letter was fixed at four ounces [122 grams] of gold, later raised to two marks or sixteen ounces [465 grams].) This would imply that Dom Afonso Henriques, with Innocent II's approval and as direct tributary of the pope, had claimed and been accorded these privileges for himself and his successors, and was exempt from any other imposition.

The last act by which Dom Afonso Henriques's independence from León was formalized took place in 1179, towards the end of his reign. Before that date diplomatic legates from Rome had avoided calling him 'king'; in that year he sent a gift of one thousand gold coins to the pontiff, after which there was no such inhibition.

7. Expansion south

Although the king of Portugal abandoned his pretensions to rule Galicia, which remained in his aunt's hands, he strengthened his grip on the territory between the Minho and Mondego and, in a series of brilliant campaigns, extended his dominion to the south.

By a bold and entirely unexpected stroke, in 1147 he seized Santarém, a place of military and economic importance commanding the rich pastures of the lower Tagus. In the same year, he tempted an army of crusaders – Teutons, English, and Bretons, *en route* to the Holy Land – to join him in attacking Lisbon, then occupied by the Moors. The city fell to him after a short siege. Among his allies, referred to as 'Franks', were several who decided to remain in Portugal, including an English priest named Gilbert of Hastings, who became the first bishop of Lisbon. Another Englishman, Osbern, wrote a 'Chronicle' describing the attack on Lisbon, which is our main contemporary source of information. With the fall of the town, numerous other strongholds gave in to Dom Afonso Henriques, among them Alenquer, Óbidos, Almada, Sintra, Sesimbra and Palmela, which enabled him to extend his frontier to the Tagus and to occupy its far bank.

Between 1165 and 1169 the theatre of action moved to the plains of the Alentejo ('beyond the Tagus'). One of his commanders, Geraldo 'Sem Pavor' (the Fearless), raised the royal standard over several fortresses there, among them the key town of Évora, which controlled what was already a vital area of grain production; he even thrust east into Estremadura (in what is now Spain).

Geraldo may have fought on his own account, as a free-booter, but he then handed over his gains to the king. Perhaps this was a ploy on behalf of Dom Afonso Henriques, for the king of Castile claimed the right of Reconquest over all lands south of the Tagus, and some respect for this claim had to be demonstrated. Matters came to a head when Geraldo attempted to seize Badajoz, capital of one of the many minor Arab kingdoms. Although Geraldo broke into the town, a counter-attack forced him and his son to take refuge in its castle, where they were besieged. As Dom Afonso Henriques marched to his help, Alfonso VIII of Castile also approached, not only with a larger contingent, but to join forces with the Moors. Dom Afonso Henriques found himself besieged and then became a prisoner of the Castilians, being released only after paying a large ransom in gold. The Moors remained masters of Badajoz.

The struggle for dominance in what are now the southern provinces of Portugal lasted a century. The Moors in the Peninsula had become decadent and divided among themselves, forming petty *taifas*, which were often obliged to pay tribute to Castile or León. At the end of the eleventh century they had turned to their co-religionists in North Africa for help, and the Almoravids, Berber tribes united by Islamic fundamentalism, then crossed the straits. Another ·dynasty, the Almohads, even more fanatic, later entered the fray, and in 1171, 1184 and 1190, successive waves of their cavalry swept north, overwhelming the Christians, and recapturing most of the territory 're-conquered'. They left a trail of destruction: razing town walls, burning churches, and taking their prisoners as slaves to Africa. Almost back to square one, the Christians had to start the whole process of Reconquest again.

The problem was not so much capturing places as retaining possession of them. With this end in view, while the king kept the important centres for himself, large grants of land re-conquered in the Alentejo were made to the various military orders of knighthood dedicated to the crusades: those of St James (Santiago), of Calatrava (later 'of Avis', where their headquarters was established), and the Hospitallers of St John, known also as the 'Order of Crato' (after another township in the Alentejo). In time, large tracts of these great estates (or *latifundi*) were leased to substantial farmers (the *lavradores*), who by working the estates maintained the knights. It was not until late in the nineteenth century that these quasi-ecclesiastical estates were secularized. The system left its mark, and to this day it is large farms which characterize the land-pattern of the Alentejo region.

8. Political events before 1245

The fifty-seven-year reign of Dom Afonso Henriques (1128–85) provided continuity and a firm basis to his State. He was peacefully succeeded by his eldest son, Dom Sancho I (1185–1211), who gained the epithet 'Povoador' (meaning that he encouraged land settlement). He continued his father's policy of administering the new kingdom through councils elected by its principal towns and villages.

But the next king, Dom Afonso II (1211–23), encountered stiff opposition from the nobility, wary of increasing royal domination, and two of his sisters refused to accept his control over castles which they had inherited from their father. Supported by a contingent from León, a high proportion of the nobility took sides against him and, in the ensuing civil war, royal forces were frequently worsted. Only the firm intervention of the pope resolved the family feud.

Yet the king was not to be deflected from consolidating monarchial authority and unifying the country. The first laws having any nation-wide application date from the first year of his reign, among them one relating to the need for ratification by the Crown of all gifts and grants by and to nobles, while from 1220 formal Inquiries were made into the legitimacy of all land holdings and into all feudal immunities claimed. He also issued the first law of mortmain: any further donations of land to the Church were prohibited (for the Church, like the nobles, claimed exemptions from numerous feudal dues and obligations). This prohibition brought Church and State into conflict, to the extent of the king's being excommunicated and his realm being placed under an anathema.

Dom Sancho II (1223–45) was still a child when he succeeded his father – always a precarious situation in feudal times. The nobles, supported by representatives of the merchant classes, were easily able to obstruct royal policies: the royal chancery was unable to give charters of self-government to a single town. Matters were to deteriorate to such an extent that by 1240 it was virtually impossible to enforce order or to dispense justice. Rival groups fought their private wars, causing turmoil throughout the country, and leaving it in chaos.

9. Social and economic development

In the period during which Portugal became established as a distinct nation, farming was still the main economic activity, the country producing grain, wine, flax, hides and beeswax, and raising cattle and sheep. Textiles were woven and leather goods were produced, and the exploitation of the country's mines enabled agricultural implements, horseshoes, nails and other iron items to be manufactured locally. Fishing boats were built in numerous shipyards; salt was mined or panned – as it had been since Roman times – to preserve produce. Encouraged by royal policies, settlements were established either by the monastic or military orders, by town councils, or by grants to free settlers; and agricultural production increased to meet the growing demand from the growing population. Foreign trade also thrived. Records confirm that goods were exported from the mouths of the rivers Douro, Mondego and Tagus, while the visitations of Crusader fleets confirm that the ports of Portugal were convenient for vessels plying between northern Europe and the Mediterranean. The Jewish population acted as intermediaries for the Christians trading with the Moors of North Africa, and prospered on the proceeds. The demands of export encouraged the cultivation of olive-groves and vineyards rather than cereals, to the advantage of the urban middle-class traders and the detriment of the great landowners, whose profits were usually geared to the production of grain.

Trade demanded a widely acceptable form of currency. In the early twelfth century commodities were still largely paid for in kind (by 'modiums' of wheat, 'lengths' of linen, and the like), but such measurements were gradually replaced by payment in coin. The first coins used in Portugal were provided from several sources, among them Arab or Leonese *maravedis*, and specie from Byzantium. Dom Afonso Henriques minted the first Portuguese *morabitanos* together with gold coins, the first produced by any European nation; in his will he left six hundred kilos of gold coins to be distributed for religious and charitable purposes. Under his successors the proportion of Portuguese currency in circulation, compared with that of foreign coins, grew steadily.

We have seen how the increase in trade encouraged the expansion of what would now be called a distinct urban middle class; but, at the time, only three divisions of society were formally recognized: the clergy, the nobility, and the rest.

The Church was a long-established and deeply-rooted organization. Parishes, grouped into dioceses, were run by the 'secular' clergy; monasteries and convents were the resort of the 'regular' clergy, divided among various Orders. This pattern, which survived the Arab occupation, had pre-dated that redistribution of Iberian territories which resulted in the creation of 'Portugal'. The pope, as head of Christendom, claimed authority over kings; and it was to him that the clergy were ultimately responsible. They were subject to ecclesiastical justice, not that meted out by kings; nor did they pay taxes to the State. Since life was brief and beset with hazards, the afterlife long and more hazardous still, the Faithful – to maintain necessary rituals, good works and intercessions – gave tithes, legacies and other gifts to the Church. The resulting and accumulated riches, privileges and power provided a ready and recurrent subject for conflict between Church and State. Such was the wealth of the Church that almost all important buildings at this time were its property: six cathedrals, two great abbeys (Santa Cruz at Coimbra, and Alcobaça), and some two hundred churches. There were no comparable secular structures, apart from royal castles.

Indeed *all* fortresses were held by the king. From as early as the reign of Dom Sancho I, nobles had been forbidden to construct or own any; and thus, much less so in Portugal than in most other feudal societies, were the nobles able to achieve any great measure of independence in the areas they dominated. It was the king, not they, who demanded military service from the peasants. Typically, Geraldo 'Sem Pavor', although the most notable commander under Dom Afonso Henriques, was not a noble. However, the socio-economic composition of Portugal was too diverse to allow a single feudal pattern to emerge. North of the Douro a 'normal' seigneurial society developed – the land being owned by the king, the Church, and the nobility – whereas to the south much of the settlement and land-holding were dependent on the military orders or on municipalities. The relatively small amount of cultivatable land in the 'seigneurial' north led to substantial migration to the south. There the earlier settlers had established municipalities and had been granted privileges equivalent to those of feudal knights, forming what might be referred to as a rural middle class. Migrants who arrived later, owning no land, formed a peasantry that was obliged to sell its labour in order to survive.

The king was well aware of the political value of those who lived in the towns or were dependent on the municipalities; they were his natural allies in any conflict with the nobility, who were forbidden to build fortresses or to set up their headquarters within town boundaries. Fostering this popular support, the king made his residence for substantial periods in such towns as Guimarães and Coimbra.

10. Dom Afonso III triumphant
With the country in the grip of anarchy in the years around 1240, Pope Innocent III found himself assailed by complaints: from bishops whose churches and monasteries had been pillaged; from the municipalities, reporting towns sacked, ships set alight, merchants imprisoned and tortured until ransoms were paid; and from many individuals.

These grave events led in 1245 to Dom Sancho II being deposed by the pope and replaced by his brother, Afonso. He was a nephew of Blanca of Castile (then Regent of France) and cousin to Louis IX, had lived in France for several years, and had married Mathilde, Countess of Boulogne-sur-Mer. Before sailing with a small army for Portugal, the future Dom Afonso III issued a proclamation in Paris in which he pledged to restore order to his kingdom, promising 'to give each person what belonged to him, without distinction between great and small, rich or poor'. Disembarking at Lisbon, he was hailed as a liberator, his cause was supported by the populace and by several nobles. As others remained loyal to Dom Sancho, it took two years of civil war before he gained control of the country, by which time Sancho, abandoned even by his queen, Dona Mécia, had taken refuge at Toledo, where he died soon after.

When Dom Afonso had first arrived in France he had been obliged to choose a feudal standard. He surrounded the five shields of the Portuguese royal house with a border of castles representing the House of Castile (that of his aunt, Blanca) thus displaying his prestigious heritage to the *noblesse*. This banner was now borne by his 'Boulonnais' army; once victory was assured, it became the national flag of Portugal.

11. The first *Cortes*: Dom Dinis reigns

Once the country was secured, [see Map 2] the reign of Dom Afonso III proved a period of peace, prosperity and rapid development (reflecting that of much of western Europe at this time) which continued well into the reign of his eldest son, Dom Dinis, who succeeded in 1279. Representatives of most of the more important towns and villages were given the right to vote in the *Cortes* or parliament, together with the clergy and nobility. The king thus rewarded those under-privileged classes of the population which had supported him in his recent struggle. The first Cortes of this more representative kind may well have met at Guimarães in 1251; more certainly, one did so at Leiria in 1254. The royal chancery revived the practice of issuing charters to towns, and of holding 'inquiries' into and 'confirmations' of the many claims to special rights too long taken for granted by the more privileged sections of society.

Lisbon, meanwhile, had grown rapidly, and from this time

became, as it has since remained, the administrative seat of government, although the king himself continued periodically to reside in either Coimbra or Almeirim, near Santarém. Between 1250 and 1300 some thirty official 'state markets' were established, the merchants who used them being exempted from paying taxes. Farm produce – chiefly wine, olive oil and honey – converged on these markets before export to France, Flanders and England. Maritime trade was thus stimulated. By 1226 over a hundred Portuguese merchants obtained an English guarantee protecting them against acts of piracy. In a charter awarded by Dom Afonso III to Vila Nova de Gaia in 1255, there occurs the first reference to a 'caravel', a new form of ship which was destined to play a critical role in the great journeys of discovery in the following centuries. And in 1293 Dom Dinis established a 'maritime exchange' for the merchants, one of the earliest insurance organizations in Europe.

Cultural life flourished under both kings. Dom Afonso had introduced the contemporary vogue for the poetry of the Provençal troubadours, devoted to courtly love, and Dom Dinis himself was to cultivate the genre. Some two thousand *cantigas d'amigo* (songs of friendship), *d'amor* (of love) and *de escárnio ou maldizer* (of mockery or slander) have survived from this period, as have traces of popular epics based on the semi-legendary feats of Dom Afonso Henriques.

The growth and power of the bourgeoisie gave culture a secular tone. The children of wealthier families might be sent to foreign universities; some are referred to in poems from this period mocking students who hoped to pass as scholars by dressing in the fashion of those attending the famous university of Montpellier. The growing demand for education led to the establishment in 1288 of a group of 'faculties' in Lisbon, which were transferred soon after to Coimbra and became the historic university which has recently celebrated its seventh centenary. Among the more remarkable figures of the time were Anthony (from Lisbon, subsequently 'of Padua'), who studied at Santa Cruz and Coimbra, taught among the Franciscans in Italy, and was canonized the year after his death in 1231; and Pedro Hispano, son of a Lisbon doctor, who became a professor of both medicine and logic at several universities and whose *Sumulaae Logicales* was a widely used text-book throughout the Middle Ages. He was elected to the papacy in 1276 as John XXI.

Portuguese kings are often given a nickname; Dom Dinis is known as 'O Lavrador' (the Husbandman, or Farmer). Many rural achievements – such as the planting of the great pine-forests near Leiria and the reclaiming of extensive marshlands – are attributed to him without much foundation; certainly, though, agriculture prospered in his reign, with landowners turning uncultivated land to arable use. This prosperity was reflected in the development of many towns and villages, as in several great buildings which survive to this day, such as the huge keep at Beja, the palatial castle at Estremoz, and the famous cloister at Alcobaça.

12. The fourteenth-century crisis
The fourteenth century proved to be a period of political turmoil, which increasingly undermined traditional society, and culminated in revolution in 1383–5.

The origin of the crisis may be traced to the later years of the reign of Dom Dinis. The Cortes had not met since 1301, and royal officials no longer held Inquiries into the arrogation of privileges; without such controls, and contrary to long-settled policy, some nobles even claimed the right to have their own vassals. With the end of the Reconquest, as it applied to Portugal, the nobles lost their role as a military caste; and although their land-rents had been commuted from crops to currency, the value of money declined and their income with it. Indeed, many were only able to retain their position in society by receiving a regular income from the king, who would otherwise have found it difficult to muster an adequate court. Meanwhile, many substantial farmers abandoned their arable land to produce olive oil and wine for export, so that food was sometimes short. The towns prospered, but conflicts of interest became increasingly apparent between the bourgeois merchants and craftsmen, and the workers.

These various tensions first broke out in a civil war which lasted from 1320 to 1323. The heir apparent (later Dom Afonso IV) accused Dom Dinis of failing to dispense justice, implying that no proper social order was being maintained. The queen, Dona Isabel of Aragon, had regularly acted as conciliator between father and son, and had mediated between rival factions, but by 1325 rebellion could be contained no longer and culminated in the bloody battle of Santarém. Dom Dinis, defeated, was forced to dismiss his more odious ministers and hand over the crown to his son. Under Dom Afonso IV, there was a return to previous policies, with the Cortes meeting frequently, and a resumption of Inquiries. The currency was devalued and in 1340, in response to popular demand, interest on loans was prohibited; indeed, in 1361 the death penalty was decreed for usury.

In 1348–9, as elsewhere in Europe, the population was decimated by the Black Death, which brutally disordered the normal patterns of life. Labour was in short supply; the traditional practice of agreeing annual contracts between master and man collapsed, to be replaced by payment – too often at scandalously low rates – negotiated daily. Many of the labourers who had survived the pestilence had inherited land, which they now preferred to sell and to seek a living in the towns. By 1349 the situation had become so acute that peasants were prohibited from leaving the countryside; but the annual reiteration of the decree suggests that such draconian measures had little effect.

In his foreign policy, Dom Afonso IV's main concern was to avoid being drawn into the wars of succession which were then ravaging neighbouring Castile, and it is in this context that the celebrated tragedy of Inês de Castro should be seen. The Castilian nobles rebelling against Pedro I (the Cruel) of Castile wanted the Portuguese *infante*, Dom Pedro, who was a grandson of Sancho IV of Castile, to claim the Castilian throne. These nobles brought pressure to bear on Inês de Castro, for she was of Galician lineage, and as Dom Pedro's long-standing mistress and mother of his three children, might persuade him to take up their cause. His father, Dom Afonso, determined not to allow Portugal to be caught up in the tangle, was persuaded by his ministers to give his tacit permission for her 'removal' from the scene. In January 1355 Inês was murdered in cold blood by three of the king's supporters.

Dom Pedro's spontaneous reaction was to raise the standard of revolt. Much of northern Portugal was ravaged, and it was only the resistance of its citizens that prevented his taking Oporto. On the death of his father in 1357, Pedro took his revenge on the assassins. Inês was buried in a magnificently carved tomb in the convent of Alcobaça; facing it is that of Dom Pedro himself, and on their tombs are inscribed the words 'Até ao fim do mundo' (Until the end of the world). The tragic tale of their love was recounted by Camões in *The Lusiads*, and has since inspired numerous other poets and playwrights in Portugal and throughout Europe.

Dom Pedro was succeeded by his son Dom Fernando (1367–83). By then, the state of the country had deteriorated even further, aggravated by the contagious effects of the Hundred Years War, such as the loss of trade with England,

France and Flanders. Two factions formed among the nobility in relation to the disputed succession of Castile: one supported the pretensions of John of Gaunt, Duke of Lancaster (for he had married a daughter of Pedro the Cruel); the other supported the claims of Enrique de Trastámara. Each of the three campaigns against the Castilians in which Dom Fernando was engaged ended disastrously.

In 1371 rioting broke out in Lisbon, partly in opposition to the king's proposed marriage to Leonor Teles (who was already married). Ostensibly bowing to this demonstration of popular discontent, Dom Fernando retired from the capital but, deviously, he then married her, before returning to carry out bloody reprisals against the leaders of the uprising. By 1373 he had made himself so unpopular that when Enrique de Trastámara (now Enrique II of Castile) marched on Lisbon, he met only token resistance from its citizens, although royal troops withstood the siege.

Despite political turmoil, Dom Fernando did his best to overhaul the administration, promulgating the 'Law of the Sesmarias' in 1375, bringing neglected land under cultivation, controlling the movement of labour, and allowing the wages paid to the peasantry to be fixed by the *homens bons* of municipal councils. In 1377 he established the 'Companhia das Naus', an association incorporating both the entrepreneurs engaged in trade and the officials who administered the royal merchant navy, which was the first attempt by the State to co-ordinate foreign trade. Regrettably, this and similar projects were rapidly overtaken by events.

13. The revolution of 1383–5: Aljubarrota
Dom Fernando died in 1383, and Beatriz, his daughter by Leonor Teles, was duly proclaimed queen, despite protest from the towns, for as Beatriz was married to Juan I of Castile, there was justifiable anxiety over whether Portugal

would remain an independent country. An influential group of nobles and merchants hatched a plot to assassinate João Fernandes Andeiro, the Count of Ourém, a leader of the Beatriz faction and by then the lover of Leonor Teles. Execution was entrusted to Dom João, an illegitimate son of Dom Pedro I and Master of the Order of Avis. Andeiro's removal from the scene sparked off a popular rising in Lisbon in support of Dom João, which spread rapidly throughout the country, notably in the Alentejo, where the rioters, seized by revolutionary fervour, sometimes mistakenly attacked those on their own side.

To assert the rights of Beatriz, her husband invaded Portugal and marched on Lisbon, where he was met by vigorous resistance from Dom João, buttressed by popular enthusiasm. Plague spread through the invading troops and the siege had to be raised. Meanwhile, Dom Nun'Álvares Pereira, a young nobleman to whom Dom João had left the defence of the Alentejan frontier, had galvanized the peasantry there into attacking a predatory squadron of Castilian cavalry, whom they slaughtered, a success which gave them confidence in their capacity to withstand these formidable and far better equipped aggressors.

In 1385 the Master of Avis assembled a Cortes at Coimbra to discuss the matter of the Portuguese succession. João das Regras, a young lawyer trained at Bologna, maintained that the throne was vacant: Dona Beatriz, and also the two sons of Dom Pedro and Inês de Castro (the Infantes Dom João and Dom Dinis), were *all* of them illegitimate, certainly no less so than the Master of Avis. While some nobles supported the claims of the Infante Dom João, the representatives of the municipalities almost unanimously declared in favour of the Master of Avis, who as Dom João was duly elected king, the first of a new dynasty.

The forces of Juan I of Castile, supported by a high proportion of the Portuguese nobility, again invaded. Meanwhile, a comparatively small but cohesive 'national' Portuguese army, together with a rapidly recruited contingent of some 800 English archers, took up position at Aljubarrota, not far from present-day Batalha, approximately a hundred kilometres north of Lisbon. Here, in the heat of mid-August 1385, the Portuguese won an overwhelming victory against much superior forces. Numerous members of the nobility who had opposed Dom João were killed in the contest. Don Juan, king of Castile, fled the field (and soon after died). The war dragged on, but further Castilian claims to the Portuguese throne were, in effect, dropped.

14. The new monarchy

The accession of Dom João I (1385–1433) inaugurated a 'new style' monarchy. The older nobility had been largely replaced by a new landed aristocracy dependent on the king, who set about establishing a more durable political system and a more broadly based social order. To strengthen the prestige and authority of the crown, Dom João negotiated a treaty of 'perpetual alliance' with Richard II of England, signed at Windsor on 9 May 1386. This – renewed and modified over the years – still remains in force, making it the longest-enduring, virtually continuous alliance between two sovereign countries. Dom João undertook to support the claims of the Duke of Lancaster (Richard's uncle) to the Castilian throne. An English expeditionary force, escorted by armed Portuguese galleys, was transported to La Coruña, but although several years were spent campaigning sporadically in the Peninsula, the English claim ultimately proved a lost cause.

Of much greater significance was Dom João's marriage in 1387 to the Duke's youngest daughter, Philippa of Lancaster. It is said that she was influential in imposing more chivalrous and formal modes of behaviour on the Portuguese court, where several English practices were adopted; at the same time she went out of her way to see that the relationship with England remained cordial. Being a cultivated woman, she ensured that her children, referred to as 'Dukes', received a thorough education. The christian names chosen for them reflected their ancestry: for example, Duarte (Edward), and Henrique (Henry, later called 'the Navigator'). Among buildings, the great abbey-church of Batalha, dedicated to St Mary of Victory, was erected near Aljubarrota, the site of that decisive encounter, and there lie Dom João and Dona Filipa, their effigies hand in hand. The magnificent cathedral shows in both the design and the detail of its Gothic architecture the influence of contemporary English 'masters of works'.

There was a great cultural revival at court. The king and at least two of his sons tried their hands as authors. Dom Duarte's *O Leal Conselheiro* can be said adequately to reflect the ideas and ideals of the time. More memorable among literary figures at the court was the chronicler Fernão Lopes. Born in 1380 into a humble family, by 1418 he had become keeper of the royal archives in the Torre do Tombo and until his death, forty-six years later, he occupied himself writing the history of Portugal. His style is direct and vigorous, and he shows a surprising appreciation of the role of ordinary people in the evolution of events – not just that of kings, nobles and clerics who so often monopolize the pages of such narratives. In particular, his account of the years 1383–5 is ranked amongst the masterpieces of medieval literature.

III *The Century of the Discoveries*

15. Political evolution during the fifteenth century
In 1433 Dom João I was succeeded by Dom Duarte, 'the Philosopher King'. Dom Duarte died only five years later, when his own eldest son, Dom Afonso V, was still a child. In his will, Dom Duarte appointed his wife Leonor of Aragon to be Regent, but while the nobility rallied to her, the inhabitants of Lisbon, as well as of other towns, preferred the succession of the late king's brother, Dom Pedro, Duke of Coimbra.

Although civil war was threatened by an insurrection in the capital and sabre-rattling in the Alentejo, a peaceful solution was found, with Dom Pedro ruling during Afonso's minority (1441–8). However, as soon as the youthful king found himself in control, he arraigned his uncle for treason; and although Dom Pedro raised a force to defend himself and attempted to occupy Lisbon, he and most of his faction were massacred by royal troops at the battle of Alfarrobeira.

Dom Afonso V was much influenced by the Braganza family, and others whom he favoured, liberally conferring titles of nobility, grants of money, and positions of power in administration. The king also embarked on several military expeditions to North Africa (which gained him the epithet 'The African'). In 1475, on the death of Enrique IV of Castile, he sent troops to support the succession of Joana, his niece and Enrique's daughter; another Castilian faction preferred

Isabel, Enrique's sister, who had married Fernando of Aragon. Dom Afonso feared that if the latter should inherit, the two powerful kingdoms of Castile and Aragon would unite and threaten the delicate balance of power in the Peninsula. Although the Portuguese forces received the backing of some Castilian nobles, they were defeated at the battle of Toro (1476). Dom Afonso then approached Louis XI of France, hoping for his support, but without result. Disillusioned and feeling left in the lurch, in 1481 he died.

By then his son Dom João (1481–95) was virtually running the country. Strong and ruthless, he was determined to re-assert royal authority: first, he ordered, after a rapid trial, the execution at Évora of the Duke of Braganza, the most eminent figure among the nobility; then, the Bishop of Évora and the Marquis of Távora were also involved in the purge; not even the Duke of Viseu, the queen's brother, was spared. Meanwhile, in 1479, peace with Castile was assured by the Treaty of Alcáçovas, with Dona Joana renouncing her claim to the succession.

This treaty had the additional importance of including the first delimitation of areas of sovereignty over future 'discoveries'. Portugal relinquished claims arising from having first discovered the Canaries, and a line was drawn along the latitude of these islands to form a boundary: territories discovered to the south would fall to Portugal; and those discovered to the north to Spain. This treaty proved short-lived, for it was superseded in 1494 by the Treaty of Tordesillas.

Dom João II's death brought an end to a period of rigorous rehabilitation. Having no legitimate offspring, he was succeeded by Dom Manuel, Duke of Beja (a grandson of Dom Duarte, and the queen's brother) and so began that illustrious era in the nation's history: the Manueline.

16. The Portuguese in North Africa

On the signing of peace with Castile in 1411, the Portuguese set about preparing a large-scale military expedition. Its destination remained top secret until 1415, when a fleet of 200 vessels containing some 20,000 troops sailed from the Tagus estuary – for Ceuta, on the African shore of the Straits of Gibraltar. The destination demonstrated the spectacular reversal that had occurred in the fortunes of the Moors since the end of their long occupation of southern Portugal, and was chosen to add lustre to Dom João I's reign. Ceuta was seized with little opposition and then massively fortified to become a base for Portuguese commerce and for further incursions into North Africa. Since the Moors controlled the hinterland, however, Ceuta had to be supplied by sea, so that within ten years it was described by the Infante Dom Pedro as 'a great drain of people, arms and money'; he added that the English also thought that it was a mistake to hang on there, but the advice was not taken and further adventures in North Africa remained on the political agenda until the end of the following century.

After the occupation of Ceuta, the next steps were to capture, first, Tangiers and then Arzila. The attempt to seize Tangiers in 1437 ended in disaster; the besiegers found themselves overwhelmed by the Moors and were only able to regain their ships after agreeing to give up Ceuta, leaving the Infante Dom Fernando, the king's youngest brother, as hostage. As the Cortes refused to ratify the surrender of Ceuta, the poor young prince was left to die in captivity.

Further North African expeditions were organized under the aegis of Dom Afonso V, which resulted in the conquest of Alcácer-Quiber (1458), Arzila and Tangiers (1471), Safim (1508), Azamor (1513), and Mazagão (1514). This was the high-water mark of Portuguese advance, for in 1515, exactly a century after their first incursion into North Africa, they again suffered a severe defeat. Dom Manuel had sent an expeditionary force to construct a stronghold at the mouth of the Mamora (near present Casablanca), which would provide a base for the projected conquest of the kingdom of Fez. In the event, the Portuguese found themselves over-powered by the counter-attacking Moors; their troops were decimated and forced to retreat with the loss of 4,000 men, 200 ships, and all their artillery.

This put paid to any further expansion in North Africa. The upkeep of the several Portuguese forts, isolated in hostile territory, became increasingly irksome and expensive. Attempts were made to live off the land but, too often, raiding parties found themselves cut off or ambushed. Few were the Portuguese families that did not count a member dead in North Africa. Yet, among the nobles, it was still considered patriotic to offer to serve there – frequently in return for a profitable command in a military order – and collective national pride demanded that, whatever the sacrifice in men and material, no foothold should be surrendered. However, when in 1541 the entire garrison of Santa Cruz do Cabo de Gué, the most southerly of the fortresses, was taken prisoner and then butchered, the king felt obliged to seek the pope's permission to abandon most of these Christian outposts, retaining only Ceuta, Tangiers and Mazagão.

The death throes of the African empire were protracted. Ceuta remained Portuguese (even if effectively it passed into Spanish hands under the joint monarchy) until 1640. Tangiers formed part of Catherine of Braganza's dowry when she married Charles II, and was ceded to the English in 1662. Mazagão (the present (El-Jadida) held out until 1769 when, besieged by the Moors, it was abandoned on Pombal's orders, and its Portuguese population transported to Brazil; there they founded a new town with the same name. Three hundred and fifty-four years had passed between the first

Portuguese landing at Ceuta and the eventual acceptance that a permanent North Africa empire was a pipe-dream.

Yet the North African adventure had important ramifications: it was there that the nobility could let off steam, pursuing their martial vocation on foreign fields rather than on home ground; and the desire to acquire fame in the African service made them dependent on royal patronage. In North Africa little trace remains of the long Portuguese presence there, apart from the relics of fortifications. Whereas at a later date the Portuguese were to intermarry with the natives of Brazil, the Orient, and in other African colonies, in North Africa Christian intolerance at the time included a prohibition against marrying a non-Christian (especially a Muslim). As a result, no 'mestizo' or half-breed population perpetuates the passage of the Portuguese.

17. Maritime expansion

From the early fifteenth century onwards, Portuguese history is punctuated by the phenomenon of overseas expansion, which took the Portuguese to East Africa, India, China, Japan and South America, with consequences which have dominated the country's development almost to the present. How can one account for this passion to colonize? What distinguishes the case of Portugal, when compared to that of other European countries, is that the voyages of discovery were not isolated actions of individual merchants or adventurers, but the result of a plan instituted by the State and carried out over many generations, whether under direct control of the Crown (as with Dom João II), or under the sponsorship of *infantes* (such as Dom Henrique, 'the Navigator', and Dom Pedro). It was this deliberate policy which made the Portuguese discoveries so far-reaching; indeed they inaugurated a new era in world history.

The original motives of the Crown in taking so active a role in maritime affairs may be sought in the long struggle with Islam [see map 4]. Once the Moors had been driven from what became modern Portugal (her present frontiers being the longest-established in Europe), the Portuguese carried the contest beyond their coasts. The war at sea was first fought by the Portuguese against Arab corsairs who raided their ports and harassed their shipping. To counteract these depredations, a royal fleet was constructed: there was certainly one by the time Dom Dinis was king, for it was during his reign that the headquarters of the Templars was transferred from Tomar, in the centre of the country, to Castro Marim, at the eastern end of the Algarve, where the combat with the Moors was particularly intense. When the Order of Crato – a continuation from the Templars – had the Infante Dom Henrique (Prince Henry the Navigator) as its 'Apostolic Administrator', its accumulated resources were directed with decisive effect towards maritime enterprise. This is how it came about that the Templar cross was blazoned on the sails of Portuguese caravels.

It was largely due to Prince Henry that what was once a desultory military activity, encouraged by the prospect of plunder, was converted to one in which a sustained programme of exploration, partly inspired by scientific curiosity, became paramount. The convergence of religious and economic interests with royal sponsorship made possible this change of emphasis. The adventure of the discoveries appealed to the growing population (many of whom had the skills of shipbuilding and the experience of navigation) for whom the pursuit provided both diversion and employment.

Involvement in the discoveries became a national preoccupation under the House of Avis, being directly promoted by Dom João I, Dom Afonso V, Dom João II, and Dom Manuel I. As we have seen, from 1420 onwards it was Prince Henry who was the guiding light of this intense maritime activity. His principal motives have been described by Gomes Eanes de Zurara, a chronicler in his service, in a way which suggests that they may have been dictated to him by 'the Navigator' himself. These were: to know – a burning curiosity – what lay beyond Cape Bojador, the extremity of the then-known world; to discover material riches and opportunities for trading; to find out the extent of the occupation of those regions by the Moors; to investigate whether any Christian prince lived in unknown African lands who might prove an ally; and the hope that, by bringing Christianity to such territories, the souls of any captured slaves might be saved.

A. The Canaries

The earliest Portuguese discovery, at some time prior to 1336, was that of the Canary Islands: Portugal's persistent claim to sovereignty over the islands was based on this early discovery. However, attempts at settlement were slight and in 1479, the Portuguese claim to the archipelago was abandoned in favour of Spain.

B. Madeira, Porto Santo and the Azores

The Madeira archipelago, like that of the Canaries, is depicted on fourteenth-century maps (among them the Dulcert chart of 1339). The date of first colonization is unknown, but it must have been around 1425, when a Portuguese fleet, having failed to land on the Canaries, landed on Madeira.

Colonists arrived soon after. In 1451 charters were issued for the settlement of Funchal and Machico; their hereditary government was granted to two of Prince Henry's entourage, João Gonçalves Zarco and Tristão Vaz Teixeira respectively. Within a few years the islands were cleared and cultivated, and used as points of supply for the Portuguese settlements on the North African coast. Towards the end of the century, sugar-cane plantations, the first in Europe, were established there and vines were planted on the steep slopes. In 1508 Funchal was granted the privileges of a town and its economic development was thereby reinforced. The island was described by Camões in *The Lusiads* as a terrestrial paradise.

The spectacular success of this colonization encouraged similar ventures elsewhere, notably the occupation of the Azores. They were drawn, even if sited inaccurately, on thirteenth-century charts. Early accounts alluded to 'darkling seas', boiling waters and ash-laden skies – descriptions which may have had their origins in volcanic eruptions taking place in the early fourteenth century.

A note on the chart of Gabriel Valséqua states that the Azores were discovered in 1427. The first document referring to human occupation – and to sheep grazing there – is dated 1439: Dom Pedro, when Regent, authorized his brother, Dom Henrique, to set about colonizing the 'seven islands of the Azores', soon after which the first officially sponsored settlers disembarked. As the islands were of volcanic origin and the ground rocky, development moved at a slower pace than in Madeira. By the fifteenth century the port of Agra had become a refuge and base for Atlantic navigators, and with the discovery of the Americas, the Azores became important as a port of call between the Old and New Worlds.

C. The African coast explored

The first expedition down the west African coast took place in 1434, with scientific enquiry high on the list of motives. It was led by Gil Eanes, a young man in Prince Henry's company, who had the temerity to sail beyond Cape Bojador.

This epic voyage was followed in each succeeding year by

other expeditions, each attempting to sail further south. As early as 1457 Dom Henrique had referred to navigators as engaged 'in trading, and bartering merchandise', and in 1496 a Lisbon merchant was granted a five-year monopoly to trade south of the dread Cape, in return for which he paid an annual fee and undertook to explore a hundred leagues of coast-line each year. In this way, in the period immediately before and after Prince Henry's death, expeditions down the African shore had become private enterprises, while the coast itself had been charted as far south as what is now Sierra Leone.

After 1474, however, control of such expeditions reverted to the State. Dom Afonso V granted the monopoly of trading with Africa to his heir apparent, the Infante Dom João, for life, and thus trade and exploration received additional momentum. In 1482 the fort of São João da Mina was constructed, becoming a base for trading over an extensive area which included Senegal, Sierra Leone, Liberia, the Ivory Coast and the Gold Coast, and as far as the Niger delta. Gold, ivory, slaves and malagueta (also called 'grains of paradise' or 'Guinea-grains' i.e. Cayenne pepper) were bought for lengths of brightly-coloured cloth, metallic trinkets, coral, and red and blue beads. The Crown retained strict control – there was a death penalty for smuggling – which may explain why there were so few Portuguese settlers in Guinea. Towards the end of the fifteenth century, traders in gold produced some seven hundred kilograms annually, which was of greater value than all the rest of the royal income.

French, Dutch, and English ships tried to break the Portuguese monopoly on several occasions, but it was not until 1637 that the Dutch seized the fort of São João da Mina, which they later surrendered to the English.

D. *The Congo reached*

A daring and somewhat bizarre project was that of 'civilizing' the natives of the Congo basin, then dominated by the 'Soba', a powerful chief. Dom João II got it into his head that the Soba might be transformed into a monarch in the European mould, who would get his Bantu subjects to adopt the Portuguese way of life. In 1490 a 'civilizing' expedition was dispatched, its vessels containing a cargo of missionaries intent on instilling Christianity, and of artisans able to demonstrate technical skills to the natives. The Soba, who duly learnt the catechism and how to dress in the European fashion, changed his name from Nazinga Nkumm to Dom João I, and filled his court with 'counts' and 'marquises'. The Portuguese 'Ordenações Manuelinas' were proclaimed the law of the land. Selected young Congolese were sent to Lisbon to learn Latin and Portuguese. Most of them proved good students: some were ordained – the Soba's son was consecrated a bishop – and one went on to teach grammar to the Portuguese attending the university at Coimbra. In the end, however, little was gained by an experiment doomed to failure since the cultural gap was far too wide to bridge; and 'civilization' did not exclude the slavers whose depredations led to the natives abandoning large areas of the country. Despite its collapse, this early attempt to impose western culture systematically on a native population remains touching and interesting. Some traces survive in the blackened walls, still standing, of the cathedral of St Saviour of the Congo, and in some curious word constructions in the Bantu languages. Near the Lelala Falls, some 160 kilometres from the mouth of the Zaire, a great rock retains a carving of the Portuguese coat of arms and the words 'This far came the caravels of the enlightened Dom João II', a record of the furthest point reached by Diogo Cão's expedition of 1482/3.

E. 'The Plan for the Indies'

It would appear that Dom João II himself dreamt up the project of establishing a direct sea link between Lisbon and the spice-rich Indies by skirting the African coast. The voyages of discovery of Diogo Cão and Bartolomeu Dias formed part of that ambitious plan.

When Diogo Cão sailed from the Tagus in 1482, he carried with him a number of *padrões*, stone pillars, which he was to set up to substantiate his discovery of any place. On his first voyage he explored 1,500 kilometres of the African coast; and on the second, having made the epic expedition up the Zaire referred to above, he sailed a further 1,300 kilometres to reach Serra Parda (22° 10' south), where he is believed to have died, although the location is disputed.

Early in 1487 another expedition, led by Bartolomeu Dias, had sailed far south when a violent storm drove it well away from the coast. When he sighted land again, he found it ran east, not south – at last, a Portuguese navigator had circled the southern cape of the vast African continent. This way lay the long-sought sea route to the Indies [see Map 3].

F. Columbus and the Treaty of Tordesillas

A proposal made by Christopher Columbus, apparently a Genovese navigator, resident in Lisbon and in the service of Dom João II, was originally put forward as part of 'The Plan for the Indies'. Since the earth was spherical, the Indies could be approached as well by sailing west as east. The alternative westward passage, Columbus argued, would prove shorter: he based his case on the calculations of Toscanelli, an eminent Florentine geographer, who had produced a terrestrial globe (on which, of course, there was no sign of the American continents) divided by him into 180 degrees, with a distance between each, at the equator, equivalent to 84 kilometres – a mere 15,120 kilometres in all (40,000 kilometres would have been nearer the mark). The king submitted Columbus' proposal to the court cosmographers, who were not impressed and advised against any investment in such a wrong-headed scheme. During the succeeding years, Columbus, with his bee in his bonnet, offered his services to the Catholic monarchs of Spain, Fernando and Isabel, who eventually, in 1492, provided him with the resources to carry out his investigations. The islands he reached, he was convinced, were the Indies; if not, then the fabled islands of Zipangu – Japan – referred to in Marco Polo's *Travels*.

Columbus called in at Lisbon on his return voyage to inform Dom João II of his discovery of this new short sea-route to the Indies. As his landfall lay south of the latitude of the Canaries, the king immediately claimed it for Portugal under the terms of the Treaty of Alcáçovas, of which Columbus was ostensibly ignorant. To resolve the disputed question of the ownership of lands discovered, a new treaty was signed at Tordesillas on 7 June 1494. It superseded the previous agreement: no longer would the division between the two great maritime nations be formed by a latitude or horizontal line, but rather by one of longitude, vertically, drawn 370° west of the Cape Verde Islands.

Historians have argued over the reasons why the Portuguese insisted on moving the line first proposed – through the Cape Verde Islands – much further west, to a position apparently chosen arbitrarily, passing through uncharted ocean. Some have argued that the Portuguese already knew of the existence of land east of the dividing longitude in the region of north-eastern Brazil, although they chose to keep the matter secret [see Map 5].

G. Vasco da Gama reaches India
Once it was agreed that lands discovered east of the

Tordesillas line would fall to Portugal, Dom João II set in motion a sea-bound expedition to India. Rather than using caravels, the fleet was to consist of heavier, purpose-built vessels known as *naus*, which could transport larger quantities of merchandise.

The king died before preparations had been completed. Dom Manuel, his successor, re-submitted the project to the Cortes, which voted against it. However, he insisted on pushing ahead, and chose as commander of the fleet a certain Vasco da Gama, the second son of a provincial official who had been employed by Dom Afonso V and had become governor of Sines. It was the first time a member of the minor bureaucratic élite had directed a voyage of discovery.

The flotilla set out from the Tagus estuary on 8 July 1497. da Gama's ship's log has survived, authenticating the route followed. Once the fleet had passed the Cape Verde Islands, it tacked west, sailing close to the Brazilian coast thereby profiting from prevailing winds and currents – previously explored by Portuguese navigations – before bearing southeast to round the Cape of Good Hope. Not until 20 May the following year did da Gama cast anchor at Calicut, one of the largest emporiums of India. He had been instructed to negotiate treaties of friendship and commerce with local rulers, but with the *Samorium*, ruler of that region, this proved exceedingly difficult: Arab traders who had long monopolized the overland route without any maritime competition raised strong objections so that any formal alliance was frustrated. Three months later, on 29 August, Vasco da Gama re-embarked. The return voyage took almost a year; a ship was lost, and half his crew died *en route*. However, the reception given to the survivors – processions and festivities were proclaimed throughout Portugal – emphasized the importance of the event, the news of which was announced by the king to sovereigns throughout Christendom.

A direct consequence of the success of this venture was the disgrace of Columbus: he was held in custody by the Catholic kings, and all the property he had formerly been awarded was confiscated.

IV *The Armillary Sphere*

18. National reconciliation

Dom Manuel I became known in history by the epithet 'The Fortunate'. His name is indissolubly linked to a period of active connection between West and East, which also produced an extraordinary burgeoning of the arts and literature. On ascending the throne, he reinstated the House of Braganza, slighted by his predecessor; in this way he propitiated the upper nobility, with whom the sovereign had been in a state of open warfare. At the same time, in 1496, he proscribed the expulsion of the Jews from the kingdom, initiating the delicate and painful settlement of the Sephardic issue.

The number of Jews in Portugal was already substantial by the time the country had become independent politically. Under the Alfonsine dynasty they had been appointed to influential administrative posts, largely financial: the royal treasurers had frequently been Jews. In 1492 the bigoted Catholic monarchs had expelled the Jews from Spain, and Dom João II had allowed many of these fugitives to take up temporary residence in Portugal on payment of substantial amounts of money. It has been estimated that as many as 100,000 Jews settled in the country, which had at the time a population of only about one million. Under strong pressure from Spain, Dom Manuel attempted to stem the flow into Portugal by not putting any shipping at the Jews' disposal (for the overland journey was hazardous). He also ordered the forcible baptism of Jewish children, a formula which would allow them to remain in his realm. He promised that all those who accepted baptism would not have the authenticity of their conversion investigated for at least two decades. While some Jews preferred to leave the country, the majority, ostensibly converted, chose to settle. But the ultimate consequences of these induced conversions were tragic: the Christians and Jews, who had formerly lived peaceably together in their separate communities, were now all considered Christians, although there was a distinction between 'Old' Christians and the 'New'; and under later rulers, the New Christians were ruthlessly persecuted if they continued secretly to observe Jewish rites.

The internal administration of the country was modernized. Among the more important steps taken were those to standardize weights and measures, to reform the *forais* or charters, and to recodify the laws (which became known as the 'Ordenações Manuelinas'). Among these reforms, that concerning the charters of privilege was closest to the interests of the populace, few of whom could make sense of the old parchments, with their Latin scripts – often corrupted or falsified when copied – which gave rise to numerous abuses. Dom João II had promised the Cortes of 1481/2 that he would look into the matter, but in the event he never did so. What is remarkable about the Manueline reforms is that, once initiated in 1497, they proceeded without interruption throughout the reign. The new ordinances gave more attention to matters of taxation and its collection than the old. These ordinances, issued by the royal presses and often very beautifully printed, are now frequently displayed in town halls as historic documents substantiating civic independence.

The Ordenações Manuelinas came into force when

published in 1512. They were systematically presented, unlike the earlier haphazard compilations. At the same time several institutions, notably the treasury and the judiciary, were drastically reformed. In 1521 a revised edition of the ordinances was published, incorporating important amendments, which provided the infrastructure of Portuguese law until it was modified by nineteenth-century liberal reforms.

Several of the reforms were initiated by Dom Manuel himself, who took a great interest in such leisurely and peaceable occupations. The setting up of a King of Arms, responsible for the blazons of nobility, was part of his heraldic reform, colourful evidence of which can be found in the *Livro do Armeiro-mor*, and in the 'Sala dos Brasões' at Sintra, with its skilfully made ceiling decorated with the coats of arms of over seventy noble families. While the king thus passed his time, his jurists produced more important statutes, among them those devoted to Towns and Villages (1502), to India and Mina (1509), to Stamp Duties (1512), to the Mint, and to the Exchequer (1514), revisions which modernized the administrative structure of the State.

19. The eastern empire

Oriental spices, of inflated economic value, had many uses: as condiments, in preserving food, in the preparation of medicines, perfumes, glues, lacquers, varnishes, dyes, in the processes of tanning, and many others. These spices reached Europe by a variety of routes, such as via the Red Sea or Persian Gulf to Alexandria, where Venetian traders would take over distribution throughout Europe. The new maritime route via the Cape, obviating caravans and a host of intermediaries, allowed the Portuguese to sell the spices at a much lower price.

A second expedition – military as much as mercantile – composed of no less than thirteen vessels, heavily armed with artillery, was set in motion, commanded by Pedro Álvares Cabral, of noble lineage, no mere squire. Instead of following the course of da Gama, it sailed further into the Atlantic, sighting Brazil. It is still being argued whether the discovery was premeditated or accidental. It is possible that the landfall was unforeseen, but there is convincing evidence that by that date the Portuguese knew of the existence of the continent.

From then on, in the spring of each year, a fleet would sail to India, with a complement of soldiers, adventurers and missionaries; and with merchandise to be bartered – for pepper on the Malabar coast, for example. In spite of the frightful rate of mortality *en route*, which might reach over 50 per cent, the numbers hankering to join increased every year [see Map 7]. India seemed to be the answer to every problem. For the king, it provided what grew to be his main source of revenue; nobles and administrators hoped to grow fat on the profits of office; and for the others it was at least employment, for at home economic activity was stagnant.

Eastern trade involved unusual difficulties, for the traffic had long been dominated by Muslims, who, not unnaturally, sought to exclude competition, and to this end would go to any lengths. At first they stirred up trouble with the Indian princes, and later solicited the support of Turkish squadrons in an attempt to chase the Portuguese intruders from their patch – the Indian Ocean. Pedro Álvares Cabral had bombarded Calicut as early as 1500 for refusing to sell him spices; but this was only the opening salvo in hostilities which were to drag on for a century and a half. The Portuguese had to counter not only local Indian forces but the Turks, and later the Dutch and English. Finally, by the mid-seventeenth century England and Holland had taken over the Portuguese position of supremacy in trading with the Orient.

[1]

[2]

Archaeologists deduce from stone hand-axe finds that tool-making humans lived in the west of the Iberian peninsula some 200,000 years ago. Thousands of rock engravings of hunted animals – horse, aurochs (wild cattle) and ibex (wild goats), constituting the largest collection of outdoor Palaeolithic figures in the world – were recently found in the Côa valley in north-central Portugal [1]. The engravings are dispersed in several clusters along 17 kilometres of the valley, the earliest dating back some 25,000 years. ¶ Numerous dolmens and caves in the north-east Alentejo region [2] show that this area was unusually populous in mid-Neolithic times (approximately 4th millennium BC).

[3]

[4]

Celts migrated into the Iberian peninsula in the 8th century BC. Their *espigueiros* – corn cribs on rock posts to deter rodents – remain effective [3]. The language spoken in north Portugal retains Celtic influences, as do numerous place names. ¶ The Romans invaded Iberia in 218 BC. Remains of their six-hundred-year occupation include those of the Temple of Diana in Évora [4] and of domestic mosaics in Conímbriga [5]. Through the Romans, too, came

[5]

[6a]

[6b]

Christianity and a basically Latin language. ¶ Subsequent occupation of Iberia by the Goths reinforced the Christian faith but left few other traces. The Islamic invasions after 711, however, were influential in intellectual life, in agriculture and irrigation, fine craftsmanship and architecture, as shown in the shape of these arches in a church in Santarém [6a] and in a tradition persisting to this day of the architectural use of tiles [6b].

[7]

[8]

Among Christian leaders engaged in the Re-conquest of Iberia from the Moors was a doughty heir to the fiefdom of Portucale (between the Minho and the Mondego rivers) called Afonso Henriques (1128–85), portrayed in this 12th-century stone effigy from Santarém [7]. He declared his independence from the King of León

[9]

[10]

and conquered lands south to Lisbon. ¶ In thank-offering he founded the abbey of Alcobaça. Begun *c*.1153, it was magnificently completed in Cistercian style in 1223 [8]. ¶ The abbey includes the superb tombs of Dom Pedro I (1357–67) [9] and Inês de Castro, placed foot to foot; romantic tradition asserted that each of the celebrated lovers wished, at the Resurrection, first to see the other. ¶ Castilian dynastic claims constantly threatened Portugal's independence. In 1387, Dom João I (1385–1433) married Philippa, daughter of John of Gaunt [10], thereby establishing firmly the alliance between Portugal and England – the longest enduring of European alliances, frequently invoked.

[11]

[12]

On 14 August 1385 the Portuguese defeated a Castilian army, much superior in numbers and *matériel*, at Aljubarrota, [11] thereby securing the country's independence. In commemoration, Dom João I built nearby the magnificent abbey of Batalha. ¶ Two of João's six sons are shown in the 'Infante's panel', part of the great retable by Nuno Gonçalves (painted *c*.1467–70). Behind the kneeling Infante, stands Dom Henrique (Henry the Navigator) [12].

¶ Henry was master of the Order of Christ (the reformed Templars)

[13]

[14]

from 1417 to 1460. Shown here is the Choir of its great monastery and castle at Tomar [13]. Henry used the Order's resources to sustain the development of ship-building and nautical skills which made possible the discoveries. Renowned for their unique expertness, Portuguese navigators – shown here in a 16th-century German woodcut [14] – were employed on expeditions and trading ventures by many nations.

[15]

[16]

The Torre de Belém [15] was built (1515–20) to protect the sea entrance to Lisbon. Nearby was the departure point of most Portuguese expeditions. ¶ The discoveries began with the exploration – for trade, gold and evangelism – of the unknown west African coast. The small manoeuvrable Portuguese *caravelas* were able to sail in shallow waters, as shown here by rock inscriptions at Yelala, well up the Congo river [16]. ¶ As the vast length of Africa was revealed, hopes grew that somewhere the continent would end, allowing a sea-route to the wealth of the Indies – a possibility confirmed by Bartolomeu Dias, the first to round the Cape, in 1487.

[17a] [17b]

[18a] [18b]

Larger vessels, the *naus*, were developed for the long, dangerous and potentially profitable journey to the Orient. The epic voyage was first completed by Vasco da Gama [18a] in 1497–9. Thereafter an annual fleet sailed to the Indies. The *Livro das Armadas* depicts the fate of successive fleets – here Cabral's (1500–2) [17a & b]. Over the 16th century fully a half of the vessels were lost. The military genius, Afonso de Albuquerque (1453–1515), established eastern footholds despite hostile princes and rival traders [18b].

[19a]

[19b]

[20]

Medieval western Christendom was obsessed with the world-wide struggle against Islam. Legend described the lost Christian kingdom, supposedly in Africa, of Prester John (= Presbyter John), a powerful potential ally against the Turks: the Portuguese achieved contact with Christian Ethiopia from 1513 and later built a fort at Gander, the then capital, and maintained a garrison. The Emperor sent a letter to King Dom João III [19a] who sent an embassy [19b] overland which reached Ethiopia in 1544. ¶ On the sea and off-shore, the Portuguese warred against the Ottoman Turks [20]. ¶ The annual *Carreira da India* fleet under Pedro Álvares Cabral (1467?–1520) reportedly blown off course, 'discovered' Brazil in

[21]

[22]

1500 [21]. ¶ Of all oriental trade goods none was more important than pepper, here shown being packed for export [22]. It was worth ten times more than any other spice in a period when meat was (inadequately) preserved by heavy salting. When the English royal navy vessel the *Mary Rose* was raised from the sea-bed in the 1980s, nearly every sailor who went down with her in 1545 was found to have owned a little bag of peppercorns. And pepper was even used as an internationally acceptable currency. When Isabella of Portugal was betrothed to the Emperor Charles V in 1521, her dowry was largely paid in quintals of pepper.

[23]

[24]

In about 1515 the Portuguese reached China by sea, but they were not allowed to establish a settlement until 1557 – and then only off-shore – at Macao. The first European enclave, it will be the last on 20 December 1999. Shown here is the surviving façade of the 17th-century Jesuit church of São Paulo [23]. ¶ In 1543 the Portuguese discovered Japan and soon controlled the very profitable trade in the pirate-ridden China seas. Japanese screens of the period brilliantly depict the arrival of the Portuguese Black Ships [24].

[25]

[26]

¶ With trade came Christianity. A hundred years after the arrival of the Portuguese, and the Jesuits they brought, there were some 300,000 Japanese converts, like the young man here portrayed [25].
¶ The Jesuits were especially active in education. Through this entrance arch [26] of the Jesuit college in Goa once passed its 3,000 students, widely ranging in age and nationality. The Portuguese language served, in the 16th and 17th centuries, as a *lingua franca* for trade and communication throughout the Orient.

[27]

[28]

Portugal's precedence in discovery and its resulting world-wide
trade, made Lisbon [27] the greatest entrepôt in Europe.
Contemporary accounts describe the presence of 400–500 ships at
a time anchored in the Tagus estuary. ¶ King Dom Manuel I, 'the
Fortunate' (1495–1521) celebrated Portuguese pre-eminence by
founding the magnificent Jerónimos monastery at Belém [28].

[29]

[30]

¶ Indeed, a distinct architectural style, the Manueline, reflected in its details both the Portuguese obsession with the sea and echoes of Portugal's oriental adventure. Shown here are the early Manueline (1494) Igreja de Jesus in Setúbal [29], designed by Diogo Boitac, and the exuberant, later Manueline window at the Convent of Christ, Tomar [30], dated c.1510–14, attributed to Diogo de Arruda.

[31–2]

Extraordinary numbers of Portuguese sailed on risky voyages of
exploration and speculative trade. Losses were enormous – at sea,
on unknown coasts, and in battles with Turks, local princes, pirates
and rival traders. Overseas, the Portuguese lived in scattered settlements, coping with strange peoples and languages... Such
experiences, and extremes of success and disaster, bred a rich and
varied literature. Its peak was the epic *Os Lusíadas* of Camões –
himself an adventurer, and now Portugal's national poet – here
shown (in the centre) in Fernando Gomes's portrait, reputedly done
from life [31]. Numerous accounts were written of the customs of
newly contacted races, of adventurous journeys, of desperate
voyages and shipwrecks. Books described new flora and fauna,
drugs and medicine; grammars of languages were published, and
treatises on nautical technology – ship-building, the mathematics of
navigation, tables of solar declination, maps and charts... In short,
new worlds spawned a new literature. Pages from a very small
sample are shown here [32]. In Latin or by translation into vernac-
ulars, such works spread throughout Europe.

A prominent figure in the early years of the struggle was Afonso de Albuquerque, who devised an ambitious plan to occupy those ports controlling trade routes to the East. His strategic plans were largely achieved: Ormuz, at the entrance of the Persian Gulf, was taken in 1507, and Malacca, commanding the shipping route east towards the Pacific, was captured in 1511. But all attempts to close the Red Sea to the Turks by seizing Aden failed, and for years the Turks continued to harry Portuguese traders both at sea and on land. The Portuguese occupied several other positions of vital importance to trade, among them Colombo, on the island of Ceylon; Pacém, on Sumatra; Ternate, in the Moluccas; and Maçaim, Damão and Diu on the western coast of the Indian peninsula [see Map 6].

20. The Portuguese in India

'India' was the topographical name at first used by the Portuguese to describe Asia and the Orient in general, from the East Africa coast to Japan. Throughout this vast area the Portuguese established settlements: these might be forts, or factories (the name applied to a trading station), or ports with which they traded and where they then chose to put down roots. The most impressive document describing the spontaneous proliferation of settlements beyond any official pattern is the *Peregrinação* of Fernão Mendes Pinto, a fascinating volume composed by an adventurer who acted out the roles of pirate, diplomat and missionary, and who was several times shipwrecked or taken prisoner.

The main seat of Portuguese power in Asia was Goa, taken by Afonso de Albuquerque in 1510, which was to remain in Portuguese hands until 1960, when it was invaded by the Indian army. The Portuguese laid out an emporium on a European plan, with renaissance churches, of which imposing remains survive. Miscegenation between the

Portuguese rank-and-file and the local women was encouraged, which rapidly generated a Catholic Indo-Portuguese population; and by the middle of the sixteenth century it was even considered the second city of Portugal, on account of its size and splendid buildings. The Jesuits made it their base for missionary activity in the Orient, erecting seminaries attended not only by Portuguese but by the natives of numerous Asian states. In 1584 an inaugural lecture was given in sixteen languages – from so many nations came the priests who taught there. An Italian Jesuit from Goa was to translate Euclid's system of geometry into Chinese; a German Jesuit was responsible for reforming the Chinese calendar... such are merely two examples of the way aspects of European culture or science were disseminated in the East as well as Catholicism.

Commercial relations with China began at an early date. Already, by 1514, Tomé Pires, a Portuguese pharmacist, had compiled a book describing China, as well as other areas such as Malaysia, Java and Sumatra; it was translated into Italian and published in 1550. In 1515 Dom Manuel dispatched an embassy to the Chinese emperor, and its delegates, after great difficulty, achieved at last an audience at Peking. Soon, however, China reverted to what became its traditionally vigilant attitude by closing all gates to the outside world and excluding all foreigners from her shores.

But by then there were numerous independent Portuguese merchants trading in the China Sea. Defying such bans, they had established clandestine contacts between the Chinese ports and those of Japan, Manilla, Siam, Malacca, India, as well as back to Europe [see Map 8]. In spite of imperial prohibitions, virtually all foreign trade with China passed into Portuguese hands, and the Chinese themselves soon came to appreciate the arrangement. In 1557 the astute mandarin of Canton found an ingenious way to circumvent the regulations by allocating to the Portuguese a small peninsula separated from the mainland by a narrow strait: Macao. Not being physically attached to China, it could carry on activities forbidden to the Chinese; what was once a small fishing-village rapidly expanded into a highly populated emporium which, until 1675, was the only 'Chinese' trading-post. From that date until the Opium War of 1839–44, the cosmopolitan port continued to play a vital role in Oriental trading with Europe. To this day Macao remains under Portuguese administration, its principal organ of government, the 'Senado da Câmara' having been established by the merchants in 1583.

The activities of merchants were closely linked to those of missionaries. In a document of 1586 Macao is referred to as 'Porto do Nome de Deus na China' – the Harbour of God's Name in China. It served not only as the centre of trade but also as the back door by which the Jesuits infiltrated China and various Pacific communities.

As with China, commercial relations with Japan were for some time a Portuguese monopoly. Portuguese adventurers had settled on the Japanese archipelago in 1540, with their principal base at Nagasaki, where the landscape, with the town facing the sea, reminded them of Lisbon. Nagasaki was also a centre of Jesuit activity. Fernão Mendes Pinto (referred to above), one of the first Portuguese engaged in the Japan trade, gave money to St Francis Xavier to build a church, the first in Japan. Missionary influence there was so great that historians have even referred to the period 1540 to 1630 as 'The Christian Century in Japan'. However, Nagasaki was destined to become known for another reason: in 1945, by an irony of history, an American plane was diverted from its original target by bad weather and dropped the last and largest atomic bomb on Nagasaki – the traditional centre of Christianity and Western influence in Japan.

Portuguese served as the international language of commerce throughout the Orient during the seventeenth century, leaving traces in many Asian languages. At this time there were numerous Portuguese traders in Africa, and Brazil had begun its astounding growth through Amazonia and to the Andes. The Portuguese language was acquiring a global spread. Today, as the official language of some 200 million users world-wide, it ranks third numerically, after English and Spanish, among European languages. [See Map 13 on p.150.]

21. The economic consequences of expansion

This widespread dispersion of the Portuguese – throughout the Atlantic islands, Brazil, in the area of Guiné, and around the Orient – had marked consequences on both their economy and attitude to life. Garcia de Resende, a secretary to Dom João II, described in his *Miscellany* the astonishing events to which he was witness. What had been a comparatively small provincial court at Lisbon had become one of the largest in Christendom (Dom Manuel provided for some 4,000 retainers). It was the honey-pot to which all flocked in the hope of obtaining advancement. Everything depended on the king; nothing could be gained without his approval. All appointments to high office among the clergy were made by him (two of Dom João II's brothers were nominated cardinals, one at seven years of age), and all grants of land and honours to the nobility were his to distribute. Royal consent was indispensable before any commercial operation abroad was undertaken. In this way the court ceased to be merely the seat of the country's government, and became the focus of every sort of activity.

With such wealth entering the country, the king was dependent no longer on taxes and services provided by the populace, who thus lost all political influence. Legal reforms put an end to the independence of councils, and provided for the centralization of administration and the standardization of all excise. The Cortes did not meet for twenty-three years (1502–25) in spite of petitions that they should do so every decade at least. The populace also denounced the parasitical court, the excessive bureaucracy, the impoverishment of the countryside, and vociferously protested their own penury.

By the mid-century the population of Lisbon had expanded to 100,000, including some 800 wealthy entrepreneurs, and 5,000 modest artisans and tradesmen; but the rest were functionaries, clerics, squires and other retainers and hangers-on of the nobility, job-hunters, and vagrants, which created a serious imbalance between producers and consumers. The active middle class suffered in consequence, being unable to keep up in the race against an illusory middle class without any economic role, surviving on appearances and hot air. With the exodus from the productive land to the sterile cities, the situation worsened, in 1521 approaching the point of actual famine, with migrating peasants dying by the roadside, while landowners attempted to put even further pressure on the farmers to make up for their falling profits. Many people were driven to take part in risky voyages of trade overseas or in outright emigration. From this period dates the maxim: 'Those wishing to remain afloat, must choose Church, Court, or Boat.'

Oriental spices had to be paid for with the local legal tender or bartered for silver, copper, lead, fine fabrics, and so on, but these materials did not originate in Portugal, and had to be imported from northern Europe via the Portuguese factory in Flanders. Lisbon could only remain the hub of Oriental trade as long as it held the monopoly of both the trade itself and the transport of goods by sea from India, which enabled costs to be kept low. But by the middle of the sixteenth century, with the re-establishment of direct trading by the city states of Italy, prices in Portugal fell substantially. Even the Flanders factory had to be closed down and, added to this disaster, the public debt showed another dramatic increase. The State, having the monopoly of the trade in spices, sold in bulk to the great capitalists, mostly foreigners, for few Portuguese could afford to enter the market. Not only had all the luxury goods in which Lisbon indulged to be imported, but also arms, gunpowder and naval tackle were bought in – indeed, entire ships. Loans and foreign letters of credit proliferated, and by the mid-century foreign debts exceeded the annual revenue, and the interest payable equalled the value of a year's income from the spice trade. The foreign debt became four times the internal debt, and the interest to be paid abroad reached 400,000 *cruzados*, while that paid to holders of government securities accounted for only 100,000. The deficit in the balance of trade continued to widen, although disguised by the re-export of foreign goods. Even if local manufacturers maintained their output, they showed no increase in produc-tion. An emergency economy set in, with the State focusing its attention on wealth originating overseas, and distancing itself from domestic problems. In the countryside the rural community found itself increasingly cut off, with its standard of living falling. Things had little changed, when in 1580, two Venetians visiting Portugal described the lower orders as surviving on a scanty fare of salty sardines, brown bread, and very little else.

22. The cultural impact

The sheer quantity and quality of its output made the sixteenth century the 'Golden Age' of Portuguese literature. Among representative figures of this cultural renaissance were Gil Vicente, both playwright and goldsmith, whose dramas acutely analysed the changing mores of the period; Fernão Mendes Pinto, previously mentioned, who, attracted by the personality of Francis Xavier, himself briefly became a Jesuit novice, and whose *Peregrinação* vividly describes his extraordinary experiences in the Orient and the contrasting characteristics of Portuguese and various Oriental cultures; and Luís de Camões (anglicized as 'Camoens'), a member of the gentry, who to avoid the backlash from amorous adventures became an expatriate in the Orient, where he composed *Os Lusíadas* (*The Lusiads*), the first modern epic, using classical forms but dealing with contemporary subject-matter. Based on the discovery of the sea-route to India, it is the very stuff of Portuguese history, and when first published in 1572 was immediately acclaimed his master-piece, although his lyric poetry is equally remarkable. Translated into most European languages, it has long been considered *the* national epic, and its reading remains obligatory in schools. The National Day of Portugal is still celebrated on the anniversary of Camões' death, the 10th of June.

But apart from these three exceptional authors, there were hundreds of others – the names of the chroniclers João de Barros, Damião de Góis, Diogo de Couto, Lopes de Castanheda, and Gaspar Correia deserve special mention – whose historical narratives or descriptions of distant lands (their exotic customs, drugs and flora), accounts of ship-wrecks, navigational treatises, grammars and dictionaries, epic poems, relations of missionary undertakings, works of moral edification and enlightenment, and the like, remain of interest and importance. Their scrutiny of the realities of the contemporary scene beyond Portugal, so different from what they were accustomed to, led to many intellectuals taking a more critical and questioning stance. To quote Garcia da Orta, a doctor: 'One can learn more with

Portuguese in one day than in a century with the Romans.' The same inquiring attitude is reflected in the works of Duarte Pacheco, Pedro Nunes, and João de Castro.

The most impressive architectural achievements characteristic of the period are the Jeronimite monastery at Belém, the Tagus-lapped 'Tower of Belém', the Manueline choir in the Convento de Cristo, Tomar, and several other churches dispersed throughout the country. In all of them the armillary sphere (*esfera*), the personal emblem of Dom Manuel, is represented as a decorative element. His contemporaries suggested that the word *esfera* alluded, punningly, to his long wait (*espera*) before ascending the throne. In fact the armillary sphere – long in use by Portuguese cosmographers, and typifying Portugal's navigational skills and world-wide geographical extension – provided an apt heraldic symbol. As exemplifying the union of the two realms, it also appeared on the standard of the United Kingdom of Portugal-Brazil. After the proclamation of the Portuguese Republic in 1910, the armillary sphere remained an element in the national ensign, symbolizing the grandeur of the country's historical expansion.

V *Faith and Defeat*

23. The reign of Dom João III

When Dom Manuel died in 1521, and his eldest son succeeded him, the country was aware neither of the magnitude of its expansion nor of the formidable difficulties which lay ahead.

Among the epithets conferred on Dom João III was 'The Pious' (or 'The Devout') which well describes both the king and his epoch. The year in which he ascended the throne was that in which Luther's condemnation of the Catholic church precipitated the Reformation; in which the Habsburg emperor Charles V declared war on Francis I of France, thus initiating a long period of hostility between the two nations; and in which the first circumnavigation of the globe was completed by ships commanded by the Portuguese navigator Fernão de Magalhães, anglicized as 'Magellan', then in the Spanish service – a voyage leading to territorial claims that were to cause further rivalry between Portugal and Spain.

Although committed to protect the unity of Catholic Europe (with the help of the Inquisition, the Jesuits, and the reform of its university), the Portuguese scrupulously avoided any involvement in the European wars, regardless of the fact that Charles V was Dom João's brother-in-law (for he had married the emperor's sister, Catarina, the parents of both being Philip 'the Handsome' and Joana 'La Loca' – the

Mad). The Portuguese preferred to broaden their zone of influence and proselytise Christianity elsewhere in the world, especially in the Far East and in Brazil.

The enormous effort required to hold together a world empire, and actively to support a militant Faith, were the two outstanding features of Portugal's evolution which – as will be described later – caused the disaster of Alcácer-Quiber, and the collapse of the Avis dynasty in 1580.

24. The Counter-Reformation

A king with such deep religious convictions as Dom João III needed little excuse to petition the pope in 1531 to introduce the Inquisition into Portugal. He had also an urgent need to procure sufficient financial backing – which the Crown then lacked – to meet the increasing cost of maintaining the empire. Since many of the larger fortunes remained in the hands of the Jews and the 'New' Christians, these might be confiscated to the Crown's advantage, under papal decrees to root out heresy.

As a consequence of the forced conversions imposed by Dom Manuel, a new community – the 'New Christians', or *Marranos*, or Crypto-Jews – had developed, whose members, ostensibly faithful adherents of the Catholic church, continued to practise Jewish rites in secret. It was within this cultured community that most practitioners of the medical, legal, and teaching professions were to be found, but their activities in financial and fiscal domains made them unpopular in general among the lower strata of society.

A Bull foisting the Inquisition onto Portugal was not issued until 1536, and then only after fierce opposition from Jews in the pope's entourage. The first *auto-da-fé* took place in Lisbon in 1541. According to the most reliable figures, in the 143 years between that date and 1684, 1,379 people were burned in Portugal. The rate of executions then noticeably decreased, although some relapsed Crypto-Jews were still being dragged to the stake seventy years later.

While the *auto-da-fé* provided the most notorious and horrifying image of the Inquisition's activities, there were many other less spectacular but equally repressive methods by which the authority of the 'Holy Office' was imposed on the population with the excuse of extirpating heresy. The book trade was closely supervised: strict control was exercised over what books might be imported, and all texts had to be scrutinized and to receive the 'Imprimatur' of the Holy Office before their publication was permitted. Books previously printed were censored; the possession or reading of any title on the 'Index' was prohibited. In this way the Inquisition, controlled by the Dominicans, was able to inhibit all intellectual activity and isolate Portugal (and Spain) from the main currents of European thought.

More constructive in its outcome was the king's personal initiative whereby the Society of Jesus (the Jesuits) was introduced into Portugal in 1537, only three years after its slender beginnings. This order devoted itself to the dissemination of Christianity in the Orient and Brazil, and to education. By the second half of the century, and in the following two centuries, secondary education, freely available to students from all strata of society, was almost entirely under their control. (Among major buildings in Lisbon once part of their property are the Hospital of São José, the Misericórdia, and the old Faculty of Science; and towns throughout the country still use their colleges and seminaries.) The propagation of some of their own publications was phenomenal: Pedro da Fonseca's *Dialectics* (1564) was reissued in every Catholic country of Europe, while the grammar compiled by Manuel Álvares went into almost five hundred editions and still served as a schoolbook in the early years of the nineteenth century.

The cultural influence of the Jesuits' prodigious missionary activity has been referred to already. Over 1,000 missionaries radiated from India; some 250 suffered martyrdom in China, Japan and the Moluccas. Over 500 were occupied propagating the Faith in Brazil; the Jesuits landed there in 1549, under the aegis of Tomé de Sousa, the first governor, and immediately set about converting the Indians. Manuel da Nóbrega, together with other members of the Society, pushed into the hinterland in order to make closer contact with the natives, and founded the college of São Paulo, a settlement that developed into the present metropolis.

In 1547, with the intention of purging impurities and possible heretical contamination, the king instigated a drastic reform of the university, founded in Lisbon during the reign of Dom Fernando but by then in sad decline. He conceived a project for transforming it into a major centre of learning which by the quality of its teaching would rank among the foremost in Europe; with this end in view its seat was transferred to Coimbra, where it settled permanently. Professors in the fields of theology, law and canon law, medicine, classical learning and the humanities, were invited to teach there. Many were Portuguese who had distinguished themselves in foreign educational establishments; and these academics were not only granted substantial privileges but paid higher salaries than those of any other peninsular university – even that of Salamanca.

Dom João III also founded a College of Arts, a form of preparatory school for those later intending to go up to the university, and André de Gouveia, then at Bordeaux, was invited to set it up. He brought with him a group of eminent scholars – among them his fellow humanist George Buchanan – and within a few months of its opening the college numbered 1,200 students. However, it was not long before some of its teachers were suspected of having

Lutheran sympathies, and the college was placed in the predatory hands of the more inflexible Jesuits.

25. Dom Sebastião, 'The Desired'

On Dom João III's death in 1557, his grandson, Dom Sebastião, aged three, inherited the throne, for his father, the Infante João, had predeceased him by a few weeks. The Portuguese had awaited the child's birth with some anxiety, for he was the king's only grandson, and the one hope of continuity for the House of Avis. He was referred to as 'O Desejado' (The Desired) even before his birth; and after his death he was also known as 'The Regretted'. His widowed mother, Catarina of Austria, acted as Regent until he was fourteen, when Cardinal Henry, a brother of Dom João III, took over. Brought up in an atmosphere dominated by bigoted and militant ecclesiastics, he came to regard himself as 'God's own captain', an instrument providentially placed to eradicate the heretics and enemies then infesting Christendom.

His personal reign lasted hardly a decade, during which problems in the Orient accumulated; even his mother had remarked that 'keeping India was indeed a miracle'. The idea of an empire in North Africa appealed to him as more viable than the one in the distant East, which was taking shape only too gradually. And North Africa awoke in him the chivalric idea of a new crusade against the Muslim. Although the foolhardy project met with strong opposition in influential governmental and court circles, as soon as the young man took over control of affairs in 1568 he surrounded himself with callow counsellors who confidently backed his rash and extravagant mission: to marshal a huge force which would land and eradicate Islam in the Maghreb and install a Christian empire in its place.

Internal dissension in the Moroccan kingdoms provided

the opportunity, for in 1576 Sherif Muley Abdelmalik, allied to the Turks of Algiers, had seized the throne; and this, in Dom Sebastião's eyes, posed a serious threat to European Christendom; his expedition, a crusade, would end it. Leading 17,000 men in person, he disembarked at Tangiers and advanced inland to Alcácer-Quibir, where awaiting him was the Moroccan king with a force of 40,000 cavalry. The Portuguese were surrounded and utterly routed. Half their number were taken prisoner; half were slaughtered; among the dead lay Dom Sebastião.

His fate profoundly unnerved the country, as it would almost certainly precipitate Portugal's loss of independence, although rumours were rife that the young king had in fact escaped, and would shortly return. Indeed, several impostors exploiting this conviction tried to pass themselves off as 'The Desired': among them were a potter's son from Alcobaça, who was condemned to the galleys; Mateus Álvares, from the Azores, fomented a rising among peasants near Torres Vedras, and was hanged; a pastry-cook from Madrigal (near Salamanca, in Spain) took up the role as part of a monkish plot to stir up a revolt against Philip II – he and Mário Túlio, an Italian adventurer who convinced several exiled Portuguese nobles, both ended on the gallows.

Much later, on 2 June 1640, when the Duke of Braganza was proclaimed king of Portugal, he promised to hand back the crown to Dom Sebastião should he ever return! 'Sebastianism' lasted long in the minds of the populace, assuming a form of messianism (particularly among the Crypto-Jews) during this period of collective distress, in expectation of some saviour who would alleviate their condition. Sebastianism also surfaced in Brazil, translated there by immigrants, and was taken up by the slave population in the north-east. One of its last dramatic manifestations took place there as late as 1897. Known as the 'war of the

Canudos', this broke out in a disaffected area, provoked by the ravings of António Conselheiro, a trouble-maker who predicted Dom Sebastião's return at the millennium, bringing justice to the hungry and destitute. It took several military expeditions to restore order, and resulted in the virtual extinction of the indigenous population.

Dom Sebastião was succeeded by Cardinal Dom Henrique, a son of Dom Manuel. His main preoccupation was with his own succession, for as he was childless, the crown would normally pass to his nephews, grandchildren of Dom Manuel. In this line of succession stood Philip II of Spain; Catarina, Duchess of Braganza (a daughter of Dom Duarte); and António, Prior of Crato (an illegitimate son of the Infante Dom Luís, whose mother was a New Christian).

Philip II was not slow to realize that this was a great opportunity to unify the Iberian Peninsula under one crown, nor did he for a moment imagine that his just claim would be contested. The majority of the Portuguese nobility surviving the Moroccan disaster thought such a union desirable, while the main entrepreneurs were in favour, foreseeing greater profits from cross-border commerce, and the powerful Spanish fleet protecting their trade routes. However, the rest of the country preferred to side with the Prior of Crato, as he was at least Portuguese, not Castilian. The decrepit cardinal-king was inclined towards the succession of Catarina of Braganza, Portuguese like himself, but to resolve the problem he summoned the Cortes to Almeirim, for this was a legal matter for them to decide. They must appoint *definidores* to advise. Unfortunately, Dom Henrique died before any decision had been made. Prior António's faction declared him king at adjacent Santarém; troops commanded by the Duke of Alba were under orders from Philip to invade and seize the country by force. Although António's forces put up some resistance at the gates of Lisbon (and received ineffective support from an English expedition), they were rapidly defeated and Alba marched into the capital. António attempted to carry on the struggle in the northern provinces. He then fled to England, and then France, from where, for some years, he obstinately but unsuccessfully continued to stir up trouble, while in Portugal several of his followers were executed.

In 1581 the Cortes, meeting at Tomar, gave in, solemnly proclaiming Philip II of Spain Philip I of Portugal.

26. The Spanish domination: 1580–1640
The 'Domínio filipino' is the name given to the sixty-year period during which the country was ruled by the Philips II, III and IV of Spain under the dual monarchy. Many Portuguese refer to these decades as the 'Spanish Captivity'.

The first Philip had assured the assembly at Tomar that he would respect the following principles: that only the Portuguese Cortes would make laws for Portugal; that both the language and the currency would remain unchanged; that the administrators would be Portuguese (and Portuguese might also be appointed to official positions in Spain); and that the African and Indian trade would remain entirely in Portuguese hands. These conditions ensured a wide margin of autonomy and, in fact, were respected by the Spaniards for several years; later, they were eroded and violated. It has been suggested that had Philip chosen to make Lisbon his capital, rather than Madrid, the future history of the Peninsula might have been very different.

Life carried on through the period of political stability and economic well-being. Trading with India continued, although less profitably, as shipping losses were on the increase and new enemies surfaced, principally the English and Dutch. But these losses were partly offset by the profits from Brazil, which had grown to become both the world's largest sugar producer and one of the main suppliers of tobacco, for smoking that weed had caught on in Europe, and provided a growing source of revenue.

Some of the more grandiose of Portuguese buildings were erected during this period, among them the New Cathedral at Coimbra, São Vicente de Fora at Lisbon, together with a number of imposing palaces put up by the nobility. In Lisbon itself there was a Viceroy, but no court as such, which had consequences of some importance: the extravagance of the former court, a frequent reason for popular complaint, ceased to burden the budget, and taxes were able to remain at their former level, even if they were no less irksome. Both nobles and the mercantile classes began to appreciate that they might gain more than lose by the sacrifice of their independence. With no court to attend, many nobles went to farm their estates, often employing slaves; but this worsened the plight of both the rural middle classes and the agricultural labourers.

Meanwhile, Spain's maritime power was repeatedly under assault. English pirates continued to prowl both the Atlantic and Pacific in pursuit of Spanish galleons. If, as was said at the time, 'the sea was an emerald in the sandal of the king of Spain, the sun a topaz in his crown', these were treasures to be plundered. Maritime rivalry was accentuated by religious differences, for Elizabeth of England supported the Protestant cause and all enemies of Spain, while Philip was the champion of Catholicism, fomenting conspiracies to reinstate Mary Stuart to the English throne; and it was the execution of Mary which precipitated war between the two powers. Philip determined to attack and seize England, but such an undertaking required a huge fleet. This fleet, which included thirty-one large Portuguese vessels, eventually assembled in the broad Tagus estuary in 1588 before weighing anchor and sailing to its destruction. Of the initial two hundred men-of-war constituting Philip's 'Invincible Armada', only fifty-one limped home. This was perhaps the first serious setback suffered by Portugal in her union with Spain, and one which had long-term repercussions.

After 1621 conditions changed dramatically. Spain, then under Philip IV, had to contend against immense difficulties. Her coffers were drained by her long involvement in European wars. The silver-mines of Peru were exhausted. Attacks made on Portuguese trading-posts became increasingly frequent. Ormuz fell to the English in 1623, and the Brazilian capital itself was occupied by the Dutch for two years before they were expelled. Between 1623 and 1638 some 500 Portuguese vessels had been seized by Spain's enemies: the English, French and Dutch. The decline of Spain brought down Portugal as well [see Map 9], a trend becoming increasingly obvious to both the mercantile and general population. It was they who paid the taxes, an attempt at raising which provoked a revolt in the Alentejo in 1637. For some months this spread unchecked, until eventually it was put down with the aid of Spanish troops.

VI *Portugal Restored*

27. The restoration

Growing dissatisfaction with the Spanish Count-Duke of Olivares's policy of centralization, which aimed at reducing the individual Iberian states to mere administrative provinces, caused insurrection in both Catalonia and Portugal.

It was after receiving orders to go and put down the Catalan rebellion that the Portuguese nobles decided to act. On the first morning of December 1640 they converged on the royal palace at Lisbon, which stood on the west side of what is now familiarly known as 'Black Horse Square', where, having overcome the guards, they assassinated Miguel de Vasconcelos, the obnoxious minister, and compelled the Duchess of Mantua, then acting as Viceroy, to order the non-interference of the Castilian garrison stationed in the castle of São Jorge.

Their plan was to place Dom João, the Duke of Braganza, resident in Vila Viçosa, on the throne. He was a grandson of the female claimant of 1580 and a descendant of Dom Afonso, a bastard of Dom João I. Well aware of the risks involved by agreeing, it was not for a fortnight after the Lisbon *coup* that he consented to be proclaimed king as Dom João IV.

The revolution sparked off an enthusiastic nationwide response, echoes of which reverberated throughout Brazil,

Angola, and other former possessions, only Ceuta voting to remain loyal to Madrid. A growing feeling of revulsion towards the domination of Spain had entered the Portuguese psyche, which was to remain a permanent feature. It was strong enough then to enable hostilities with Spain to be sustained until 1668. The optional use of Portuguese or Castilian, whether spoken or written, common during the late sixteenth century, was certainly no longer tolerated after the Restoration. In the words of a popular maxim: 'Do not expect either a good wind or a good marriage from Spain.'

28. The struggle for a place in Europe

Among the more serious problems posed by placing the Braganzas on the throne was Portugal's position in the context of European conflicts and interests. During the Spanish domination, Portugal was part of the powerful Habsburg inheritance, so that its enemies were France, England and Holland; but once the Portuguese had shaken off the Spanish yoke, they attempted, at first unsuccessfully, to obtain the support of these traditional adversaries of Spain.

Different procedures were followed in dealings with different courts – those of Rome, Paris, London and Amsterdam. In Rome, Spanish influence was still strong enough to prevent Dom João IV being recognized until peace with Spain had been made in 1668. However, the Portuguese had great hopes, in view of Cardinal Richelieu's promises, of gaining the support of France. Due to political machinations in Paris, negotiations failed to achieve any agreement. The idea of a formal league, which might be the basis of future foreign policy, was quashed; instead, in 1656, France signed a peace treaty with Spain at St Jean de Luz in which France still accepted Spain's sovereignty over Portugal as long as the Spanish agreed to an amnesty by which the rebel province and the Duke of Braganza would be pardoned. Deviously, at the same time, France allowed troops to be raised on her territory to assist the Portuguese; 500 officers and artillerymen, led by the Count of Schomberg, entered Portugal and entirely reorganized Portuguese forces – an intervention that was to prove vital to the successful outcome of continuing hostilities between Portugal and her neighbour.

As far as England was concerned, in 1642 António de Sousa de Macedo, the Portuguese ambassador, had little difficulty in getting the new government accredited; but then, not long after, he took the side of Charles I in his struggle against Parliament, which threatened retaliation. Portuguese support for the Stuarts led in 1649 to Prince Rupert and his brother Maurice making the Tagus estuary the base of the Royalist squadron in the naval war against the Parliamentarians, from which they preyed on English merchant shipping. Cromwell retaliated by dispatching a flotilla under Admiral Blake to blockade the mouth of the Tagus, but the Royalists eventually escaped into the Mediterranean. Partly in reprisal, in 1654 the Parliamentarians imposed the Treaty of Westminster on Portugal, demanding the right to trade with the Portuguese colonies, freedom of worship for British subjects in Portugal, and freedom from arrest without compensation, unless with the consent of the Judge Conservador. Dom João, having religious scruples, hesitated to ratify the treaty, but great pressure was brought to bear.

Happily, the temporary frigidity between the two countries melted on the restoration of the Stuarts. Charles II had not forgotten the services rendered to his father by the former Portuguese ambassador, and in gratitude honoured one of his sons with a baronetcy. In this cordial context a marriage was arranged between Charles and the daughter of

Dom João IV, Catherine 'of Braganza', with her dowry fixed at two million *cruzados* and the gift of both Tangiers and Bombay. This, and the Treaty of Alliance of 23 June 1661, brought about a return to the amicable relationship that the two powers had enjoyed in the sixteenth century.

As for Holland, a peace negotiated in 1641 was disrupted by Dutch attacks in Brazil, Africa, São Tomé, India and Ceylon. For years Portuguese and Dutch diplomats coped with the incompatible situation of peace in Europe and intermittent hostilities around the world, until 1657, when a Dutch fleet sailed to Lisbon with a formal declaration of war (although prevented from actually entering the Tagus by the presence there of an English squadron). It was not until 1661 that peace was achieved with an agreement by which the Portuguese retained their Brazilian and African possessions but ceded territories in the Orient. It took several years to offset the war debt.

29. The Revolution of 1668

The House of Braganza ruled from 1640, with the accession of Dom João IV, until the proclamation of the Republic in 1910. At the very start, in 1641, it was beset by severe economic and political problems. That part of the nobility which had collaborated with the Spaniards, together with some of the higher-ranking clergy, set out to topple the monarchy. The revolt was put down boldly by beheading those that led it, among them the Duke of Caminha and the Marquis of Vila Real and his son. Not long after, Francisco de Lucena, the minister of state responsible for carrying out these executions, was himself put to death for his involvement in another plot. The healthy Portuguese reaction to Spanish domination made it impossible for any absolutist regime to rule without opposition.

Dom João IV died in 1656, when Dom Afonso VI was still

a minor, and during the next six years his mother, Dona Luísa de Gusmão, ruled firmly but with moderation. However, the young king suffered severe physical disabilities and was mentally disturbed, making him scarcely fit to govern. In 1662 the Count of Castelo Melhor, an ambitious young noble, brought pressure to bear on the Regent to withdraw from the scene and installed himself as prime minister.

His government showed some energy in carrying on the war of independence from Spain during a vital phase. Portuguese troops won several decisive combats, for Spain was exhausted after defeats on the European battlefields, and could no longer take the offensive, even against a comparatively weak adversary. Castelo Melhor considered the time was ripe to redouble military efforts in order to gain substantial advantages when peace came. To martial exertions he added diplomatic activity and as a ploy to attract French co-operation he arranged for the king to marry Maria-Francisca-Isabel of Savoy (or Mademoiselle d'Aumale), daughter of the Duc de Nemours. In 1667, the year after the marriage by proxy, a military alliance with France was concluded.

The marriage was to cause a domestic crisis. The nobles, tiring of the war he persevered in carrying on, had tired of Castelo Melhor. There were rumours too that the king was impotent, which would put Portuguese independence at risk again. As it was unlikely that there would be any prince from that quarter, the nobility rallied round the king's virile brother, Dom Pedro, who would in any case inherit the crown in the absence of a legitimate son. The unsatisfied queen and Dom Pedro came to an understanding: first, she persuaded the king to dismiss Castelo Melhor; next she fled the palace to take refuge in a convent, from there insisting that the cathedral chapter annul her marriage on the grounds of her husband's impotence. Thus abandoned, the king was compelled to sign a document relinquishing his kingdom in favour of Dom Pedro and his legitimate children, with the proviso that he would receive an annual income of 100,000 *cruzados*. He was then shipped to the Azores, and from there, after several years under duress, was brought back to the mainland, to be kept in virtual isolation at the royal palace at Sintra. The *azulejo* floor of his chamber is said to have been worn away by his incessant pacing. He died in 1683.

Meanwhile, the chapter having declared her former marriage void on the grounds of non-consummation, the queen married Dom Pedro, who remained Regent until his brother's demise. It has been suggested that these extraordinary events were instigated by the 'French cabal' at court (political agents who had entered Portugal with the queen), and the whole episode has given rise to much speculation. Whatever the truth, the overriding factor was a desire for the maintenance of independence, although rivalry amongst the nobles surfaced again as soon as Castelo Melhor had left the political arena.

In 1668 a peace treaty was signed between Portugal and Spain, in which her independence was recognized, and all villages and prisoners seized during the war were exchanged. Only Ceuta continued Spanish, as it had voted to do in 1640, and has since remained.

30. The reign of Dom Pedro II
On succeeding to the throne in 1683, Dom Pedro II found himself beset by serious domestic problems. The defence of Portugal's overseas settlements against the Dutch (and others) had undermined State finances and taxes were increased. Rural distress led to increased emigration, chiefly to Brazil, which the government tried in vain to restrain.

Brazil was becoming increasingly rich from agricultural

exports, especially sugar, but the consequent demand for European goods did little to boost Portuguese manufacture because colonial imports could be exchanged for goods imported from elsewhere.

In 1675 a book entitled *O Discurso Sobre a Introdução das Artes no Reino* (A Discourse on the Introduction of the Arts into the Kingdom – 'arts' in this context meaning 'industries') caused a sensation. Its author, Duarte Ribeiro de Macedo, was a Portuguese diplomat resident in France. He expounded Colbert's policy: the State should intervene actively to promote national manufacture and production so that the value of its exports would exceed that of all imports, as reckoned in gold.

In that same year the Count of Ericeira was appointed Chancellor of the Exchequer, and tried to introduce this 'Mercantilist' system. The production of woollen goods was revived in areas where it had formerly flourished (at Covilhã, Fundão, and Estremoz), with the State recruiting skilled workers and, to protect internal production, banning (or at least making extremely difficult) the importation of foreign cloth. Within a few years there were 400 weavers at work in Covilhã. Tanneries, glass-works, and silk-spinning mills were set up. One of the suburbs of Lisbon was even called 'Amoreiras' after its mulberry plantations, and the government distributed prizes to those who planted the largest numbers of these trees, as one way in which to stimulate the breeding of silk-worms.

Significant changes were noticeable in the countryside: for example, maize was introduced throughout the provinces north of the Douro, replacing rye in the making of bread, so that maize bread became a staple in peasant diet; and vineyards were extended in the region of the Douro, so that by the end of the seventeenth century wine, particularly Port wine, had become one of Portugal's main exports, its marketing handled by English factors who supervised its production and transport direct to England.

31. The War of the Spanish Succession

As for foreign policy, the government aligned itself with England as long as this did not clash with Portugal's European interests.

One major example of this alignment occurred in the War of the Spanish Succession. Carlos II of Spain had died in 1700, which gave rise to a long-anticipated problem. He had two sisters, one married to Louis XIV of France, the other to the Habsburg emperor, Leopold I. Both these powers laid claim to succession to the Spanish throne. Although, after much shilly-shallying, in his will Carlos had named Philip, Duke of Anjou, Louis XIV's grandson, as his successor, this decision was unacceptable to Leopold, who declared war.

Initially Portugal sided with the French bloc; however, 'The Grand Alliance' had been formed, in which England, the Low Countries and Austria united against France, and after two years Portugal was drawn into this league. To reinforce the English connection, the government signed the Methuen Treaty in 1703, which gave Britain exceptional trade privileges and had far-reaching consequences for Portugal.

Military operations on the Portuguese-Spanish frontier, starting in 1704, dragged on for eight years; in 1706 an Anglo-Portuguese army entered Madrid, where the Habsburg pretender, the Archduke Charles III, one of Leopold's sons, although acclaimed king, was defeated soon after at Almansa. The Treaty of Utrecht brought the conflict to an end in 1713. This brought some advantages to Portugal, notably in Brazil where, in the north, Portuguese rights to both banks of the Amazon were recognized (French claims being withdrawn), while in the south the frontier was extended to the River Plate (Spanish claims to the colony of Sacramento being abandoned).

32. Brazilian gold
In the meantime, gold had been discovered in Brazil. After a century of prospecting, rich deposits had been located some 400 kilometres from the coast in the region of the present state of Minas Gerais. Being alluvial gold, its exploitation could be carried out in the most elementary way.

The first cargo – some 500 kilograms – reached Lisbon in 1699. Deliveries increased dramatically during the following years, in 1720 totalling 25,000 kilograms. No accurate data survives of the overall amount which entered the capital, but it has been estimated at 1,000–3,000 tonnes. In 1730 diamond mines were discovered and by the end of the century production had amounted to over 2 million carats [see Map 10].

The exploitation of these precious commodities was undertaken by private companies, the State only imposing a tax, originally fixed at a fifth of the amount extracted, but as the miners would evade paying this by all possible means its collection was never easy. Repressive measures taken to put a stop to smuggling were naturally resented, provoking the first anti-Portuguese demonstrations, and proving a source of constant discontent.

VII *The Reforms of the Eighteenth Century*

33. The reign of Dom João V

The influx of Brazilian gold enabled Dom João V to carry out policies to raise the prestige of the monarchy, which had suffered in the vicissitudes of its Restoration.

From a social standpoint, the nation had kept up with the general development of western Europe during the first half of the seventeenth century and, in spite of problems caused by the hounding of New Christians, the mercantile bourgeoisie had prospered and their future influence in politics was to be more pronounced, notably during the government of the Marquis de Pombal. Politically, the State was by then imbued with the philosophy of absolutism current at that period, although in Portugal this was manifest largely in courtly ceremonial and grandiloquent formulae rather than in any regal authority asserted by the king. The epoch is characterized by the lethargy and inefficiency of governmental institutions, by the king's supine failure to curb the sway of the Inquisition, by the increasing prominence of the privileged classes, and by the diminishing effectiveness of the central administration. Its external politics were guided by a wish to avoid involvement in international disputes and to enhance the tarnished prestige of the House of Braganza. Culturally, the first half of the eighteenth century was characterized by conservatism, but also by a growing interest in the scientific and literary activity then proliferating throughout Europe. Material evidence of the gold boom may be seen in the extravagantly gilded woodwork (*talha*) of numerous baroque churches and in the erection of the gigantic royal convent-palace at Mafra, a monument only to the temporal power and ostentation of the Church, not to the country as a whole.

The Turks at this time had occupied the Peloponnese and threatened to blockade the Adriatic. Induced by Pope Clement XI, the Portuguese attacked the Turkish navy and won a resounding victory at Matapan (1717). In Lisbon this was hailed as a national triumph but essentially served only to enhance Dom João's international prestige.

As the mid-century approached, an increasing awareness grew among the élite that it was time for radical changes in Portuguese society and culture. The Jesuits still dominated education, following routines virtually unchanged since the sixteenth century, and the Inquisition still retained its position of power, insulating the country from the bracing winds of change blowing from Europe. Many Portuguese who lived in exile due to religious intolerance, and others, such as diplomats in foreign capitals, openly supported any scheme to modernize the country and bring it into line with the rest of Europe. They were referred to as the *estrangeirados*, the foreignized.

Among the more distinguished were Luís António Verney, author of the famous *True Method of Study* (1747), in which he advocated not only a radical change in the whole philosophy of teaching but also a radical change in the Portuguese 'mentality'. But the *estrangeirado* who made the most profound impression was Sebastião José de Carvalho e Melo, a former diplomat in both London and Vienna, who was invited to enter the government in 1750, the year Dom José succeeded his father Dom João V. He became better known to history by his title when ennobled: the Marquês de Pombal.

34. The government of Pombal

During his time in London, Pombal had been much impressed by the progress made by the English middle class and by their commercial organization. He had likewise absorbed the ideals of enlightened absolutism when in Austria (and his wife was Austrian). A man of immense energy, it was not long before he entirely dominated Dom José, who handed over to him the reigns of government.

In 1755 a violent earthquake shattered Lisbon, razing large areas. Although several palaces and other grand buildings partly survived the widespread destruction, Pombal would not permit their restoration: indeed, his enemies have said that his demolitions caused more damage than had the earthquake. Pombaline Lisbon reflected the Pombaline State. The rebuilding of the capital by a team of architects under Pombal's direction was designed as if on entirely level ground, in an authoritarian manner on a rectilineal plan, with the same design imposed on all edifices built for private use. No external display was allowed which might indicate the social status of the occupant, while the heights of church façades were not to exceed those of adjacent structures. A range of government offices, with shops at ground level, were constructed on the site of the former water-lapped royal palace – the old Paço da Ribeira – and flanked three sides of the adjacent square, with the Tagus on the fourth. And even the name of the square was changed, from the time-honoured Terreiro do Paço to Praça do Comércio (although frequently known as 'Black Horse Square'). Commerce, in Pombal's ideology, was the basis of the nation's strength.

Any opposition to royal authority was ruthlessly crushed. An attempt to assassinate Dom José in 1758 served as a pretext to execute, with exemplary but needless cruelty, several members of the higher-ranking nobility. The Jesuits, accused of complicity, were expelled, and their immense wealth confiscated. By this *coup* the all-powerful minister won his long struggle with the Jesuits in Portugal, and subsequently, by expulsion, in Brazil as well. But that was not enough. With the support of Spain and France he urged that Pope Clement XIV abolish the Society altogether, and he even submitted the Bull of abolition to the king in advance of its promulgation.

Several legal and fiscal reforms were carried out, and all distinction between 'Old' and 'New' Christians was obliterated. Although the Inquisition lost its former authority, control by censorship was transferred to the 'Real Mesa Censória', a body accountable to the State, and as the work of such authors as Hobbes, Voltaire and Rousseau remained prohibited, little change took place in this respect.

The reorganization of commercial processes was carried out through the agency of large, privately financed companies, whose monopolies were guaranteed by the State. Some of these attempted to integrate the Portuguese economy with that of her colonies, notably Brazil. It is not unreasonable to credit Pombal with having created a Portuguese 'commonwealth'. Trade was deemed a noble activity, with entrepreneurs being awarded coats of arms; and an 'Aula de Comércio' was set up, a prestigious business school at which mathematics, accountancy, and aspects of banking such as currency exchange were taught to employees.

Among his more important interventions was the setting up in 1756 of the 'Companhia de Agricultura das Vinhas do Alto Douro', to restrict the area of Port wine vineyards, which had expanded in an entirely uncontrolled way during previous decades, and thus protect the larger Portuguese entrepreneurs and encourage them to compete with the British exporters in Oporto.

Important reforms also took place in the field of education.

With the expulsion of the Jesuits, State-funded primary and secondary schools were established throughout the country. In 1772 a radical reform of the university took place, which was considered in advance of its time, in which the progressive innovations of the *estrangeirados* were taken up (even if many of them were not yet allowed to return).

These various programmes of reform were rigorously enforced in the face of strong opposition. The jails were crammed with political prisoners, principally nobles who had objected and found themselves detained indefinitely.

35. Volte-face

The only authority sustaining Pombal, and enabling him to push through these reforms at absolute discretion, was that of the king. And when Dom José became seriously ill towards the end of 1776 and Dona Maria became Regent, Pombal's days were numbered. Before his death, the king had made two requests to his daughter: that all political prisoners should be amnestied, and that she should protect all those who had served him faithfully during his reign. The period of transition which followed became known as the *Viradeira*, the volte-face. Pombal's adversaries assumed that his removal from the scene would mean an immediate and fundamental about-turn in Portuguese politics, but the queen remained cautious. Other ministers – even Pombal's son, who was the 'Presidente do Senado da Câmara de Lisboa' – retained their posts. However, demonstrators in the streets of the capital clamoured for the despotic statesman's death. The coach trundling him to exile in his home town of Pombal (south-west of Coimbra) was stoned. The exultant mob broke open prison gates, liberating some 800 of those confined, and the fort of Junqueira, one of the main places of incarceration, was razed by the rioters.

Among matters requiring urgent attention were the alle-

[33]

[34]

The young Dom Sebastião (1557–78) led a crusade against the Muslim Berbers in Morocco. The Christians, mostly Portuguese, were disastrously defeated (1578) in the sands of Alcácer-Quibir [33]. The king was killed, Portugal ruined. Two years later, King Philip II of Spain 'united' Spain and Portugal. ¶ Spanish Dominicans enforced a rigorous Inquisition [34] in which – despite Jesuit advocacy – New Christians (converted Jews), on whose financial and mercantile skills and connections much of Portugal's trading prosperity relied, were particularly afflicted. Some were burnt; many were ruined and emigrated. The handling of Portugal's entrepôt trade (and its profits) passed substantially into the hands of foreigners, notably those of the British.

[35]

[36]

Under Philip II, the relatively open trading enterprise of Lisbon was subordinated to the rigid control and fanaticism of Madrid. Iberian resources – finance, ship-building, expert mariners and soldiers – were poured into warfare in the Netherlands and into creating the 'Invincible Armada' against England. The destruction of the great armada [35] (1588) and three subsequent armadas, as well as other disasters, left Portuguese administrators and factors overseas without any supplies or reinforcements to meet increasing Dutch and English attacks.

[37]

[38]

¶ These attacks were stimulated by Jan van Linschoten. Before Spain's take-over, he was secretary to the Portuguese Bishop of Goa. In his influential *Itinerario* he portrayed the riches of *Ásia Portuguesa* [36], ripe for plucking, and revealed the invaluable Portuguese 'rutters' – most secret instructions for piloting eastern seas and harbours. ¶ The Dutch displaced the Portuguese in the East Indies, Ceylon and the Cape, and seized ports and forts on the Guinea coast (here Annobon [37]). They occupied a substantial part of Brazil [38] until finally expelled in 1654.

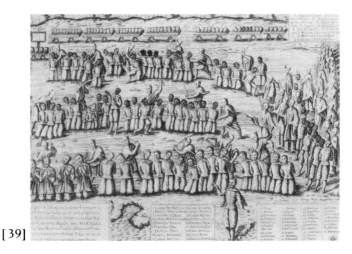

[39]

[40]

That mighty Portugal should be defeated by Muslim forces and occupied by another European power, encouraged local rulers and traders, as well as foreign rivals, to contest her dominance. The Persians, assisted by English ships, re-captured Hormuz (1622). The Japanese, who doubted the patriotism of converts to Christianity, martyred and expelled foreign priests and closed the country to foreigners for 200 years. Members of a last Portuguese embassy (1640) were executed, except those allowed to convey the news [39]. ¶ In 1640, the Portuguese rebelled against their 'Babylonian

[41]

[42]

captivity' by Spain. The Duke of Braganza, precariously, became king. To secure support against Spain, his daughter Catherine [40] was married in 1662 to the impecunious Charles II of England. Money apart, her rich dowry included Bombay [41], reluctantly surrendered by the Portuguese viceroy who foresaw English expansion in India. Portugal's independence was finally accepted by Spain in 1666. By 1700, when this view of Lisbon was engraved [42] the port was prosperous again, this time chiefly from the fast expanding trade of Brazil.

[43]

[44]

The settlement of Brazil in the 1530s, aimed (uniquely among South American colonies) at agricultural development. Settlers did not expect, though, to toil unaided in the heat, and sugar – the most profitable crop – was extremely laborious to plant, harvest and process [43]. The Amerindians, however, were hunter-gatherers; they found regular work for wages meaningless, and proved acutely susceptible to European diseases. Moreover, they were protected by the influential Jesuit, António Vieira [44] and other missionaries – with partial success – from forced labour and exploitation by the

[45]

[46]

planters, chiefly by being collected into mission villages. Traders then diverted across the Atlantic part of the ancient, cruel African slave trade, previously conducted overland north and east to Islamic countries [45]. ¶ From the early 17th century, the *bandeirantes* (bands of mixed races) undertook extraordinary explorations into the vast, unknown interior of Brazil, discovering alluvial gold in the 1730s [46], then diamonds and other precious stones, and in the process opening up the country to missionary, planter, cattleman and merchant.

[47]

[48]

The riches of Brazil made Dom João V the wealthiest monarch in Europe. He spent lavishly, especially on architectural monuments, such as the vast convent-cathedral-palace of Mafra and the exquisite library he gave to the University of Coimbra [47]. ¶ Lisbon had become 'the most visibly rich of cities' when it was struck by the Great Earthquake of 1755 – the worst ever experienced in Europe. Some 15,000 people were killed. Many survivors commemorated their salvation in votive *milagres* given to churches [48]. The tidal wave which followed the earthquake, and the fires that continued for a week, destroyed a third of the city.

[49]

[50]

¶ The Marquis of Pombal (1699–1782) – to use his subsequent, familiar title – was given dictatorial powers by the king to deal with the crisis: besides immediate measures to secure order and succour, he organized the re-building of the city [49]. ¶ Pombal reduced the powers of the nobility, the privileges of foreign traders (chiefly British), expelled the Jesuits and revived Portugal's industry, agriculture and finances. Many fine edifices were built in his time in a Portuguese-Baroque style, a typical, modest example being this church in Viseu begun in 1775 [50] designed by António da Costa Faro.

[51]

[52]

In 1807 Britain alone still opposed Napoleon and Portugal alone refused to close her ports to British trade. A French army of 25,000 invaded Portugal; only 2,000 reached Lisbon: a scorched earth policy, effectively employed for the first time against the French, and fierce guerrilla activity, inflicted unprecedented losses. The French arrived in time to see the Portuguese navy and larger merchant ships – much needed after Trafalgar – set sail for Brazil with the king and court who set up a government-in-exile there. [51] ¶ Evicted from Lisbon by Wellington (to use his subsequent title), the French still seemed secure in 1809, under Soult in Oporto [52]. Its citizens, however, helped Wellington's vanguard to cross the Douro and then – when the French, outflanked, withdrew behind the city walls – transhipped the main army in every sort of local boat. Soult's army fled. ¶ From 1808, General Beresford [54], appointed a Portuguese

[53]

[54]

marshal, trained a new Portuguese army in British tactics. At the
battle of Buçaco [53], the Portuguese proved so effective that
Wellington, declaring them 'worthy of contending in the same ranks
as British troops', formed a fully integrated force. One or two
Portuguese brigades placed in each allied division, comprised a third
to a half of the army at subsequent engagements. The Allied army
won a succession of extraordinary victories against much larger
French forces, to the final battle of Toulouse in France in 1814.

[55]

[56]

After the Peninsular War, Portugal became a fashionable place to visit. 'The village of Sintra', declared Lord Byron 'is in every respect the most delightful in Europe...' [55]. Beckford rebuilt Fonthill on the model of the abbey of Alcobaça. Marshal Beresford remained as commander of the Portuguese army and exercised viceregal powers on behalf of Dom João VI for seven years, pending the king's tardy return from Brazil. ¶ These were anxious years, made difficult in Portugal (as elsewhere in Europe) by tensions between reactionaries and liberals, tensions embodied in Portugal in rival members of the royal family and culminating in 'The War of Two Brothers' (1832–4). Many British (and French) Peninsular veterans joined the

[57]

[58]

Portuguese liberal army to fight for constitutional Dom Pedro until the 'absolutist' Dom Miguel was finally driven from Santarém [56] into exile. ¶ The group portrait of 35 British and nine Portuguese port wine factors (1834) in Oporto's Rua dos Ingleses [57] is a reminder of the depth of British involvement in Portuguese trade. ¶ Eça de Queirós [58], Portugal's greatest novelist, held diplomatic posts in Britain and France. With other members of 'The generation of 1870', he was strongly rationalist, European, anti-conservative and anti-clerical in his earlier works: later he became more attracted to Portuguese rural backwardness, less confident about the direction of French progress and British material prosperity.

[59]

[60]

From the 'Scramble for Africa' among European powers Portugal finally acquired extensive new territories, a third empire to add to remnants from the first and second. This early 20th-century Portuguese cartoon [59] shows an elderly Portuguese father out walking with his daughters (China, Indonesia, Mozambique, Angola) while two 'mashers' (Britain, Germany) circle round to take the girls off his hands. ¶ The early years of the century witnessed in Portugal, as elsewhere, violent industrial unrest and revolutionary movements. In 1908 the king and crown prince were assassinated;

[61]

[62]

in 1910, following a wave of strikes and riots, Dom Manuel II abdicated and a republic was declared [60]. ¶ The dismantling of the old order stimulated the energies and aspirations of a brilliant group of Portuguese writers and artists. 'First Modernism' included the astonishing Fernando Pessoa [61], anticipator of many European literary developments, and the multi-talented Almada Negreiros – artist, writer, impresario – seen here [62] in a self-portrait, with friends, in the café *A Brasileira*.

[63]

[64]

In the 1914–18 war, Portugal fought on the allied side. By the time it ended, Portugal's overseas trade was in tatters, its public finances ruined. Social and industrial turbulence followed, and in 1926 military dictatorship. An austere Coimbra professor of economics, António de Oliveira Salazar, joined the government to restore financial order, gradually acquiring dictatorial powers, which he then projected into his *Estado Novo*. In the Second World War, at the urgent request of Churchill, who feared a premature second front, Portugal remained neutral. At a meeting in Seville [63] Salazar helped to persuade Franco also to stay out of the war. ¶ The ageing Salazar was incapacitated after 1968. His deputy, and after 1970 successor, Marcello Caetano, struggled against ultra-right opposition to liberalize the regime and to modernize its colonial policies, with slight effect. The *Estado Novo* was overthrown bloodlessly by a military coup supported by popular demonstrations on 25 April 1974 [64]. Portugal, its democracy restored, joined the Common Market in 1986.

gations made against the former administration: Pombal's personal accountability for his tyrannical regime was investigated; the families condemned for their involvement in the conspiracy against Dom José pleaded innocence and demanded the return of their confiscated fortunes. The queen, in a quandary as to what measures she should take in view of her father's plea for clemency for those who had supported him, gave way to stronger influences, and instituted proceedings against the former minister, who defended himself by arguing that he had done no more than carry out his sovereign's orders. In 1781 a verdict was reached, that in view of his age Pombal should be spared bodily punishment, and that banishment to a distance of twenty leagues from the Court would suffice. He died at Pombal the following year.

Meanwhile, the government committed itself to extricate the country from the grave situation in which it found itself, for which – according to the then prevailing faction – Pombal was responsible. Among the first measures were those to remedy the parlous state of the treasury by restricting expenditure. Mass dismissals were made among workers at the arsenal. Bull-fighting was banned and the bulls sold off, together with the gorgeous coaches used in processions, also some 2,000 horses and mules in the royal stables. Public works were suspended, including many far from finished projects for the reconstruction of the capital. Such measures merely created unemployment and dampened any enthusiasm the populace might have had for the new regime. Well might they say *'mal por mal, antes Pombal'* ('evil for evil, better Pombal'), an epigram which entered the language.

Governmental measures also inclined towards liberalization of both economic and political fields. With Pombal's disciplinarian methods of implementing his undertakings relaxed, several institutions relapsed into lethargy. State control of the economy and its entrepreneurial role in business were features of the administration that were gradually shelved. The grand monopolistic companies were dismantled, and trading with Brazil was opened to all comers; most of the state-owned industries passed into private hands, with managerial command giving way to fiscal incentive. However, a programme of road-building which had been postponed was implemented, with the construction of a highway linking Lisbon and Oporto passing through the main towns *en route*: Caldas, Leiria and Coimbra. The first regular stage-coach service was inaugurated in 1798 between the two cities, although lack of demand was to cause its suspension in 1804. The road was later extended from Oporto to Guimarães.

Two important establishments in Lisbon – the Royal Academy of Sciences, and the Casa Pia (the Royal Orphanage) – were founded during Dona Maria's reign; both acquired great prestige and have lasted to this day.

In foreign affairs, Portugal had to face issues arising from Anglo-Spanish rivalry. In 1776 the American struggle for independence received encouragement from both France and Spain; the latter, taking advantage of England's predicament, hoped to recover Gibraltar. The sea off the Portuguese coast was of vital importance to the English fleet during these hostilities, and in spite of Portugal's official neutrality, English ships continued to use the Tagus estuary as a base from which to keep an eye on the manoeuvres of hostile squadrons. Some English merchants in Lisbon not only kept these ships supplied and armed, but also sold any prizes taken. In 1780 there was a row over the re-equipment there of two captured French vessels, which were rigged out as warships to harass the Spanish coast. The Spanish promised their support in case of any reprisals by Britain should the Portuguese take action by prohibiting these ships from leaving the port, expelling the factors responsible, and closing the Tagus to English shipping. Instead, a privateer entering the estuary not long after this incident was impounded and its crew arrested. In such half-hearted ways, Portugal applied a neutrality imposed by her neighbours.

Then a clash with France developed over the matter of Cabilda, north of the mouth of the Zaire, where both French and English ships frequently landed to acquire cargoes of slaves. To safeguard her sovereignty, Portugal built, armed and garrisoned a fort there. The French claimed that the area was not part of Portugal's zone of influence and, while their diplomats were arguing the case, sent in a flotilla to Cabilda, and demolished the fort (1784). Spain intervened energetically on behalf of Portugal, and demanded French recognition of Portuguese sovereignty over that part of Africa. In response, Louis XIV threw the blame for the incident on the excessive zeal of the French naval commander, but the matter was only settled by the signing of an agreement in Madrid, with the mediation of Spain, whereby France accepted Portugal's right to Cabilda, while Portugal agreed not to interfere with French maritime trade. In the same year Luso-Spanish collaboration was demonstrated by their joint descent on the port of Algiers, the lair of privateers, who had caused more than enough damage to Iberian shipping and coastal villages. This retaliatory expedition led to an agreement between Spain and Turkey (for Algiers then formed part of her empire), whereby the Eastern Mediterranean was opened up to Spanish shipping; but in spite of the representations of her ambassador, who had sailed to Constantinople with that intent, Portugal was not included in the agreement. Nevertheless, ties between Portugal and her neighbour were strengthened in 1785 by the marriage of two *infantes*, Dom João and Dona Mariana Augusta, to two scions of the Spanish royal house.

VIII *The End of the Old Regime*

36. Facing the European crisis

A dramatic series of events in Paris led to the outbreak of the French Revolution in 1789. After apprehensive hesitation, the European monarchies determined to intervene, not only to try to save royal lives but to check the spread of democratic ideas, which in the words of the Portuguese ambassador in London, 'threatened general peace in Europe, and the toppling of all established governments'.

Portugal chose to align itself with England and Spain and, while declaring its strict neutrality in the fighting which had already broken out, endeavoured to persuade its two allies to form a triple alliance that would best suit its own interests, for if Portugal entered the war without the backing of England or without an understanding with her Spanish neighbour, she would not only risk the loss of Brazil, but lay herself open to invasion by land.

The execution of Louis XVI in January 1793 shocked the governments of Europe and – apart from Switzerland and the Scandinavian states – they formed the First Coalition to mount a general offensive against revolutionary France. In that March France declared war on Spain which, unknown to Portugal, then entered into an agreement with England. At the same time, the Convention government in France sent a representative to Lisbon in an attempt to establish diplomatic relations and be given the assurance of Portugal's continued neutrality, vital to France, as the port of Lisbon would thus be kept open to French ships trading with America. In the event, the Portuguese government refused to accept the French envoy's credentials, and he was bundled onto an American ship bound for Le Havre. This was intercepted by an English warship and the diplomat taken prisoner, which accentuated the gravity of the incident.

With the failure of its allies to agree to a triple alliance, Portugal signed separate treaties with Spain and England (on 15 July and 28 September 1793, respectively) whereby she entered the war on the side of both those powers. Portuguese troops sailed to Catalonia to join forces with Spanish troops then operating in Roussillon.

French reactions to invasion were violent, and before long the Coalition forces found themselves in retreat on all fronts in the face of the armies of the Convention. But even before the setback to the joint Spanish and Portuguese offensive, Spain had sued for peace with France (Treaty of Basle, 22 July 1795), negotiated without the knowledge of her ally Portugal. Finding herself thus isolated and in urgent need of making peace with France, Portugal would have made a deal but for her treaty obligations with England, and her reliance on England to protect her trade with Brazil – facts which made a separate peace unacceptable to France. Portugal had little alternative but to keep up the diplomatic balancing-trick, which lasted for some time, of maintaining peaceful relations simultaneously with England, Spain and France.

Meanwhile, the government in Lisbon, using as justification Portugal's old alliance, continued to collaborate with England. Late in 1797, precisely when the projected Treaty of Paris was under discussion, a Portuguese squadron was entering the Mediterranean to join Nelson, whose warships were soon after to destroy the French fleet in the Battle of the Nile. The Portuguese ships reached Aboukir Bay when the combat was already over, but they then sailed on to blockade Malta, recently seized by the French.

In 1801 France and Spain signed another treaty, by which both countries stipulated that Portugal should abandon the English alliance, open its ports to French and Spanish shipping, close them to that of England, and hand over to Spain one or more of its overseas possessions. Spain would undertake to see that these obligations were carried out.

The Portuguese government, determined to resist, requested further military support from its remaining ally, but the British government, under pressure elsewhere, was then of the opinion that any such intervention was inopportune, and in fact withdrew two of its regiments stationed in Lisbon.

In May 1801 a Spanish army crossed the border into the Alentejo and occupied the villages of Olivença and Juromenha. The bloodless operation, derisively referred to as 'the War of the Oranges', was soon over but, under threat, an agreement was signed whereby Portugal undertook to close her ports to British shipping, and hand over several border villages, which were east of the Guadiana, to Spain. (By the Treaty of Paris in 1814 these villages should have been handed back to Portugal, but they never were.)

After the short-lived Peace of Amiens (1802), war broke out again between France and Britain. Under the pretext of protecting them against likely French attack, the British occupied Goa and Madeira, which did not affect Anglo-Portuguese relations. The Portuguese government again declared its 'inviolable position of neutrality', and with this excuse prohibited English privateers entering its ports. This stance was accepted by Britain at its face value. It was a solution which best suited Portugal, for it enabled her to maintain a trade already increased by the war in Europe. Exports to England exceeded 10,000 *contos* (or 10 million *escudos*) in 1803, the high-point in an average of 8,000 *contos* per annum between 1800 and 1807. Imports were also high, reaching sums averaging 5,000 *contos* a year. A proportion of these imported goods was then exported to Spain and France, Lisbon acting as an 'economic lung' for the warring nations, and useful to all so long as she remained neutral.

Meanwhile, Napoleon was intensifying his offensive against England. To achieve absolute victory he needed larger naval forces than those available to him. One reason for his alliance with Spain was that this made Spanish naval resources accessible to him for the proposed invasion of England, but Nelson, though heavily outnumbered, virtually destroyed the Franco-Spanish fleet off Cape Trafalgar on 21 October 1805.

The English blockaded the mouth of the Mediterranean by basing themselves on Portuguese ports, and the Portuguese in granting this facility and otherwise supplying the British stretched their neutrality as far as they could. Portuguese vessels stationed off the Algarve coast, under the pretext of defending it from incursions by Algerian corsairs, gave British shipping any protection needed should hostile squadrons menace.

Increasingly, the conflict took on the aspect of an economic war. On 21 November 1806 a French ordinance declared the British Isles 'in a state of blockade', prohibited any trading with them, and ordered the interception of all shipping sailing from British colonies. Britain responded by decreeing a continental blockade, in which 'All the ports and garrisons of France and its allies, or any other State at war with Great Britain, as well as those European countries from which the British flag has been banned, even if not at war with Great Britain, will be subject to restrictions of trade and shipping as if they were blockaded in the strictest sense; all trading in produce or manufactured goods from the aforementioned

States will be considered illegal, and any shipping coming from, or leaving for, those destinations will be legally seized, and both ship and cargo will be allotted to their captors.'

Control of Portuguese ports was vital to Britain if she was firmly to impose a continental blockade, just as it was to France if she was to isolate the British Isles. In mid-1807 Napoleon instructed Talleyrand, his minister of foreign affairs, to insist that Portugal adhere to the blockade or face occupation by a Spanish army. At the same time Portuguese vessels delivering colonial or manufactured English goods to the ports of Caen, Cherbourg, Nantes, Bayonne and Antwerp, were confiscated.

37. The Peninsular War
As a French – not Spanish – army approached Lisbon, the royal family and its entourage, the government and the administrative hierarchy with their hangers-on, a total of some 10,000 people, embarked on a fleet of all the seaworthy ships that could be assembled in the Tagus estuary, and sailed for Brazil. (The idea of translating the Court to the far side of the Atlantic was not new: the celebrated Father António Vieira had aired it in the seventeenth century.)

Before weighing anchor, Dom João, the Prince Regent, recommended that those remaining should give the French a peaceful reception. Even before the *fait accompli* of the invasion, the Portuguese were doing their best to keep up the appearance of neutrality. As General Junot's troops marched into the capital, the rearmost sails of the Portuguese fleet, weighed down with fugitives, and escorted by British men-of-war, could still be discerned on the horizon.

Junot, together with his small court, was resident in Lisbon for a few months only. In May 1808 there had been a popular revolt against the French occupation of Madrid, for Spanish pride would not tolerate Napoleon's scheme of replacing their king, who had been decoyed to France, by his brother Joseph Bonaparte. Before long the revolt had spread throughout Spain, and reached Portugal.

The British government were quick to seize the opportunity to invade the Continent. An expeditionary force was transported to the Portuguese coast and landed on beaches near Figueira da Foz, west of Coimbra. It included a well-equipped contingent of cavalry, together with artillery. The disembarkation was carried out methodically and smoothly over a period of eight days, uninterrupted by the French, who had a popular rising in Lisbon to occupy them. Commanded by General Sir Arthur Wellesley (later, and better known, as Wellington), the British marched south towards the capital. The French moved north in an attempt to hold them at bay, but they were outgeneralled and totally defeated by Wellesley at both Roliça (just south of Óbidos) and Vimeiro (further south-west) on 17 and 21 August respectively. An armistice, known as the Convention of Cintra, was signed on the 30th, whereby all remaining French forces (together with much artistic plunder) was transported back to France in British ships. The British then peacefully occupied Lisbon.

The complexities of the next six years of warfare in the Peninsula can only be briefly outlined here. In the spring of 1809, following General Moore's disastrous retreat from central Spain and his death at La Coruña, General Soult entered the north of Portugal and occupied Oporto. Many of its inhabitants, fleeing south, were drowned when the bridge of boats crossing the Douro gave way.

Meanwhile, Wellesley had returned to London to face a parliamentary inquiry into the unpopular Convention of Cintra. Once in Portugal again, Wellesley expelled Soult from Oporto (12 May) and northern Portugal, and then entered Spain. He retired to the Alentejan frontier area after the bloody battle of Talavera (after which he became Viscount Wellington). Beresford, a general possessing great organizational ability, was appointed commander of the Portuguese army, and before long he was able to assemble a fighting force able to take its place beside the British in all their future peninsular battles. They were to show their sterling qualities, first at Buçaco, where, in equal numbers and with equal casualties, they joined British regiments in a notable victory (27 September 1810) against a French army of 65,000 men, led by Masséna, which had crossed the frontier near Almeida. Wellington then withdrew behind a series of formidable fortifications known as 'The Lines of Torres Vedras', which, unknown to the French, had been carefully prepared during previous months between the Tagus and the Atlantic, not far north of Lisbon. The Lines were to prove an insurmountable barrier. As Wellington had put into effect a 'scorched-earth' policy north of these lines, virtual starvation forced the French to retreat. The importance of the 'Lines' in defeating Masséna has been underestimated. Although little actual fighting took place there, total French losses in the campaign (for which they received 10,000 reinforcements during the winter), have been estimated at some 30,000, while the Allied losses were only a few hundred. If it had been a 'battle', it would have been celebrated as one of the most decisive ever fought as far as comparative losses were concerned. When the French retreated in the following March, the Anglo-Portuguese forces chased them to the frontier, winning bloody battles at Fuentes de Oñoro, Albuera and Salamanca (July 1812). Not until May 1813 were the French finally driven from Portuguese soil, to be defeated again at Vitoria (21 June).

The French invasions of Portugal had serious repercussions. It has been estimated that over 100,000 Portuguese – even more civilians than soldiers – lost their lives in the struggle;

the land was largely abandoned and laid waste; commerce and maritime trade were at a standstill [see Map 11].

38. The absent court

Having reached Brazil, the Prince Regent gave instructions that Brazilian ports should allow the ships of all friendly nations to enter, and embargoes on imported goods were lifted. This measure complied with the assurances given to Britain during the negotiations of 1807, and in effect gave Brazil economic independence, for from then on all former 'colonial' restrictions were abolished. The building of 'factories' was encouraged; the Bank of Brazil, with a mint, was established; a military academy was set up and institutes of higher education were founded which were to fill the administrative ranks of an independent Brazil. All the processes for rapid economic growth were thus activated and, at the same time, aspirations to political separation from Portugal became apparent, encouraged by the example of North American independence.

Although Rio de Janeiro was the governmental capital, the administration of the huge country was in effect carried out locally by a *junta* of governors. They were answerable to Rio, but distance from the centre weakened their authority, and real power was exercised by the military commanders of each region.

Once the war against Napoleon had ended, Portugal itself was left with a large army of about 100,000 men, the maintenance of which absorbed almost all the national income. Economists in Lisbon were of the opinion that the situation of the mother country would be improved by the reversion of Brazil to the status of a colony, and the politicians in Lisbon wanted the Court to come home. An intellectual coterie, aware of the political changes taking place in Europe, aimed at the modernization of the State's structure and, more specifically, urged the adoption of a Constitution. The military establishment wanted its higher ranks to be in Portuguese rather than British hands.

In 1817 Marshal Beresford, still in command of the Portuguese forces and with the authority of a viceroy, became aware of a conspiracy among army officers and informed the government, which crushed the plot with excessive severity. Those implicated were hanged, among them General Gomes Freire de Andrade, a prestigious figure in military circles and sympathetic to fresh ideas. Public opinion blamed Beresford for the executions. Some curious aspects of the inquiry into the plot, and other evidence, point to the government itself being involved in the affair.

39. The 1820 Revolution

A revolution was fomented by a small group of intellectuals from Oporto who, in 1818, had set up an underground organization known as the 'Sinédrio'. Among its more notorious members were Fernando Tomás, the son of a fisherman from Figueira da Foz, who had rendered substantial services to the British when they landed there in 1808, and Ferreira Borges, who had supported the French invasion and had collaborated actively with Soult.

The Sinédrio gained the support of some military units among garrisons in northern Portugal. On 24 August 1820 an artillery regiment left its barracks to attend an open-air mass, after which a twenty-one-gun salvo provided the first salute to the success of the Revolution. Although there is evidence that preparations had been made in advance for a march on the capital, this proved unnecessary, as Lisbon garrisons joined the movement. A provisional *junta* took power, and a 'Constitutional Cortes' was assembled which, by drawing up a modern constitution, aimed to provide the State with a suitable structure.

40. Constitution and reaction

The deputies elected for this Constitutional Cortes were largely indoctrinated academics, together with those landowners and ecclesiastics already receptive to the liberal ideological theories of the time. They saw their work as hammering out a pristine and uncompromising constitutional system of government whereby sovereignty was invested in a 'Soberano Congresso' or parliament, with the king himself relegated to a subordinate position, entirely dependent on the parliamentary vote.

The radicalism of this Constitution was not justified by social or economic realities. Portugal lacked the middle class which elsewhere in Europe constituted the basis of liberal regimes. The most influential elements in society remained the traditionalist land-owning nobility, interested in maintaining the *status quo* and their privileges, and the conservative Catholic Church, equally suspicious of change. Both soon found themselves in head-on collision with the constituent deputies, with their free-thinking and jacobinical notions.

Further complications in an already complex state of affairs arose from the conflicting attitudes within the royal family in Brazil. In 1821 the Cortes summoned Dom João VI (king since 1816) back to Lisbon. Disembarking with all his retainers after an absence of almost fourteen years, he swore on 4 June 1821 to accept the Constitution. Carlota-Joaquina, the queen, refused to do so, and was therefore confined in the convent of Ramalhão, near Sintra. The Infante Dom Pedro, heir to the crown, had remained in Brazil, but as the Cortes was reluctant to allow any member of the royal house to remain in a former colony, he was ordered home, where he might complete his education in the more cultured ambience of Europe. He chose to ignore the summons, and on 7 September 1822, in an act of open rebellion, made the famous declaration known as the *grito do Iparanga*: 'Independence or Death!' Just over a month later Dom Pedro was proclaimed 'Emperor of Brazil' in an outburst of nationalist enthusiasm. Portuguese troops made token opposition only, and the independence of Brazil from the mother country became an accomplished and irreversible fact.

Reaction to the revolutionary changes in Portugal was demonstrated by the Count of Amarante pronouncing against the Constitution in January 1823, but this rising in the northern provinces was subdued by the army – professedly obeying parliamentary orders – after several skirmishes. On 23 May that year, another of the royal princes, the Infante Dom Miguel, put himself at the head of the disillusioned troops and marched on Santarém with the aim of assembling sufficient forces with which to restore 'inalienable rights' (*inauferíveis direitos*), an expression memorable at the time, referring to what was seen as the usurpation by parliamentarians of the monarch's authority – sacrosanct, and an inherent right which could not be surrendered to any other institution.

Every regiment in succession, followed by ministers, senior officials, and groups of civilians, flocked towards Vila Franca de Xira, the first stop on the road to Santarém. Dom João VI himself at first decided to join the demonstration of solidarity, then returned to his capital to declare the Constitution abolished. There was no opposition to the *coup* anywhere in the country. The revolution had been premature, and not sufficiently widely based to withstand the power of vested interests.

In the April of the following year the fervent Dom Miguel attempted to follow a more right-radical and ultra-royalist course of action known as the 'Abrilada', but his *coup* failed through lack of support. Ordered to leave the country, he exiled himself to Vienna.

41. The constitutional charter

By 1826 the situation in Portugal would seem to have reached a reasonable equilibrium, politically; then Dom João VI died. It was anticipated that his eldest son, Dom Pedro, Emperor of Brazil, would succeed to the throne. Instead, professing that he did not wish to hurt the feelings of independent Brazil by wearing both crowns, Dom Pedro submitted a Constitutional Charter for Portugal and abdicated the crown of Portugal in favour of his seven-year-old daughter, Dona Maria da Glória. The young *infanta* was to marry her uncle, Dom Miguel who, if he agreed to adopt and stand by the Charter, could act as Regent during her minority.

The Charter was a carbon copy of the Brazilian Constitution, which in turn was based on the French Charter of 1814. Its main characteristic was the re-introduction of firm monarchial rule, referred to as 'a moderating power'. The sovereign had the right to dissolve parliament at will, veto its decisions, and appoint or dismiss governments; the Constitution was granted by him, not imposed on him by his subjects. In this way the face of absolutism was saved, and at the same time it gave hope to the Liberals since the Charter included provision for some parliamentary participation in government.

Despite its autocratic nature, the Charter provoked strong opposition, with demonstrations and mutinies in Trás-os-Montes, in Beira and in the Alentejo, where partisans took up the cudgels on behalf of Don Miguel. Spain abetted these reactions against the Lisbon government, which was powerless to suppress them.

At the request of the Portuguese ambassador in London, the British government, with Lord Canning at the helm, dispatched a division to Lisbon, commanded by General Clinton, with the assignment of enforcing the Charter.

In February 1828 the Infante Dom Miguel returned from Austria to Lisbon, where he was received with rapture. Demonstrations in support of absolutism were rampant throughout Portugal. On 13 March Dom Miguel dissolved the Cortes, and on 25 April he was proclaimed absolute king, a gambit referred to as 'Restoration' by his supporters, and as 'Usurpation' by his opponents.

Since 1820 liberal ideas had gained numerous supporters, especially through the medium of the periodical press, which had an extensive circulation among intellectuals and the Masonic lodges, and had found many sympathizers, particularly in military circles. Dom Miguel's arrogation of power was repudiated by the liberals who precipitated several uprisings in the Algarve, on Terceira in the Azores, and especially in Oporto, where widespread military unrest was evident in May 1828. However, the revolt was put down; numerous politicians and members of the armed forces went into exile, being welcomed in England, whose foreign policy, opposed to that of the Holy Alliance, was sympathetic to liberal movements. Some 3,000 Portuguese émigrés found shelter in Plymouth, where they were to form the nucleus of a Liberal army.

42. Civil war

Terceira, in the Azores, was the first Portuguese territory to have the Constitutional Charter declared (25 May 1828). A government flotilla sent to put down this mutiny was frustrated. The following year saw a steady flow of liberal émigrés to the island, and in 1830 the Duke of Palmela set up a Council of Regency there, which received the sanction of Dom Pedro in Brazil. Within the next year or two the Liberals, growing in strength, were to occupy most of the archipelago.

In April 1831 Dom Pedro, faced with insurmountable

political obstacles in Brazil, chose to abdicate the imperial crown and sail for Europe. On 3 March 1832 the ex-emperor, now preferring to be known as the Duke of Braganza, disembarked at Terceira, proclaiming himself Regent and protector of his daughter's rights, and finalized the preparations in train to launch a combined naval and military expedition to the mainland.

On 8 July a Liberal army of some 7,000 men landed at Mindelo and next day forced its way into Oporto, to be besieged by a Miguelite army of 13,000. Among those landing were Almeida Garrett, the author and future liberal politician, and Alexandre Herculano, the future poet and historian. Although the immediate nation-wide support they had anticipated was not forthcoming, their defences, partly manned by a British 'international brigade', were able to resist the besiegers, although the city suffered serious deprivation. Ten months later the opposing forces had increased to 17,000 Liberals holding out against 24,000 Miguelites. Although a small British flotilla patrolled the river mouth, keeping a weather eye on British interests, it was unable to stop the Miguelites, when they eventually retreated, from destroying several of the Port-wine lodges at Vila Nova de Gaia, across the river from Oporto proper, as a parting shot. One witness to this event was young Joseph James Forrester, later an influential figure among the British Port exporters.

The Liberal cause in Oporto looked as though it would be jeopardized by the exodus of a sizeable contingent which had sailed to the Algarve. In the event it disembarked in June 1833 and, led by the Duke of Terceira, marched rapidly north, meeting no real resistance. It traversed the Alentejo, and entered Lisbon on 24 July. The capture of the capital was decisive. The demoralized Miguelite forces were defeated at both Almoster and Asseiceira, but it was not until 26 May of the following year that a convention was signed at Evoramonte, north-east of Evora, that put an end to hostilities. The Convention banned Dom Miguel from the country, and so put an end to the *ancien régime* in Portugal.

IX *Monarchical Constitutionalism*

43. Chartists versus Constitutionalists

The constitutional system was established in Portugal at a time of great economic depression. The Civil or Miguelite War (or War of the Two Brothers) did nothing to improve this, and the standard of living was further eroded by disturbances caused by bands of partisans who, while settling scores with rival factions, depended for their survival on looting and raiding, with consequences which were to be felt for several years.

Mousinho da Silveira's revolutionary legislation had abolished all forms of tithes, privileges, monopolies and feudal obligations, but there had been little time in which to organize their replacement, and implementation by new legislation. Sources of governmental income were exhausted and trade and industry was at a standstill. The State survived on the proceeds of confiscations of property from the monarchy, the nobility and the Church. In 1834 the abolition of the religious orders was decreed. These owned about a third of all property, both urban and rural, the sale of which was put into immediate effect. The expression *devorista* entered the political vocabulary, frequently used by the opposition to castigate governments which survived only by devouring national property. Another cause for depression was demobilization for, with peace, the rank and file of the armies of both sides – some 100,000 men – returned to their homes to find themselves without employment. This state of affairs, combined with the stagnant economy, was to cause serious political crises which took years to resolve.

In September 1836 groups of dissidents took part in anti-governmental demonstrations in riverside areas of Lisbon. The National Guard, ordered out to disperse the mobs, joined the movement, which brought down the administration. The radicals, shouting 'Death to the Charter; long live the Constitution', in what came to be called 'the September Revolution' were known as 'Vintists' or Septembrists: their opponents, adhering to the more moderate faction whose political creed was symbolized by the Charter, were referred to as 'Cartistas'.

The new government, headed by Manuel Passos, suspended the Charter and introduced a dictatorship, which was to last until a new constitutional text had been prepared. The period was memorable as one in which a certain amount of progressive legislation took place: grammar schools were founded, providing a wider education for the growing middle class, and so was a National Academy of Fine Arts. The navy acquired its first steam-powered warships.

A new Constitution was promulgated in April 1838. It was a compromise document that aimed at balancing the radical tone of the Constitution of 1822 with the more sober pater-nalism of the Charter. Objections to this formula were voiced in the main by a group of radicals known as the 'Arsenalistas', because they used to meet at Lisbon's naval arsenal. However, in that October they were dispersed by government troops and the Constitution of 1838 remained in force until early 1842. A more middle-class or bourgeois way of life took root in Portugal, and the stability of these few years contributed to the country's economic recovery.

Characteristic of the architecture of the era is the 'Gothick' castle, 'da Pena', overlooking Sintra, built for Dom Fernando

(Ferdinand of Saxe-Coburg-Gotha, the second consort of Dona Maria II, and a cousin of Prince Albert), as is the interior decoration of the Palácio da Ajuda, above Belém.

44. 'Cabralismo'

By 1844 the current of opinion demanding a return to the basically monarchist Charter was already strong; it was the queen's preference too, with which she identified her reign. The National Anthem was known as the 'Hino da Carta' (Hymn of the Charter), and a certain romantic glamour still surrounded the text approved in 1826.

António Bernardo da Costa Cabral, the Minister of Justice, was the stage-manager behind the political scene at this time. From Oporto, he pronounced the Charter restored, and very soon gained Lisbon's support. So many were the measures given effect by this dynamic statesman that the era was called 'Cabralismo'. Among these measures were fiscal reform; the reorganization of the judiciary; the publication of a new Code of Administration, directed towards more centralization; the foundation of the Theatre Dona Maria II; the setting up of the Imprensa Nacional (the National Printing-house); the rehabilitation of the national archives in the Torre do Tombo; the revision of the system of public education; the spanning of the Douro at Oporto with a suspension-bridge; the construction of more roads to improve communications; the setting up of a register of rural property, and the banning of burials within churches. The last two measures caused a wave of unrest among the peasantry in the Minho.

Not unnaturally, Costa Cabral's domineering personality provoked political antagonism from all parties, and the agitation in the Minho was used by the opposition as a lever to oust him. Officers from units ordered to quell the disturbance refused to take action and his government fell. The riots, known as the 'Revolta da Maria da Fonte', after a peasant alleged to have led them, gave rise to one of the curious myths of recent history, for everything suggests that no such person existed – an invention to conceal those really responsible for fomenting the disturbances.

Political events accelerated dramatically. Costa Cabral, now sporting the title of Count of Tomar, went into exile, and a new ministry was formed by the influential and experienced Duke of Palmela. But he was then unseated by a *coup d'état* to which the Palace was a party, and the Duke of Saldanha took over the reins of government. The latter personified a return to 'Cartismo'. A revolt hatched by Septembrists broke out in Oporto, where a provisional government was established. Both sides took up arms in a civil war, lasting ten months, known as the 'Patuleia'. Troops were approaching Lisbon when the British government decided to intervene, blockading the mouth of the Douro and taking prisoner the troops of the Count das Antas. Meanwhile, a Spanish division entered the country, and reinstated royal authority in Oporto. The Convention of Gramido, putting an end to the war, was eventually signed on 24 June 1847.

These events further aggravated the disturbed state of the country and, although the Count of Tomar was reappointed President of the Council in 1849, dissatisfaction continued to simmer, even if all sections of the community longed for an end to a political turmoil which had lasted ever since the days of French occupation.

45. Regeneration, and the new parties

Marshal Saldanha, commanding yet another self-declared military *pronunciamento* in Oporto, was then called upon to head a new administration – the start of the 'Regeneration' movement.

This party, opposed to Costa Cabral, was to split into two

factions: the 'Regenerators' and the 'Historicals', both professing to be the legitimate representatives of the former Progressive party which had brought down the 'Cabrais'. The political debate continued between these two factions.

The Regenerators were led by Fontes Pereira de Melo and, after his death, by Hintz Ribeiro, and they carried on their campaigning until the proclamation of the Republic. Leader of the Historicals was the Duke of Loulé, a man of considerable prestige, the son of the Marquis of Loulé, counsellor to Dom João VI, who had been murdered in the royal palace in mysterious circumstances (according to rumour, on Dom Miguel's orders). For this reason, the duke supported Dom Pedro (who was also his brother-in-law, for he had married the Infanta Dona Ana, a sister of the Duke of Braganza). He had seen action during the siege of Oporto, had been a Septembrist, and was among the leaders of the Patuleia. Although he then became leader of the Historicals, and took up their cause with fervour, he was unable to disassociate himself entirely from privileged society: he was a Rightist speaking the language of the Left. The party lost much of its strength at his death in 1875, and so in the following year the Historicals merged with the Reformists, a new dissident group which had surfaced under the aggressive leadership of António Alves Martins, bishop of Viseu. The merger took place at Praia da Granja, and with the so-called 'Pact of Granja' a new Progressive Party was born, among whose eminent future leaders were Anselmo Braancamp and José Luciano de Castro. From 1879 until 1906 the Progressives and the Regenerators were to share power alternately.

Social conditions in Portugal – still on the periphery of any effective 'industrial revolution' and with a largely illiterate population – were such that the masses were unable to take any responsible part in the programmes of political parties; and so a network of agents, usually people of local influence known as *caciques*, had developed between the party leaders and the electorate. Naturally, each party tried to attract to themselves the largest possible number of these political bosses, whose support was repaid by favours. Inevitably, the government in power controlled the majority of these *caciques*, for in a small country like Portugal there were few other bodies who were in a position to grant any favours.

The torpid *status quo* was periodically interrupted by intervention by the king, who, whenever he sensed a deterioration under the existing party, would appoint a new government and dissolve Parliament. It was a foregone conclusion that the new government in power would win the election.

This alternating system, with the king acting as arbitrator, worked well enough until the end of the century, and provided a long period of stability in which the country, by now better provided with roads and railways, was able to recover the ground it had lost during earlier decades and resume a more normal pace of development. The civil service expanded; the middle classes extended; and literacy gradually became more general. Among the more eminent writers of this era were Camilo Castelo Branco and Eça de Queirós. Newspapers increased their circulation, and there was a widespread aspiration, particularly among the intellectuals and in university circles, for the reform both of society and of political life. As time passed, the alternating system came into disrepute, and growing pressure groups sought a new path to follow, which resulted in the formation of a Socialist Party and, inspired by it, an active although small Republican Party. Socialist projects for social reform were overtaken by the much simpler proposal of toppling the monarchy.

In 1901, inspired by these developing movements, a splinter group among the Regenerators gave birth to the Liberal Regenerating Party, led by João Franco, with a much more dynamic programme of social and economic policies than the dominating parties. Then in 1905 a split developed within the Progressives, with one faction headed by José de Alpoim allying itself with the Republicans in their efforts to overthrow the monarchy.

There were therefore, at this pre-Republican period, five political groups in Portugal: the older Regenerators, the Progressives, the Liberal Regenerators led by Franco, the Socialists led by Alpoim, and the Republicans.

46. The end of the monarchy

The Republican Party was supported largely by city-dwellers – journalists, students, non-commissioned officers, minor civil servants, businessmen. Its influence was noticeably increased at the time of the 'British Ultimatum' of 1890. In the European 'Scramble for Africa', British aspirations for a continuous link north to south – 'Cairo to the Cape' – clashed with Portuguese attempts to link their territories west to east – Angola to Mozambique. A conflict of interests occurred in what is now Malawi. The Portuguese proposed international arbitration; the British refused and issued an ultimatum. The Portuguese were forced to withdraw. The Republicans took it upon themselves to lead a movement of popular reaction, denouncing the government and the king in particular, as responsible for national humiliation [see Map 12]. On 31 January 1891 a Republican rebellion broke out in Oporto which, although put down by the municipal guard without too much trouble, made a great impression throughout the country.

Republican agitation continued; there were street riots and bomb-throwing incidents; the press intensified its attacks on the government; questions were raised in Parliament about the payments made by the public treasury to the royal household, the repercussions of which had an enormous effect on public opinion.

In 1906 Dom Carlos tried hard to halt what appeared to be an inevitable move towards a republic; João Franco, with authoritarian and progressive views inspired by the 'state socialism' then in vogue (with which the king had some sympathy), was invited to join the government. Republicans joined other dissidents in fomenting a revolt, which failed. Its principal leaders were arrested, and were about to be exiled when, on 2 February 1908, a group of activists (*carbonários*) assassinated both Dom Carlos and the Infante Dom Luís Filipe in the Terreiro do Paço of Lisbon. The king's younger son, who escaped the assassins' bullets, assumed the throne as Dom Manuel II.

This entirely unexpected regicide – for the king had the backing of his army – left politicians paralysed with fear. João Franco was dismissed. Succeeding governments, of which seven were appointed during the thirty months of Dom Manuel II's reign, tried unsuccessfully to generate a climate of national reconciliation.

The republican revolution eventually took place on the night of 3 October 1910. It was mounted by numerous elements from the Lisbon garrison supported by large groups of civilians armed by the *carbonária*. After two days of indecision the navy allied itself with the republican cause; Dom Manuel abdicated and sailed away to exile in England. The revolution had triumphed.

X *The Three Republics*

47. The First Republic

The Republic was proclaimed from the balcony of Lisbon's Town Hall, when the names of the members of the first provisional government were announced.

Elections did not take place for six months, and then only Republicans ran for parliament, for other parties had been disbanded. Thus an unacceptable and increasing gap was produced between the social foundations and the political heights. This maladjustment caused friction, several factions springing up and striking alliances with military or revolutionary civilian groups.

In August 1911 the first republican Constitution, strongly parliamentary and democratic in character, was approved. Although all members of parliament were Republican, before very long divergent tendencies developed, which led to the setting up of additional parties, such as Evolutionists and Unionists; but it was Afonso Costa's Democratic Party which was the most energetic, had the broadest parliamentary backing, and was able to retain power until 1914.

Although the first Republican administration produced some progressive legislation, it soon disillusioned the majority of those who had pinned their hopes on it. No economic improvement was noticed, nor any improvement in the standard of living among either civil servants or the populace in general. There was a significant increase in the numbers emigrating. The promised freedom did not materialize to any extent; anti-clerical policies upset the conservative community. Growing discontent led Manuel de Arriaga, the first elected President of the Republic, to dismiss the Democratic government and hand the leadership of the executive to General Pimenta de Castro, whom he trusted. This was the first of a series of attempts to bring conservative influences closer to the centre of decision-making. But the Democratic Party was not to be brushed aside so easily: it resorted to arms to regain power, and several hundred people were killed in the clash.

Meanwhile, the First World War had broken out.

The Democratic Party, led by Afonso Costa, believed it would be in the best national and political interest to intervene on the side of the Allies. This would prevent any encroachment on Portuguese colonies by the side likely to prove victorious ultimately and, by entering the struggle on an equal footing with the great powers, the Republic would rise in international stature. Conservative elements were in favour of keeping out of a conflict in which Portuguese interests were not involved.

In 1916 the government seized seventy German ships anchored in Portuguese harbours, which sparked off a German declaration of war. A Portuguese contingent was dispatched to the French front, where it remained until the armistice of 1918. The Portuguese 'Tomb of the Unknown Soldiers' (one from Africa, one from Flanders) is at Batalha.

Popular discontent and political malaise continued to mount. Disturbances, including the looting of shops, took place in Lisbon throughout 1917, and were put down with severity. Thirty died in the clashes that May alone. The distribution of food had been badly organized, leaving the cities almost in a state of famine, and the government's unpopularity increased yet further.

On 5 December 1917 a military *coup* placed a general, Sidónio Pais, in power, and elections confirmed him as President. The Constitution was altered to provide the President with more power. He called the new regime the 'New Republic'. Among its basic principles would be the guaranteeing of law and order, social justice and national independence. Among its main supporters were conservative Catholics, former monarchists, the lower middle class (unnerved by all the recent changes), and those military circles who had opposed intervention in the war.

The 'New Republic' came to an abrupt end in December 1918 with the assassination of Sidónio Pais. Not long after, a monarchist rising in the conservative north of the country went so far as to proclaim the monarchy reinstated, but this merely mobilized popular support for the Democratic Party, which soon regained dominance.

However, Afonso Costa, the party leader and best political strategist, disenchanted by disunity within his own party, left the country. Constant squabbling between different parliamentary factions produced a highly volatile situation. In the elections of 1921 the conservative wing of the Republicans won seventy-nine seats as opposed to fifty-four for the Democrats. On 19 October of that year another military rebellion toppled the government. This was followed by the assassination of António Granjo, the prime minister, together with several other eminent politicians, including Carlos da Maia and Machado dos Santos, both accused of being 'Sidonistas'. This tragic and alarming episode not only affected the political situation profoundly, but provoked foreign condemnation and even the stationing of warships in the Tagus for several weeks.

The post-war world depression only exacerbated matters. Wages effectively decreased as the currency was devalued. Workers, often involved in trade-union organizations with anarchistic tendencies, fought for their rights by striking and bomb-throwing. Bourgeois circles, alarmed by such events as the Russian Revolution of 1917, demanded a 'strong hand' to control further terrorist and subversive activity. Gradually, the conviction spread that only the urgent imposition of a dictatorship would restore social tranquillity and political harmony.

48. The military dictatorship, 1926–33

A plan of action, which met with the support of the army, was hatched in Braga on 28 May 1926. Political parties expected this development. The President of the Republic, Bernardino Machado, himself invited one of the leaders of the movement, Commandant Cabeçadas, to form an administration which reflected revolutionary aspirations. However, the military establishment in the north of the country not only intended to topple the Democratic party but demanded the replacement of the existing system of parliamentary parties by a national non-party government. They thus presented themselves as a 'National Revolution', an expression which was to become a slogan in the propaganda of the subsequent regime.

But, apart from its concern with the maintenance of law and order, the new regime had no clear-cut programme, and in February 1927 members of the former parties, collaborating with other military units, stirred up rebellion in both Lisbon and Oporto, only to be put down after three days of street-fighting in which many lives were lost. All activity by these politicians was ruthlessly suppressed; some 600 were arrested and deported to the Azores, Cape Verde, and Angola. Many others left the country of their own accord and organized themselves into dissident groups abroad. The military dictatorship remained in force until 1933, with each successive government presided over by a general.

However, Portugal's financial crisis intensified and, in 1928, in an attempt to solve it, General Carmona invited António de Oliveira Salazar, Professor of Political Economy at Coimbra since 1918, to join his administration as Minister of Finance. His inaugural speech – 'I know very well what I want and where I am going, but I cannot be asked to accomplish it in a few months' – reflected his strong personality, which effectively imposed itself on the military clique in power, and in 1932 they entrusted him with forming a new government.

49. The Constitution of 1933

As Prime Minister, Salazar's first move was to distance himself from the previous military dictatorship by drafting a new Constitution which, submitted to a plebiscite, was approved in March 1933. With it, and the fundamental laws which it incorporated, the era known as the 'New State' was inaugurated.

The Constitution of 1933, while drawing its inspiration directly from the Constitutional Charter, was permeated by the right-wing philosophies of the 1930s – anti-parliamentary, anti-communist, nationalistic. It emphasized the power of the executive, subjecting the market economy to State control. State and society were together to comprise a united 'corporation'.

'Presidentialism' might well describe the political formula adopted. The President of the Republic was elected by direct and universal suffrage, and the government was directly answerable to him and was not dependent on parliament. There was a parliament (or national assembly), elected by direct and universal suffrage, but its sphere of influence was very restricted; the making of legislative decisions rested entirely with the government. In the absence of political parties, the choice of candidates to Parliament was made by the 'União Nacional' (National Union), which the government maintained was not a party since it was open to all Portuguese regardless of their ideologies. In reality, and despite the inclusion of many independent names not registered with the União Nacional, the parliament always acted in accordance with the directives of the executive and, while complete freedom to criticize was ostensibly enjoyed by the deputies, parliaments never opposed governmental measures.

50. The New State, 1933–74

The 'New State', as the Portuguese Second Republic was commonly named, followed the same ideological line as the 'Ideia Nova' of Oliveira Martins and the 'República Nova' of Sidónio Pais: all three movements aimed at achieving a programme of 'national renewal', with strong governments buttressed by conservative elements in the community.

The forty-two-year period in which the country was dominated by merely two people – Salazar from 1932 to 1968, and Marcelo Caetano from 1968 until 1974 – may have given the country some political stability, but the cost was high.

Politically, the regime was characterized by the inflexibility of what was an entirely authoritarian State. Severe repression was exerted by a political police, the PIDE (Polícia Internacional e de Defensa do Estado), particularly when dealing with members of the Communist party or those affiliated to workers' organizations. Censorship of the press persisted throughout the period, which prevented any free discussion of governmental decisions, one of the main causes of the New State's unpopularity among the intelligentsia. Fernando Pessoa, the greatest of Portugal's modern poets, wrote in 1932: 'I don't want to get drawn into discussions of the New Constitution and the Corporate State; I accept them both as disciplines. I keep myself clear of them because I don't agree with them.' No attempt to start a political party was permitted. So-called 'secret societies' were banned in 1935 (including Freemasonry, which had many adherents among intellectuals and politicians); Pessoa wrote vigorously in opposition. Local trade unions were strictly controlled, and lacked any proper representation at national level. Working-class opposition formed clandestine organizations, almost all of which were controlled by the Communist Party, which continued to operate, though illegal.

The regime made many social and economic changes. The tight administration of public funds made it possible to implement an important programme of public works: the network of roads, on which no money had been spent for decades, was partly rehabilitated and adapted for motor traffic; long-postponed projects were carried out, such as two bridges spanning the Douro, and one over the Tagus. Public offices and services – law courts, hospitals, barracks, post-offices, schools, libraries, museums and the like – long accommodated in former church buildings, were provided with their own new buildings; sports-grounds and airports were laid out, harbour installations were modernized, and new dams and power-stations were constructed. The policy of paying low wages in a period of stability allowed industry to develop, and production rose steadily. Urbanization increased; Portugal ceased to be an essentially rural country. The urban middle class expanded greatly.

Opposition to the regime grew at the same pace as the industrial and mercantile working- and middle-classes expanded. Whereas in the 1920s the crises had made state autocracy welcome, increasing stability made the people impatient for the establishment of a liberal democratic 'norm'. But, despite occasional show elections, the absence of political parties made organized opposition impossible.

As far as foreign policy was concerned, the regime

continued to follow a course of intransigent nationalism, maintaining (with Churchill's encouragement) neutrality during the Second World War, and carrying on a prolonged diplomatic and military campaign to retain Portugal's overseas territories. In 1936 Salazar had supported the nationalist military rising in Spain, led by General Franco, and cultivated close relations with his dictatorial regime. Salazar was sympathetic towards the Allies, allowing them to place bases in the Azores in 1943; on the other hand, to play safe, he continued supplying wolfram to Germany until 1944.

Colonial problems took on an international pattern after the Second World War. The Charter of the United Nations defined the legitimacy or otherwise of colonization, defending the rights of peoples to self-determination, an expression which rapidly became synonymous with independence. In 1955 Portugal was asked whether she had fulfilled Article 73 of the Charter when administering any non-autonomous territory. Naturally, the Portuguese answer unleashed strong reactions among Soviet and Afro-Asian blocs, which no longer recognized the legitimacy of the Portuguese government. Long drawn out diplomatic wrangling, which did not end until 1974, was marked by high-minded declarations of principles on the part of Portugal, which were not observed in practice, in answer to successive condemnations of her colonial policies. Her specious arguments were that overseas territories were a part of Portugal, not merely colonies; moreover, post-war anti-colonial invective was merely a smoke-screen behind which powerful nations intended to take effective economic advantage of countries given political independence but unable to sustain it. Until 1961 the offensive against Portuguese colonialism had the United Nations as its headquarters, with speeches and resolutions as their only weapons. But in that year (which coincided with Kennedy's election as President

of the USA) the struggle entered a new phase, that of guerrilla warfare.

The first waves of violence occurred in that February. In
Luanda, police-stations and jails were attacked, followed in
March 1961 by bloody rioting, then by calculated terrorism
with the massacre of settlers near the frontier with the
Republic of Congo. These events were entirely unexpected,
observers having no advance warning of any trouble
brewing in the interior. There were no forces available in the
vicinity to combat the violence, and panic ensued. Only with
the arrival of troops from Lisbon was the situation
temporarily stabilized. This was only the beginning of an
anti-guerrilla campaign which was to last thirteen years,
with momentous political repercussions not only in the
African colonies but at home in Portugal. In 1963 there was
a revolt in Guinea; and in the following year guerrilla
warfare erupted in northern Mozambique. Finding itself
involved in a colonial war on three distinct and distant
fronts, Portugal had to mobilize forces on a large scale.

The direct consequence of the African wars, around which
political attacks on the regime now centred, was the fall of
the Second Republic. The escalating expense of carrying on
the wars naturally slowed down dramatically the rate of
investment in the public sector and therefore in overall
development. Intellectual circles and university students in
particular were vocal in their protest against military service;
their conscription into the officer-training corps interrupted
their education, delayed for years the start to a career, and
caused intense hostility towards war and militarism in
general. Many chose to continue their studies abroad. War-
weariness set in among the professional army, who saw no
end to a struggle in which guerrilla warfare broke out again
whenever vigilance lapsed for a moment. Ultimate defeat
seemed likely, but opinion was divided over what action to

take. Die-hard Salazarists in Lisbon were all for carrying on a policy of giving no concession, believing firmness would eventually win through. Many others now opted for the alternative: a negotiated political solution.

In 1968 Salazar, incapacitated by ill-health, retired and was succeeded by Marcelo Caetano, a Professor of Administrative Law, who was considered to be the natural heir to Salazar by the liberal wing of the regime. Caetano announced that the line he intended to follow was one of 'evolution within continuity', to bring about change without disruption. His administration was received sympathetically, being thought of as a step towards the return of party democracy and, in military circles, as perhaps able to bring an end to the colonial wars.

Under Caetano's aegis there was some speeding up of economic growth; the Sines complex and motorways were constructed; the country was opened up to foreign investment; restrictive policies in industry were ended. Social benefits were extended to rural communities and to domestic employees.

Attempts to democratize institutions were met on one hand by tight-lipped resistance from conservatives, and on the other with impatience from progressives. It was still impossible to set up political parties. In the legislative elections of 1973 only members from the National Union took their seats, for the opposition refused to contest the election at all.

However, it was the continuing colonial war which was to bring down the New State, and the youth of the nation took a decisive part in its fall. The United Nations continued to reiterate opposition to Portugal's colonial policy, while the major powers gave moral and political support to the guerrillas. Discontent among the military culminated in the 'Armed Forces Movement' (Movimento das Forças

Armadas, or MFA). The ensuing bloodless revolution of 25 April 1974 was led by a group of army captains; it met with no resistance, and toppled with ease the regime which had oppressed the country for almost half a century.

The merits or otherwise of the New State and its impact on society remain the subject of debate, with no unanimous verdict. Some have condemned it as an obnoxious era, with unjustified authoritarian restrictions imposed on a society given no democratic freedom of action; others have seen it as a necessary and fruitful phase in the evolution of Portuguese society, in which a broadly based middle class burgeoned, without which the democratic institutions of today would not have been able to develop.

51. The Third Republic

After the military *coup* of 25 April, power was exercised by a military 'Junta of National Salvation' presided over by General António de Spínola, which then elected him President of the Republic.

A power struggle among rival factions now developed between the Armed Forces Movement, the Communist Party, and left-wing groups of an anarcho-populist character under the leadership of Major Otelo Saraiva de Carvalho. At first, owing to the lack of organized political parties, the military supervised matters, but the Communists, although formerly a clandestine body, were better organized, and successfully demanded a place in the administration, forming the Aliança Povo/MFA. Command of the armed forces was entrusted to Otelo Saraiva de Carvalho (not a Communist, but actively radical) who had distinguished himself in preparing the military *coup* of 25 April. The COPCON (Comando Operacional do Continente, *continente* meaning 'mainland Portugal'), given both political and military authority to keep order, set about exercising its functions in a way which shocked public opinion by such outrages as the forcible occupation of private houses and offices, the establishment of 'residents' committees', the purging of companies' senior staff, setting fire to the Spanish Embassy in Lisbon, and the like. In September 1974 General Spínola renounced the Presidency with the excuse that he felt restricted in the exercise of his functions. General enthusiasm for the revolution flagged. A return to normal routines was what the general public wanted, with the restoration of law and order and the protection of vested interests. The government, by distancing itself from grass-roots opinion, had succeeded in creating an atmosphere of instability: the state of affairs apparent in 1820 and 1910 was repeating itself. On 25 November 1975 the forces of the MFA (without arousing Communist intervention) were able to check an anarcho-populist attempt to gain control. Order was restored in both streets and barracks, the events of that day marking an end to a period of anxiety and disorientation.

The authors of the April Revolution had divided views as to what policy to pursue with regard to the overseas territories. General Spínola, among the more moderate, was of the opinion that their self-determination should be a gradual process, which would allow time for the establishment of a new order in the ex-colonies. The Communists wanted independence to be granted immediately. In the event this was implemented in the case of Guinea, Cape Verde, São Tomé and Principe, and Mozambique. The situation in Angola was complicated by the fact that three rival movements contended for supremacy (MPLA, Movimento Popular de Libertação de Angola; UNITA, União Nacional para a Independencia Total de Angola; and FNLA, Frente Nacional para a Libertação de Angola), each with opposing ideologies. On 15 February 1975 the Portuguese government signed the Agreements of Alvor with representatives of all three factions, providing for a period of transition and setting the following 11 November as Independence Day. Making good use of the military equipment left behind by the Portuguese, the MPLA seized power on the agreed date, having rapidly overwhelmed their opponents. Not only in Angola, but also in Mozambique, independence degenerated into chaos, and protracted civil or tribal warfare followed.

Meanwhile, new political parties had been instituted, which demanded the transfer of power into their hands from those of the armed forces. The elections of April 1975 reflected a marked trend towards the centre: the Left (the Communists and fellow-travellers) gained less than 20 per cent of the votes, the Centre (PS or Socialist Party, and PSDH or Social Democrats) 64 per cent. The deputies drew up the Third Republican Constitution, based on the aspiration for social reform and with a political system which aimed at balancing presidentialism with parliamentarianism. Once new institutions had come into operation, there was a continued consolidation of the Centre, which grew at the expense of extremist groups. The Constitution was revised in 1982 and the Council of Revolution (a residual military body which, in the 1976 Constitution, had authority to certify every proposed law as true to the revolution or not) was replaced by a Constitutional Tribunal. In a further revision (1989) any references to socialism, to transition towards a classless society, and to the irreversibility of nationalization, were omitted. The re-privatisation of enterprises which had been nationalized in 1975 immediately took effect.

Within the post-revolutionary Constitution in Portugal, democratic institutions, as regulated by parliament, came into operation. Elections were properly conducted, without the accuracy of the results being questioned on any occasion. A degree of civic maturity and political awareness – understandably absent in the election of the First Republic –

became evident. From successive free elections, contested with enthusiasm, emerged governments of coalition or compromise, until 1987, when the Social Democrats (PSDH) obtained a large majority. This enabled them to govern in a climate of stability and to re-vitalize the economy. Màrio Soares, the first civilian head of State for sixty years, was sworn in as president in 1986.

Negotiations began soon after the revolution for Portugal to join the European Economic Community (as it was then named). On 1 July 1985 the formal act of admission was signed in a ceremony taking place at the Mosteiro dos Jerónimos at Belém, and came into force the following January. Since then Portugal's centuries-old overseas enterprise has been replaced by the European enterprise, with expansionist dreams of empire abandoned and Portugal restored to the physical extent of her original state. She is now adapting her economic structure to co-exist in a wider community, but without renouncing those distinctive characteristics which have developed and matured during eight centuries of dramatic history.

MAPS

Map 1 A–D: *Early occupants of the Iberian peninsula 218–737*

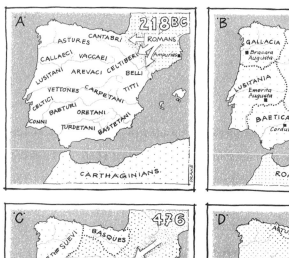

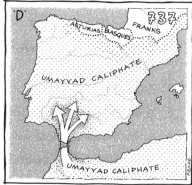

Experts believe that the first tool-making humans, presumably from Africa, settled in the Iberian peninsula (including that part now labelled Portugal) some 200,000 years ago. Subsequent 'pre-historic' development has been traced from archaeological remains. ☐ In 'historic' times, Celtic tribes are thought to have entered the Iberian peninsula from the 9th century BC onwards. Some seven centuries later they were named and placed in approximate locations by Roman historians, as shown in Map A. ☐ The Romans had entered the north-east of the Iberian peninsula in 218 BC in order to cut the lines of communication of their Carthaginian enemies. They slowly gained control over the whole peninsula, except the region inhabited by the Basques. In AD 300 the Emperor Diocletian re-organized the whole Roman empire for more efficient administration. The Iberian provinces at that time, each with its capital, are shown in Map B. ☐ The Roman practice was to use troops from one part of their empire to control the inhabitants in another. Germanic tribes were extensively used in Iberia. After the Roman withdrawal in the 5th century, various Germanic kingdoms were established in Iberia within boundaries broadly indicated in Map C. ☐ In the 7th century a new inheritor to Roman territory arose in Arabia: the Muslims. The new religion spread with astonishing speed. Populations to the east and then the south of the Mediterranean were swiftly over-run and converted to Islam. In 711, Muslim Berbers crossed the straits, landing at *Gebel Taric* (Gibraltar). Very soon they had conquered the whole Iberian peninsula, except for the mountainous region along the northwest coast. They invaded the territories of the Franks across the Pyrenees and were not turned back until defeated by Charles Martel at Poitiers, in central France (732). The Muslim kingdoms in Iberia as they were in 737 are shown in Map D.

Map 2 A–D: *The 'Reconquest' and the formation of Portugal 1000–1267*

The Moors occupied different parts of Iberia for different periods – in all for nearly 800 years. During that long period, Muslim princes – like their Christian counterparts – quarrelled and fought, sometimes among themselves, sometimes against theological adversaries, with frequent shifts of alliance that often disregarded religion. Some stages in what Christian historians call the Reconquest are shown in the four maps opposite. The final surrender, that of Granada, didn't occur until 1492. Such Christian success was not matched by the parallel crusades in Palestine. □ In the course of the Reconquest, a doughty heir to the fiefdom of Portucale, Afonso Henriques, holding lands between the Minho and the Mondego rivers from the King of León, asserted his independence. He extended his territory south in battles with the Moors. Crusaders from northern Europe, *en route* for Palestine, helped him conquer Lisbon in 1147. □ Afonso Henriques' successors steadily pushed beyond the Tagus down to the Algarve coast. The pope formally recognized the ruler of Portugal as an independent king in 1179. The present boundaries of the kingdom had been established, and were widely recognized, by 1267. Changed only in minor detail since, these boundaries are the oldest of any of Europe's present nation states.

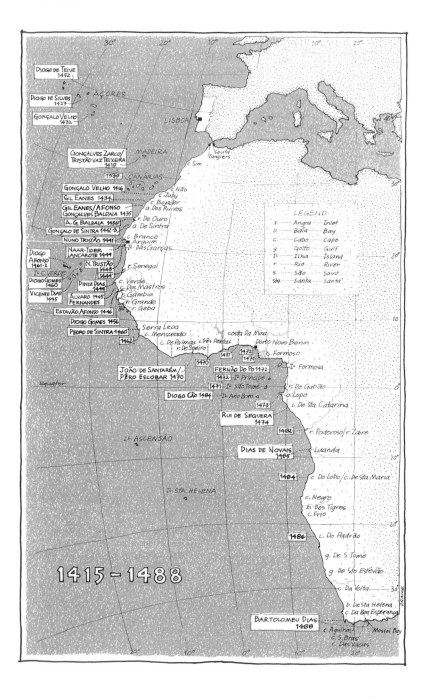

DIOGO DE TEIVE 1452

DIOGO DE SILVES 1427

GONÇALO VELHO 1432

AÇORES

LISBOA

GONÇALVES ZARCO/ TRISTÃO VAZ TEIXEIRA 1419

MADEIRA

Ceuta
Tangiers

c. Sim

1339 CANÁRIAS

GONÇALO VELHO 1416
c. Não
c. Juby

GIL EANES 1434
c. Bojador
a. Dos Ruivos

GIL EANES/AFONSO GONÇALVES BALDAIA 1435
r. De Ouro

A. G. BALDAIA 1436
a. De Sintra

GONÇALO DE SINTRA 1442-3
c. Branco

NUNO TRISTÃO 1441
Arguim
I. Das Garças

NAAR-TIDER LANCAROTE 1444

DIOGO AFONSO 1461-2

N. TRISTÃO 1443
I. C. VERDE

DIOGO GOMES 1460

DINIZ DIAS 1444
1444

r. Senegal
c. Verde
r. Dos Mastros

VICENTE DIAS 1445

ÁLVARO 1445 FERNANDES
r. Gambia
r. Grande
r. Geba

ESTAVÃO AFONSO 1446

DIOGO GOMES 1456
Serra Leoa

PEDRO DE SINTRA 1460
c. Mensurado

1462

c. De Palmas c. Três Pontas
r. De Sueiro

costa Da Mina

Porto Novo Benin

1472
1471

1471
1470

G. Formoso

I. Formosa

JOÃO DE SANTARÉM/ PÊRO ESCOBAR 1470

FERNÃO DO PÓ 1472

1472 I. Principe

r. Do Gabão

DIOGO CÃO 1484

1471 I. São Tomé
I. Ano Bom

c. Lopo
c. De Sta. Catarina

RUI DE SEQUERA 1474

1473

I. ASCENSÃO

1482 r. Poderoso/ r. Zaire

DIAS DE NOVAIS 1485
Luanda

1484 c. Do Lobo/ c. De Sta Maria

I. STA. HELENA

c. Negro
b. Dos Tigres
c. Frio

Equator

1486 c. Do Padrão

g. De S. Tomé

g. De Sto Estêvão

c. Da Volta

b. Desta Helena
c. Da Boa Esperança

BARTOLOMEU DIAS 1488
c. Agulhas   Mossel Bay
c. S. Bras
r. Das Vacas

1415 – 1488

LEGEND

a.	Angra	Inlet
b.	Baía	Bay
c.	Cabo	Cape
g.	Golfo	Gulf
I.	Ilha	Island
r.	Rio	River
s.	São	Saint
sta.	Santa	Santa'

Map 3: *Atlantic and African explorations* c.1400–88

Having expelled the Moors from the territories that now comprised their kingdom, the Portuguese carried their crusade across the straits into north Africa, seizing and fortifying Ceuta (opposite Gibraltar) in 1415. □ Under the leadership of Prince Dom Henrique – dubbed 'Henry the Navigator' by 19th-century historians – Portuguese captains sailed westward into the Atlantic, making additional discoveries among the Madeira, Azores and Canary groups of islands. They began to explore the north-western African coast (then known only vaguely and from the landward side). Contemporary cosmographers, following Ptolemy, believed the coast soon turned west to enclose the Atlantic like a lake. Motives for these explorations included: crusading evangelism; wresting, by sea, the trade of west Africa – including gold – from the Muslim traders who then monopolized it overland; and sheer scientific curiosity. A turning point in southward exploration was the rounding of the dangerous, legend-haunted Cape Bojador (1434), the limit of the then known world. The first permanent Portuguese trading post and fort was established on the island of Arguim (1449). □ Henry's successors continued his policies. The Portuguese persisted in their search down the vast coast-line of Africa, at first inching down, later – as improved navigational techniques allowed – advancing in broader sweeps. Hopes increased that somewhere the coast would finally turn east and north, leaving a passage for a route by sea to the riches of the Indies. In 1487 Bartolomeu Dias at last rounded the end of the continent, naming it 'The Cape of Storms', which Dom João II corrected to 'The Cape of Good Hope'.

Map 4: *Western Christendom hemmed in by Islam 1485*

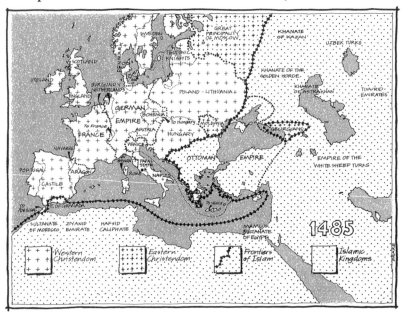

Islam in the 7th century had extinguished the Christian kingdoms of the Middle East, those in Armenia and Ethiopia surviving by their inaccessibility. Christian communities yet further east similarly withered, leaving small residues such as some Nestorian Christians in China and some followers of St Thomas in south India, cut off from the West. Further, the Ottoman Turks steadily diminished the great Byzantine Empire, which had been for most of a thousand years the dominant centre of Christendom – theologically the bitter rival of western Catholicism. By their capture of Constantinople itself in 1453, the Turks reduced Orthodox Christianity in Europe to the status of a dependent religious community, and further tightened Islamic control over all overland routes to 'the rest of the known world, confining Catholic Christendom to western Europe. That situation is represented in Map 4. □ Then, at the end of the 15th century, in a single decade, the fortunes of western Christendom enjoyed an astonishing transformation. In 1487 Bartolomeu Dias rounded Africa and opened the possibility of Christian access to the Indies by sea; in 1492 Christopher Columbus believed he had found a shorter route to the Indies – and stumbled upon a continent; in 1497–9 Vasco da Gama established the workable route to the Indies, which at last opened the wealth and high civilizations of the Orient to the West. □ After eight centuries, the Islamic monopoly of trade and conversion beyond Europe had been broached. The worldwide expansion of Europe had begun.

Map 5: *Dividing the world 1479–1529*

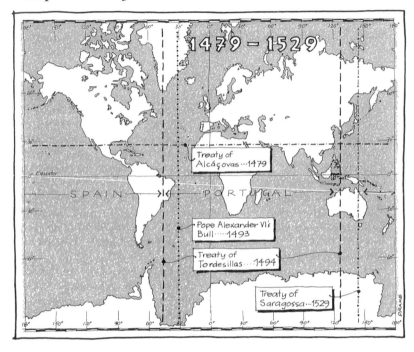

1479 – 1529

Treaty of Alcáçovas ···1479

Pope Alexander VI's Bull ····1493

Treaty of Tordesillas ···1494

Treaty of Saragossa···1529

Equator

S·PAIN   P·O·R·T·U·G·A·L

The princes of Spain did not finally expel the Moors until the surrender of Granada in 1492 – two centuries later than the expulsion from Portugal. During that interval the Portuguese had explored extensively in the Atlantic and down the west coast of Africa. □ Spain and Portugal, the leading maritime powers of the 15th century, were frequently embroiled in dynastic quarrels and the warfare common between neighbours. An attempt was made to reduce conflict, at least in overseas exploration, by designating spheres of influence through the Treaty of Alcáçova (1479). Atlantic sea-routes and discoveries north of a line drawn east and west below the Canary islands were to be Spanish, those south Portuguese. □ Despite his (falsified) logs and charts, Columbus' sailing route and his land-fall in the Antilles fell, the Portuguese argued, within their sector. The Spanish pope, Alexander VI, proposed a new line, this time running north and south – Spanish to the west, Portuguese to the east (see the Bull *inter Caetera* line on the map). Surprisingly, the Portuguese insisted on the line being moved much further west (370 leagues west of the Cape Verde islands) still in apparently blank sea. Only then would they sign the Treaty of Tordesillas (1496). Four years later Brazil was officially 'discovered' by the Portuguese – within their sector. □ The Tordesillas line was supposed to extend around the globe. Where exactly it ran in relation to the distant and very valuable Spice Islands, the Moluccas – 'discovered' by the Portuguese by eastward sailing through their own sector – remained obscure. That mattered little until the Portuguese Fernão de Magalhães ('Magellan') – in Portuguese service for many years in far eastern waters but then employed by Spain – reached the islands in 1520 by sailing westward with Spanish ships through the Spanish sector. At negotiations, the Spaniards – under the Emperor Charles V the paramount power in Europe – set the Moluccas (wrongly) on their side of the line. To preserve their spice monopoly, the Portuguese paid a large sum to the Spaniards (then involved in expensive military operations in their extended territories). The Treaty of Saragossa (1529) was then agreed. Map 5 shows the newly agreed line, but with the islands placed correctly. □ Such legal niceties as these had some point so long as the rivalry in 'discovery', and consequent trade monopoly, concerned only Portugal and Spain, and while both accepted the moral authority of the pope and of their mutual treaties. Such relative stability was undermined by the Reformation, and the rise of Holland and England as naval and mercantile powers, vigorously anti-Catholic.

131

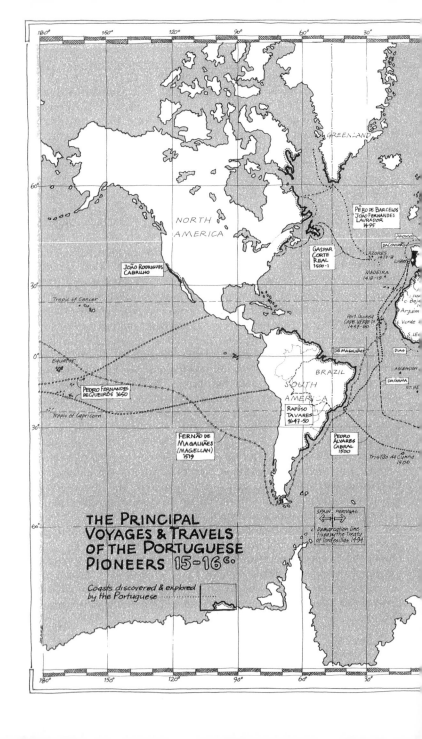

PÈRO DE BARCELOS
JOÃO FERNANDES
LAVRADOR
1495

GREENLAND

NORTH
AMERICA

AFONSO
DA COVILHÃ

AZORES
1431-2

Lisboa

GASPAR
CORTE
REAL
1500-1

MADEIRA
1418-19

JOÃO RODRIGUES
CABRILHO

Tropic of Cancer
80

C. Bojador

Arguim

Port. Guinea
CAPE VERDE Is.
1457-60

Verde Is.

S. Leone

Equator

DE MAGALHÃES

DIAS

BRAZIL

ASCENSION

PEDRO FERNANDES
DE QUEIRÓS 1650

DAGAMA

SOUTH
AMERICA

ST. HELE

Tropic of Capricorn

RAPÔSO
TAVARES
1647-50

FERNÃO DE
MAGALHÃES
(MAGELLAN)
1519

PEDRO
ALVARES
CABRAL
1500

Tristão da Cunha
1506

40

SPAIN PORTUGAL
⟵⟶

c Demarcation line
fixed by the Treaty
of Tordesillas 1494

THE PRINCIPAL
VOYAGES & TRAVELS
OF THE PORTUGUESE
PIONEERS 15-16ᶜ·

Coasts discovered & explored
by the Portuguese . . . .

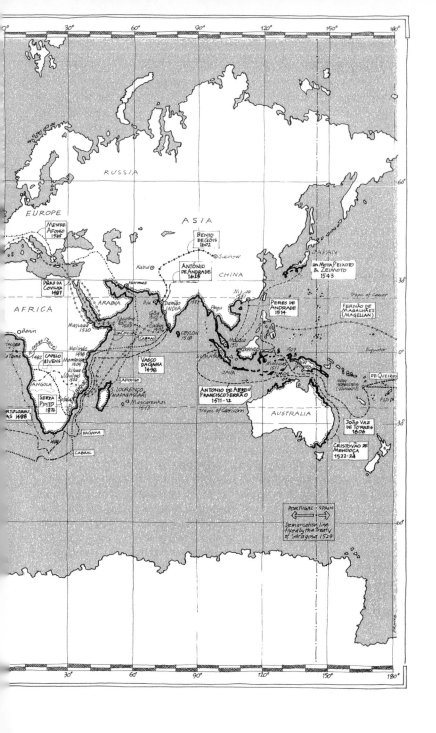

Map 6: *The principal voyages and travels of the Portuguese pioneers (chiefly 15th and 16th centuries)*

□ The map shows those places and coasts explored by Portuguese pioneers, sometimes overland but generally by sea. These journeys are referred to in history as the Discoveries – meaning, of course, that the relevant places were then discovered/revealed to western Europeans. The importance of the discoveries lay in the establishment of a world-wide network of connections, and in the initiation of that extraordinary expansion of European influence which has marked history since the late 15th century. □ Maps showing the extent of Portuguese discoveries quite often vary in detail, for new evidence still surfaces and historians assess the old evidence differently. For early explorations could not be confidently registered in some international court, able to adjudicate between rivals. Besides, the finding of yet more land was not in itself of particular importance: what mattered was whether it yielded something valuable at once (such as gold) or likely to be valuable soon (by way of trade). The Portuguese regarded their discoveries as trade secrets: the first port of call for returning navigators was the *Casa da Índia* where log-books and charts were deposited under a seal of security. There too a secret 'planisphere'/world map was maintained, constantly adjusted by a team of map-makers and cosmographical experts. The *Casa da Índia,* a part of the royal palace, was on the bank of the Tagus in Lisbon. It was destroyed, with all its priceless records, by the Great Earthquake of 1755 – the collapse of the building, the devastating fires, the tidal waves. □ The loss of the primary, direct evidence of the journeys of the Portuguese pioneers means that historians have had to rely on oblique references and pirated documents. Thus, a voyage to Greenland and probably Northern Canada (Barcelos and Lavrador 1492–5) is known to have occurred – not from log-books but from the records of a law-suit in 1506. Don Antonio Lombardo, sailing round the world with Magellan, wrote in his diary in 1520 about the intricate passage through the Straits of Magellan: 'Had it not been for the Captain General, we would not have found the strait, and we all thought and said it was closed on all sides. But he himself knew full well where to sail to find the well-hidden strait, which he had seen depicted on a map in the Treasury of the King of Portugal, which was made by that excellent man, Martin Behaim.' Had someone, one wonders, indeed ventured so far south and previously reported the position of the strait to the Casa da Índia? A planisphere by

Behaim still exists; embodying some Portuguese discoveries; it was made in 1492 on commission for the merchants of Nuremberg. Such pirating of Portuguese maps (theoretically punishable by death) was a considerable business. Bartolomeo Columbus, who worked in the Lisbon royal map workshop, joined his brother Christopher in Spain before 1489, bringing a copy of the secret world map, smuggled out on eleven sheets of paper, which he then sold in Italy to raise funds. Alberto Cantino, sent by Duke Ercole d'Este of Ferrara and posing as a purchaser of pure bred horses, obtained a copy of the secret Lisbon world map, by bribery, in 1502. His version surfaced in an Italian library – but only 450 years later. Even in the 1990s, Australian historians re-examining the 'Dieppe' maps (made by a school of copyists producing French versions of smuggled Portuguese originals) concluded that the Portuguese had explored at any rate the north-west coast of Australia (and some evidence points to the north-east and south-west coast as well) early in the 16th century. □ In sum, any map of the discoveries such as Map 6, may strive for accuracy but cannot be regarded as certain, still less as final.

Map 7: *Sailing to the Indies 1497…*

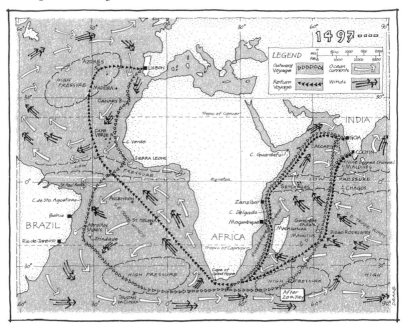

Map 6 shows routes between Portugal and India and some factors which determined them. □ Vasco da Gama's long and dangerous voyage to the Indies and back – three times longer and much more intricate than the journey across the Atlantic – was a technical triumph of seamanship. Sailing vessels, powered solely by natural forces, are subject still to hazards of wind and sea; in addition, reefs, island outcrops and coastal obtrusions, now thoroughly mapped, were then little known; patterns of dominant currents and prevailing winds – shifting radically in the course of the year – had still to be established; longitude could not be fixed with much accuracy, and latitude only by the painstaking compilation of tables of the sun's declination, seasonally, at different points on the globe; the movement of stars in unfamiliar southern skies had still to be plotted... and so on. □ The reduction of some of these hazards occupied Portuguese nautical science in the ten years between Dias finding open sea beyond the Cape and da Gama sailing for the Indies. In that period also the Portuguese, who had used tiny, manoeuvrable *caravels* for their early explorations, developed the *nau*, a much larger, well-armed vessel, suited to carrying substantial trade cargoes over long distances. □ Once da Gama had shown the way, a regular annual trading fleet – the *Carreira da Índia* – sailed from Lisbon to India on a two-year round trip. Additional trading posts were rapidly established down India's Malabar and Cochin coasts and the Portuguese swarmed throughout the East, within thirty years reaching China. □ Of these Asian developments, Adam Smith wrote, in *An Inquiry into the Nature and Causes of the Wealth of Nations* (1776): 'The discovery of America, and that of a passage to the East Indies by the Cape of Good Hope, are the two greatest and most important events recorded in the history of mankind... the empires of China, Indostan, Japan, as well as several others in the East Indies, without having richer mines of gold or silver, were in every respect much richer, better cultivated and more advanced in all arts and manufactures than either Mexico or Peru... rich and civilized nations can always exchange to a much greater value with one another, than with savages and barbarians.' □ The influence of the East in the development of the West was varied and great: in civility and thought, in the introduction of economic and decorative plants, in medicine, in craftsmanship; above all, in the creation of numerous trade goods – spices, fine cloth, jewels, porcelain... which triggered that rapid growth in the wealth of the West, and that sense of new horizons, and new opportunities, which sparked the High Renaissance.

137

Map 8: *Portuguese trade in Asia (16th and 17th centuries)*

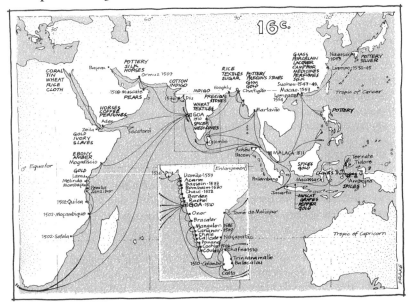

Portugal's first empire in Asia was based on control of trade: territorial occupation was generally limited to the seizure of key emporiums and entrepôts, such as Mombasa and Malacca, and the fortification of strategic towns, such as Goa and Hormuz. From these secure places, Portuguese armed ships patrolled the established sea lanes used by oriental merchants (in some places even issuing licences for a fee), attacking pirates (a serious, widespread, hazard to trade) and extending a protective arm over numerous Portuguese 'factories' – communities of merchants – settled in the countries of the East. Portuguese became the *lingua franca* among traders of all races throughout the region, as widespread linguistic traces of Portuguese words testify to this day. □ Map 8 shows the principal Portuguese forts and trading settlements and the main commodities handled by the Portuguese in *Ásia Portuguesa*. In the 16th century, Portugal's superiority in ships, guns and navigational technique, the success of her soldiers and her merchants, enabled the Portuguese to dominate trade both within the region (for example, between distant China and Japan) and also between the region and Europe.

138

Map 9: *A world-wide war 1603–98*

Portuguese monopolies in overseas trade, resulting from prior discovery and swift exploitation, were viewed with mounting envy by other European powers. The Reformation undermined the authority of the pope as arbiter of 'rightful' monopolies and added *odium theologicum* to the attacks of Dutch, Danish, and English rivals abroad (whatever the relationships within Europe). These attacks became the more frequent and fervent when Spain and Portugal became a joint kingdom (1580), Spain, then the paramount power in Europe, being plainly the dominant partner. Thus Portugal was drawn into the eighty-year-long struggle between the Spaniards and the Dutch, and into Spanish dynastic claims on England. Portugal's empire became hostage to Spain's fortunes. □ Spain had 'acquired' Portugal as the result of the stunning Portuguese defeat of Alcácer-Quibir, in the sands of north Africa, the end of a last, futile crusade against the Moors (1578). The news of this victory of Muslim forces, and the subsequent domination of Portugal by Spain, electrified Asian princes into hopes of casting off Portuguese control. Ten years later, the building, and then the total destruction, of the 'Invincible Armada' (1588), and three subsequent armadas, utterly exhausted Iberian resources – ships, guns, deep-sea mariners, funds. For lack of normal supply and reinforcement, Portuguese commanders abroad had to rely exclusively through much of the 17th century on their own local initiative to repel frequent attacks. □ Map 9 provides some scant impression of this first world-wide war (seldom declared) extending over five continents. The main beneficiaries were the Dutch. As Willem Bosman remarked, the Portuguese overseas had acted as 'setting dogs to spring the game, which as soon as they had done, was seized by others'. Additional opponents included English, Danes, French, Congolese, Persians, Indonesians, Cambodians, Japanese… By the end of the century, the Portuguese had lost all their dominance throughout Asia (keeping only a few outposts); had lost some, and retained some, of their African positions; and, thanks to vigorous local support, had repelled numerous foreign attempts to gain a permanent foothold in Brazil. □ The Portuguese blamed the destruction of their supreme position in overseas trade on their 'Babylonian captivity' to Spain. From the end of 1640 began Portugal's re-assertion of its independence, which was finally recognized by Spain in 1668.

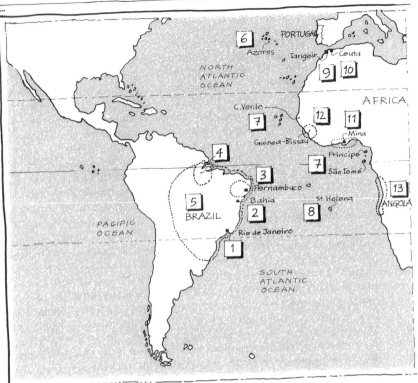

—BRAZIL—

1] French occupy 'France Antartique' (around Rio de Janeiro); expelled 1615.

2] Dutch occupy Bahia; expelled 1625.

3] Dutch colonize Pernambuco & inland for 25 years; finally defeated 1654.

4] British repulsed from Amazonia 1625.

5] Portuguese and Brazilians vigorously explore and expand Brazil.

—ATLANTIC ISLANDS—

6] The Azores repeatedly attacked by French, British, Dutch·····repelled.

7] Dutch capture São Tomé 1641, then expelled; repulsed from Príncipe and··

·····Cape Verde Islands.

8] British acquire St. Helena.

—NORTH AFRICA—

9] Tangier ceded to Britain 1662······ (Catherine of Braganza's dowry).

10] Spanish retain Ceuta 1668 when Portuguese regain independence.

—WEST AFRICA—

11] Dutch capture Mina 1637 and other Guinea coast forts.

12] To compensate,··· Portuguese develop area of Guinea-Bissau.

13] Dutch capture Angola coastal forts 1640 but expelled in 1648.

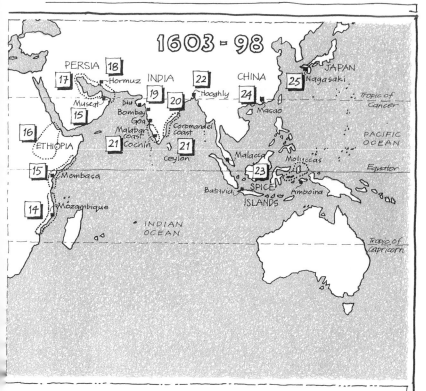

1603-98

PERSIA 18
17
Hormuz INDIA 22
19 20 Hooghly CHINA 24 25 Nagasaki JAPAN
Muscat Diu Macao
15 Bombay
16 Goa
ETHIOPIA Malabar coast Coromandel coast PACIFIC OCEAN
21 Cochin 21
15 Mombasa Ceylon Malacca Moluccas Equator
Batavia SPICE Amboina
14 Mozambique ISLANDS

INDIAN OCEAN

Tropic of Cancer

Tropic of Capricorn

SOUTH-EAST AFRICA

14 Portuguese repel strong Dutch attacks on Mozambique and coast.

EAST AFRICA / PERSIA

15 Omanis, with British & Dutch help, take Muscat, & Mombasa 1698 & Zanzibar coast.

16 Portuguese expelled from Ethiopia 1634.

17 By 1650 Portuguese ousted from Persian Gulf.

18 Persians, with British help, occupy Hormuz 1622.

INDIA

19 Portuguese repel Dutch attacks on Goa and Diu. 1603 + 1610.

20 Bombay ceded to British 1662 ·········· (Catherine of Braganza's dowry).

21 Dutch take Cochin & other Malabar coast settlements 1662, then Coromandel coast settl'm'ts 1663 & occupy Ceylon by 1668.

22 Mogul's troops take Hooghly 1632.

EAST INDIES

23 Dutch take Spice Islands 1605, Batavia, Moluccas, Malacca 1641, Amboina 1665. Repelled from Timor. Dutch dominate East Indies and spice trade.

FAR EAST

24 Portuguese repel Dutch from Macao 1622+26.

25 Japanese expel Portuguese 1639, & close to the West, except some Dutch contact.

16 C.

- ◇ JOÃO DE BARROS & AIRES DA CUNHA (PARÁ)
- ◇ FERNÃO ÁLVARES DE ANDRADE (MARANHÃO)
- ◇ ANTÔNIO CARDOSO DE BARROS (PIAUHY)
- ◇ JOÃO DE BARROS & AIRES DA CUNHA
- ◇ PERO LOPES DA SOUSA (ITAMARACÁ)
- ◇ DUARTE COELHO (PERNAMBUCO)
- ◇ FRANCISCO PEREIRA COUTINHO (BAHIA)
- ◇ JORGE FIGUEIREDO CORREIA (ILHÉUS)
- ◇ PERO DO CAMPO TOURINHO (PORTO SEGURO)
- ◇ VASCO FERNANDES COUTINHO (ESP. SANTO)
- ◇ PERO DE GÓIS (S. TOMÉ)
- ◇ MARTIM AFONSO DE SOUSA (R. DE JANEIRO)
- ◇ PERO LOPES DE SOUSA (SANTO AMARO)
- ◇ MARTIM AFONSO DE SOUSA (S. VICENTE)
- ◇ PERO LOPES DE SOUSA (SANT'ANA)

MERIDIANO DE TORDESILLAS

'A'

17 + 18 C.

1650

MANAUS   BELÉM   S. LUÍS

RECIFE

SALVADOR

RAPOSO TAVARES

PAULISTAS

BAIANAS

PERNAMBUCANAS

MARANHENSES

AMAZONENSES

R. DE JANEIRO
SANTOS
S. PAULO

RAPOSO TAVARES (START)... 1647

'B'

19 + 20 C.

BRAZIL

'C'

LEGEND

1 FRENCH GUIANA
2 SURINAM
3 GUYANA
4 VENEZUELA
5 COLUMBIA
6 ECUADOR
7 PERU
8 BOLIVIA
9 CHILE
10 PARAGUAY
11 URUGUAY
12 ARGENTINA

DISTANCE
0   500   MLS   1000
0   1000 KM.

DRAKE

Map 10: *The development of Brazil c.1550–c.1750*

Brazil was officially 'discovered' in 1500 by Pedro Álvares Cabral, blown off course en route for India. Serious settlement, however, did not begin until the 1550s. Hereditary rights over wide stretches of territory in Brazil were allocated to selected 'captains', operating under royal licence. The original captaincies are shown in Map A opposite. □ Spanish colonization in South America followed the search for gold and plunder: the chief aim of Brazilian colonization after 1550 was agricultural production – sugar, tobacco, cotton, nuts, coffee, tea, hides, oils, wood and dyes... The plantations required labour; the indigenous Indians, however, were raiders and hunters to whom regular agricultural labour for wages was meaningless and repugnant. Moreover, Jesuit missionaries, notably the remarkable António Vieira, protected them from exploitation by the settlers, partly through forming co-operative Indian settlements, the *aldeias*. In the long run, Portuguese intrusions and raids and, above all, European diseases, decimated the Indians. In their place African slaves were bought from Arab and African dealers and imported in large numbers to supply the labour required. □ Map B indicates the extraordinary explorations into the vast interior by the *bandeirantes*. These bands, formed under a 'captain' and comprising Portuguese, creoles, mulattos, mestizos, freed negroes and friendly Indians, penetrated far beyond the official Tordesillas boundary. One such epic journey, led by António Rapôso Tavares (1647–51), is shown by way of an example on Map B; the main thrusts of the many other expeditions are broadly indicated. These journeys yielded alluvial gold (from 1693–5), and then silver and precious stones, including diamonds, all of which helped make João V (1689–1750) the richest monarch in Europe. Much of the wealth from Brazilian and other overseas trade passed, however, to those who handled onward exports from Lisbon to the rest of Europe, notably the British. □ The territorial 'discoveries' of the *bandeirantes* and subsequent pioneering settlement in the interior led to Portuguese claims over enormous areas of the continent, which were successfully sustained against attacks by Dutch and French rivals and in countless boundary disputes with the Spanish, colonies. By the Treaty of Madrid (1750) Brazil achieved its present boundaries – bar minor adjustments. This single, multi-racial country, fifth largest in the world, accounts for half the land and population of the whole continent, the equal of all the ten Spanish colonies put together, a position shown in Map C. Brazil achieved independence in 1822, retaining links to Portugal through language, religion, culture, history, inter-marriage and immigration.

143

Map 11: *Portugal and the Peninsular War 1807–14*

After victories at Austerlitz, Iena, Eylau, Friedland, and the conclusion of the Treaty of Tilsit (1807) with Russia, Napoleon was supreme on the Continent. Britain remained implacable. All markets were to be closed to that 'nation of shopkeepers'. In all Europe there was only one accredited British envoy – in Lisbon. Threats having failed, Napoleon decided on invasion to close this leak in his 'Continental System'; an 'Army of Observation' under Junot prepared for 'an armed parade, not a war'. The Spanish were supportive (French allies since 1795). Junot duly arrived in Lisbon in 1807 – in time to catch the distant prospect of the king, court and the Portuguese fleet (much needed after Trafalgar) sailing for Brazil with a British escort. Junot's army had moved rapidly; it could do so because it was unhindered by any baggage train, living instead off the country. However, in Portugal the French encountered for the first time a fully effective scorched earth policy. A French officer wrote: 'We found not a single peasant in his hut. Many men met their deaths through sheer misery – or at the hands of the peasantry. We received rations only when we reached Lisbon.' Of 25,000 men that crossed the border only 2,000 reached Lisbon. □ Subsequent military campaigns of the Peninsular War can be traced in Map 11. However, whereas British actions were those of an expeditionary army, the Portuguese contribution in its war of national liberation was multilayered, in ways which cannot be mapped and which therefore require other reference. For example: *Through popular involvement:* scorched earth (see above); guerrilla attacks on flanks and lines of communication; constant flow of intelligence to Allied armies. Some highlights: (1807) Coimbra students and some peasants seized the fort at Mondego Bay thereby enabling the British under Wellington to land unopposed; the Bishop of Oporto raised 5,000 horses and mules for Wellington's army; (1809) Wellington moved north rapidly to attack Soult in Oporto. Local people had concealed four barges in the reeds; with these, Wellington's vanguard crossed the Douro. Outflanked, the French withdrew behind the city walls, whereupon the populace flocked to the riverside to bring the main British and Portuguese forces across in every sort of small boat; (1811) Masséna was forced to lift his siege of Lisbon by scorched earth starvation. □ *Through the militia:* every peasant, having destroyed his farm, was required to serve in the militia. This fulfilled many of the reserve and protective functions for which the French had to use regular troops, thereby releasing trained soldiers for the front line. (1810) Some highlights from Masséna's invasion: capture of artillery train and 800 men; surprise seizure of Coimbra (Masséna's base) and 5,000 French soldiers; all messengers sent to France and Spain were captured. 'Not a single letter has reached the French since they entered Portugal' wrote Wellington. Masséna was finally driven to employ General Foy with an armed escort of 600 men to make contact with Spain. Thirty thousand men, mostly militia, manned the Torres Vedras forts, the army resting in tactical reserve. □ *Through trained soldiers:* at no time in the Napoleonic War did Britain – relying on volunteers – field an army of more than 40,000 soldiers (plus 130,000 sailors commanding the seas); the French – relying on the *levée-en-masse* – committed 365,000 to the Peninsula alone. For all his brilliance, Wellington was chronically, desperately, in need of troops. In 1809 General Beresford was appointed to train Portuguese recruits in British field tactics and manoeuvres under fire. After their disciplined effectiveness in the victory at Buçaco (1810) Wellington, judging them 'worthy of contending in the same ranks as British troops', fully integrated the Portuguese and British armies – one, sometimes two, Portuguese brigades in each division – in a genuinely Allied army (a degree of co-ordination not remotely paralleled elsewhere in Europe in the armies of the five successive, quarrelsome, coalitions). In 1809 Wellington commanded 20,000 British, 30,000 Portuguese (and 40,000 Portuguese militia). The Allied army with which he crossed into France in 1813 numbered 36,000 British, 23,000 Portuguese and 4,000 Spanish (figures at the Battle of Nivelle) with many thousands more Portuguese securing the army's lines of supply and communication. Of the Portuguese, Wellington wrote in July 1813 'No troops could behave better; nothing could equal their forwardness now, and their ready willing temper'. Before Waterloo, Wellington urgently sent for 14,000 of his 'trusty Portuguese' but the speed of Napoleon's advance overtook response.

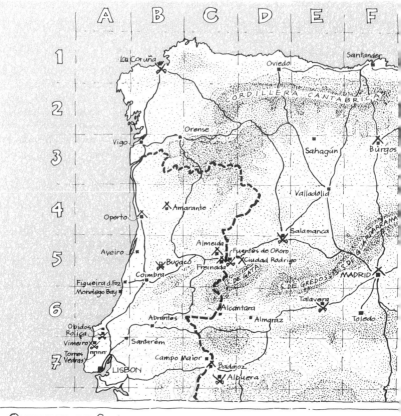

OUTLINE OF CAMPAIGNS

1807 French gather at Bayonne [H1], cross Spain (French ally since 1795) into Portugal, severe losses from 'scorched earth' policy, occupy Lisbon [A7]. Portuguese king, court, navy etc. sail to Brazil.

1808 French usurp Spanish monarchy -Joseph Bonaparte crowned king. National risings Madrid [F5] and Lisbon. Wellington lands Mondego Bay [A6], south to ✗ Óbidos [A6], ✗ Roliça [A6], ✗ Vimeiro [A7]. Wellington replaced. French evacuate Lisbon (Convention of Cintra). Beresford begins training Portuguese recruits in British tactics. Moore invades Spain from Portugal to divert Napoleon's advance on Madrid.

From Saragún [E1], he retreated to ✗ Coruña [B1]. 5/6 of British forces evacuated. Soult winters in Oporto [B4] - cut off by Portuguese and Spanish guerrilla activity

1809 Wellington returns, takes Oporto. Soult retreats, blocked by Portuguese at Amarante [B4], pursued across mountainous route, with severe losses, to Orense [B3] British victory ✗ Talavera [E6].

1810 Masséna commands 140,000 Army of Portugal, takes Almeida [C5] en-route for Lisbon, British and Portuguese rear-guard action ✗ Buçaco [B5]. _Henceforward British and Portuguese amalgamated into fully integrated Allied army._ Masséna unable to penetrate Torres

LEGEND

□ General location or site of conflict.

■ City or town.

✗ Place occupied or taken by siege by Allied army

✗ Location of battle.

- - ·· National border

— Main road/route

Distance

1807-14

Vedras lines of hill-top forts [A7], 'scorched earth' policy starvation and cut off by Portuguese guerillas.

1811 March, French retreat (by then losses 25,000), ✗ Fuentes de Oñoro [C5], ✗ Albuera [C7],

1812 (Napoleon withdraws 27,000 men for Russian war). ✗ Ciudad Rodrigo [D5], Badajoz taken [C7], severe French defeat ✗ Salamanca [D4/5]. Wellington briefly enters Madrid, withdraws to winter at Freinada [C5]. (French still 200,000 effectives, Allied army 56,000 ··· Napoleon begins retreat from Moscow)

1813 Allies retake Salamanca, Valladolid [E4] but not Burgos [F3]. Spanish guerillas also active. King Joseph retreating to France with vast train of refugees and plunder, severely defeated ✗ Vitoria [G1], (news of Vitoria brings Austria into the war). Allies take Saragossa [I3], Pamplona [H2], (news nine day ✗ Pyrenees/Roncevalles [H2], ✗ San Sebastian [H1]. Oct. 7 Allied army enter France. ✗ river Nivelle, take St. Pée. (Napoleon defeated battle of Leipzig). King Ferdinand of Spain makes separate treaty with Napoleon. ✗ river Nive.

1814 Allied army takes Bayonne [H1], occupies Bordeaux [north off map] ✗ Orthez [I1], ✗ Vic-Bigorre [I1], April 10 final victory ✗ Toulouse. News arrives of Napoleon's April 6th abdication.

Map 12: *Portugal and The Scramble for Africa 1880–91*

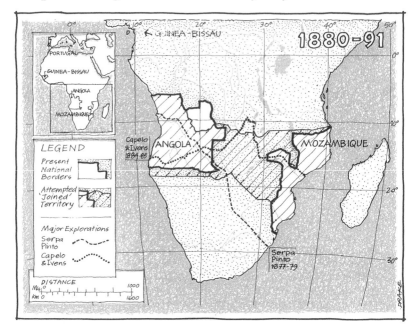

The second half of the 19th century saw growing rivalry between the European powers in the scramble for Africa. Portugal had long been established on the coasts of Guinea, Angola and Mozambique, and numerous expeditions had been undertaken, by military officers, scientists and merchants to explore the interior between latitudes 7° and 27° South, in the regions now called Zambia, Malawi, Zimbabwe and Zaire. A few of the more important expeditions are shown on Map 12. ☐ At the Berlin Conference (1884–5) the rival powers decided that effective occupation, not prior discovery, should constitute justifiable claims. This did not suit the Portuguese, whose effective occupations scarcely extended beyond the coast and hinterland and along the Zambesi river. Attempts were made to promote rapid African settlement but with little success – Brazil and the USA were stronger magnets for emigrants. Nonetheless, in 1887, the 'Pink Map' showed claims to a Portuguese Meridional Africa – as shown on Map 12 – joining Angola and Mozambique east and west and cutting across British ambitions for

148

continuous territory south to north, Cape to Cairo. On 11 January Lord Salisbury's government issued an ultimatum demanding the immediate withdrawal of Portuguese forces from the disputed areas. □ This ultimatum from so old an ally deeply shocked public opinion in Portugal, which demanded war. In the event, matters were settled by a treaty in 1890 and then by a further treaty in 1891 partitioning the Congo Free State. This allocated new and vast areas east of the Congo river to Portugal and resulted in a much enlarged Angola. □ Guinea-Bissau, Angola and Mozambique are all now independent, but retain linguistic and many other ties with Portugal.

Map 13: *The Portuguese language around the world*

Map 13 overleaf shows where Portuguese is spoken (excluding a dozen or so regions where argots of a Portuguese patois and an earlier indigenous language persist, for example, in Goa and Timor). □ This world-wide distribution of Portuguese is the result chiefly of Portugal having established the first sea-borne empire of any European power, and the marked propensity of the Portuguese ever since the 16th century to migrate, settle and inter-marry abroad, whether in countries of Portuguese culture or under other dispensations: for example, Paris is believed to contain the largest numbers of Portuguese of any city in Europe outside Lisbon and Oporto. In 1997, 4,639,000 Portuguese citizens were registerd as living abroad – nearly half as many as live in Portugal itself. □ The map distinguishes between these Portuguese migrants and the populations in countries where Portuguese is the official language – for example in Portugal, Brazil, Angola etc. □ In international tables listing population numbers world-wide according to their use of particular official languages, Portuguese, with nearly 200 million official users – 156 million in Brazil alone – ranks third, after English and Spanish, among European languages.

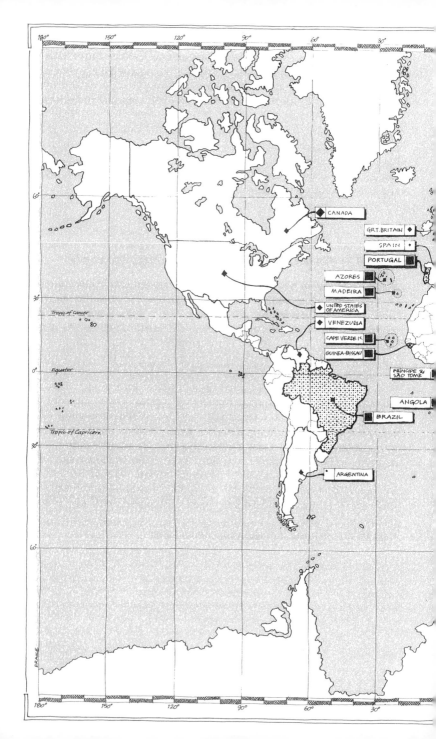

CANADA

GRT. BRITAIN ◆

SPAIN ◆

PORTUGAL

AZORES

MADEIRA

UNITED STATES
OF AMERICA

VENEZUELA

CAPE VERDE IS.

GUINEA-BISSAU

PRÍNCIPE &
SÃO TOMÉ

ANGOLA

BRAZIL

ARGENTINA

Tropic of Cancer

Equator

Tropic of Capricorn

180°   150°   120°   90°   60°   30°

60°

30°

0°

30°

60°

FRAME

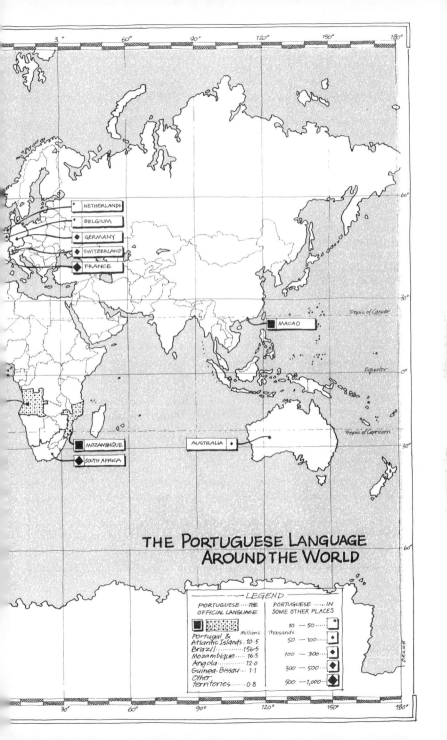

NETHERLANDS

BELGIUM

GERMANY

SWITZERLAND

FRANCE

MACAO

MOZAMBIQUE

AUSTRALIA

SOUTH AFRICA

Tropic of Cancer

Equator

Tropic of Capricorn

THE PORTUGUESE LANGUAGE
AROUND THE WORLD

--- LEGEND ---

PORTUGUESE ···· THE OFFICIAL LANGUAGE	PORTUGUESE ······ IN SOME OTHER PLACES

Portugal & Atlantic Islands ·· 10·5
Brazil ·············· 156·5
Mozambique ····· 16·5
Angola ············· 12·0
Guinea-Bissau ···· 1·1
Other territories ······· 0·8

Millions

Thousands.

10 — 50 ····
50 — 100 ····
100 — 300 ····
300 — 500 ····
500 —1,000 ····

DRAKE

Map 14: *Portugal – regions*

Map 14 shows the names and the boundaries of the historic regions of Portugal – those likely to be referred to in conversation and in literature. However, Salazar re-organized the administration of continental Portugal into eighteen administrative districts; the map shows their capitals. The best pattern for regional devolution is currently again under discussion.

Chronologies

Some of the more oft-quoted nicknames are given; dates in brackets indicate the year of marriages.

House of Burgundy (or Afonsin Dynasty)

1128/39–85 Afonso (Henriques) I *m.* Mafalda of Maurienne and Savoy (1146)

1185–1211 Sancho I *m.* Dulce of Aragon (1174)

1211–23 Afonso II *m.* Urraca (1208), daughter of Alfonso VIII of Castile and Eleanor Plantagenet

1223–48 Sancho II *m.* Mécia López de Haro

1248–79 Afonso III *m.* 1) Matilde, Countess of Boulogne (1235) *m.* 2) Beatriz de Guillén (1253), daughter of Alfonso X of Castile

1279–1325 Dinis, 'O Lavrador' (the husbandman) *m.* Isabel of Aragon (1282)

1325–57 Afonso IV *m.* Beatriz of Castile (1309), daughter of Sancho IV of Castile

1357–67 Pedro I (the Justiciero) *m.* 1) Blanca of Castile (1328) *m.* 2) Constanza of Castile (1340) *m.* 3) Inês de Castro (1354?)

1367–83 Fernando *m.* Leonor Teles (1372)

1383–5 (Interregnum)

House of Avis

1385–1433 João I *m.* Philippa of Lancaster (1387)

1433–8 Duarte (Edward) *m.* Leonor of Aragón (1428)

1438–81 Afonso V (the African) *m.* Isabel of Portugal (1441)

1481–95 João II *m.* Leonor of Portugal (1471)

1495–1521 Manuel I ('the Fortunate') *m.* 1) Isabel of Castile (1497) *m.* 2) Maria of Castile (1500) *m.* 3) Leonor of Spain (1518)

1521–57 João III *m.* Catarina of Spain (1525)

1557–78 Sebastião ('the Regretted')

| 1578–80 | Henrique, the Cardinal-king |
| 1580 | António, Prior of Crato |

House of Austria (Spanish usurpation)
1580–98	Felipe II of Spain (I of Portugal)
1598–1621	Felipe III of Spain (II of Portugal)
1621–40	Felipe IV of Spain (III of Portugal)

House of Braganza
1640–56	João IV *m.* Luisa de Guzmán (1633)
1656–83	Afonso VI *m.* Maria-Francisca-Isabel d'Aumale of Savoy (1661; unconsummated)
1683–1706	Pedro II (Regent from 1668) *m.* 1) Isabel d'Aumale (1668) *m.* 2) Maria-Sofia-Isabel of Neuberg (1687)
1706–50	João V ('the Magnificent') *m.* Maria-Ana of Austria (1708)
1750–77	José *m.* Mariana-Victoria of Spain (1729)
1777–1816	Maria (Francisca) I *m.* Pedro III (her uncle; in 1760)
1816–26	João VI (Regent from 1792; formally from 1799) *m.* Carlota-Joaquina of Spain (1784)
1826	Pedro IV (who abdicated, leaving the kingdom to his daughter, Maria) *m.* 1) Maria Leopoldina of Austria (1817) *m.* 2) Maria Amelia of Leuchtenberg (1829)
1828–34	Usurpation of Dom Miguel *m.* Adelaide-Sofia of Loewenstein-Rosenberg (1851)
1834–53	Maria II ('da Glória') *m.* 1) August of Leuchtenberg (1834) *m.* 2) Ferdinand of Saxe-Coburg-Gotha (1836)
1853–61	Pedro V *m.* Stéphanie of Hohenzollern-Sigmaringen (1858)
1861–89	Luís *m.* Maria-Pia of Savoy (1862)
1889–1908	Carlos *m.* Marie-Amelie of Orléans (1886)
1908–10	Manuel II ('the Unfortunate') *m.* Augusta-Victoria of Sigmaringen

Republic
Presidents or heads of provisional governments
1910	Teófilo Braga
1911–15	Manuel de Arriaga
1915	Teófilo Braga

1915–17	Bernardino Machado
1917–18	Sidónio Pais
1918–19	Admiral João de Canto e Castro
1919–23	António José de Almeida
1923–5	Manuel Teixeira Gomes
1925–6	Bernardino Machado
1926	Commander Mendes Cabeçadas
1926	General Gomes da Costa
1926–51	General António Óscar de Fragoso Carmona (with António de Oliveira Salazar as prime minister from 1932 to 1968)
1951–8	General Francisco Higino Craveiro Lopes
1958–74	Admiral Américo de Deus Rodrigues Tomás (with Marcelo Caetano as prime minister from 1968 to 1974)
1974	General António Sebastião Ribeiro de Spinola
1974–6	General Francisco da Costa Gomes
1976–86	General António dos Santos Ramalho Eanes
1986–96	Mário Alberto Nobre Lopes Soares
1996	Jorge Sampaio

CHRONOLOGICAL TABLE

c.1100 BC	Phoenicians active in southern Portugal
c.1000 BC	Northern Portugal invaded by Celtic tribes
c.600 BC	Greek traders reach Portugal
c.535 BC	Carthaginians in control
218–202 BC	The Second Punic War, after which Iberia was dominated by the Romans, and Portugal formed part of the province of Hispania Ulterior
154 BC	The Lusitani revolt; their leader Viriatus is assassinated in 139 BC
138–136 BC	Expedition into Gallaecia under Decimus Junius Brutus, who then establishes his capital at Olisipo (Lisbon), as does Julius Caesar in 60 BC
19 BC	The territory which now constitutes 'Portugal' is pacified by the Romans
AD 409	Northern Gallaecia and Baetica invaded by the Vandals, and Lusitania occupied by the Alans (in c. 429 crossing to Africa)

c.411	The Suevi settle between the Minho and Douro. Their king, Rechiarus (448–57), was killed by the Visigoths
c.415	The Visigoths enter the peninsula
585	Leovigild suppresses the Suevic kingdom; Recared, his successor, is converted to Catholicism (589)
711	Muslims led by Taric ibn Ziyad invade the peninsula from Africa; Portugal south of the Mondego occupied by *c*.716
868	Oporto reconquered by the Christians; the area between the Minho and Douro first referred to as 'Portucale' in 883
1073	Alfonso VI king of Castile, Galicia and Portugal. His daughter Urraca marries Raymond of Burgundy, who by 1095 is also lord of Galicia and count of Coimbra
1097	Raymond's cousin, Henry, given the County of Portucale and Coimbra. On his death (1112/14) his wife Teresa (an illegitimate daughter of Alfonso VI) becomes regent for their son, Afonso Henriques
c.1099	The Almoravids settle in the Algarve (al-Gharbh al-Andalus), followed by the Almohads in 1146
1128	The battle of São Mamede (Guimarães) won by Afonso Henriques
1139	The Moors decisively defeated at Ourique
1143	By the Treaty of Zamora, Afonso (Henriques) I is recognized as king of Portugal by Alfonso VII, and formally by Pope Alexander III in 1179
1146	Afonso Henriques marries Mafalda of Maurienne and Savoy. Lisbon falls to him in 1147
1153	The Cistercians given land at Alcobaça; their monastery built between 1178 and 1223
1158	Alcácer do Sal taken; and Beja and Évora in 1162 and 1165
1171	The Christians pushed back to Santarém by the Almohads
1185–1211	Sancho I, second ruler of the House of Burgundy or Afonsin dynasty, captures Silves in 1189, but territory south of the Tagus is lost to al-Mansur the following year

1208	The future Afonso II marries Urraca, daughter of Alfonso VIII of Castile and Eleanor Plantagenet
1211	The first *Cortes* held at Coimbra
1212	The battle of Las Navas de Tolosa in Spain, a watershed in the Reconquest of the Peninsula as a whole
1223–48	Sancho II
1248–79	Afonso III
1267	Castile gives up any claim to the Algarve, completing territorial integration of Portugal
1279–1325	Dinis, 'O Lavrador'
1297	Frontier with Castile endorsed by the Treaty of Alcañices
1319	The Order of Christ founded
1325–57	Afonso IV
1340	Afonso, allied with Alfonso XI of Castile, defeats the Moors at the battle of Salado
1357–67	Pedro I, the Justiciero
1355	Inês de Castro murdered
1367–83	Fernando
1373	Lisbon sacked; and an Anglo-Portuguese alliance was signed
1381	Edmund of Cambridge's troops land at Lisbon
1383–5	Interregnum of Leonor Teles
1385	The battle of Aljubarrota (14 August). João of Avis proclaimed king, and reigns until 1433
1386	The Treaty of Windsor signed with England
1387	João I marries Philippa of Lancaster, daughter of John of Gaunt, at Oporto
1388	Construction of Batalha commenced
1415	Ceuta captured
1419–27	Madeira and the Azores discovered or rediscovered
1437	Tangier expedition fails
1433–8	Duarte (Edward)
1438–81	Afonso V, 'the African'
1445	First 'factory 'on African coast established, at Arguim
1449	The battle of Alfarrobeira, in which the Duke of Coimbra is killed
*c.*1457	Cape Verde Islands discovered
1460	Death of Prince Henry the Navigator, who had instigated much maritime exploration

1471	Tangier eventually taken
1476	Indecisive battle of Toro against the Castilians
1479	Portugal cedes Canary Islands to Spain
1481–95	João II
1482	São João da Mina fort built on the Gold Coast; Diogo Cão reaches the Congo river
1487/8	The Cape of Good Hope rounded by Bartolomeu Dias
1492	Some 60,000 Jews expelled from Spain take refuge in Portugal
1494	The Treaty of Tordesillas divides the new discoveries between Spain and Portugal
1495–1521	Manuel I, 'the Fortunate'
1497–8	Vasco da Gama discovers the sea-route to India
1499–1502	Newfoundland, Labrador and Nova Scotia reached by Gaspar and Miguel Corte Real
1500	Brazil discovered by Pedro Álvares Cabral; Madagascar discovered
c.1501	Fishing settlement established on Newfoundland
1507	Fort built at Mozambique
1510–15	Goa, Malacca and Ormuz occupied by Afonso de Albuquerque
1514	First Portuguese trade mission to China
1518	Fort built in Colombo, Ceylon
1519–22	The surviving ship of Magellan's expedition, commanded by Elcano, sailing under the Castilian flag, circumnavigates the globe
1521–57	João III
1531	The Inquisition introduced into Portugal
1537	Diu ceded to the Portuguese
1542/43	The Portuguese reach Japan; a mission founded there by Francis Xavier, S.J., in 1549
1549	Portuguese governor-general takes up his post in Brazil
1557	Trading post established at Macao
1557–78	Sebastião, 'the Regretted'; he is killed at the disaster of Alcácer-Quibir in 1578
1571	Portuguese established at Nagasaki
1572	Camões' *Os Lusíadas* published; he dies in 1580
1578–80	Henrique, the Cardinal-king
1580	António, Prior of Crato, proclaims himself king, but

	is defeated by the Duke of Alba at Alcântara
1580–1640	Castilian usurpation – the 'Sixty Years Captivity'
1581	The Cortes at Tomar proclaims Felipe II of Spain as King Felipe I of Portugal
1588	Most of the Spanish 'Armada' sails from Lisbon
1598–1621	Felipe II (III of Spain)
1606	The New Hebrides discovered
1621–40	Felipe III (IV of Spain)
1630–54	Dutch occupation of much of north-eastern Brazil
1637	Revolt at Évora
1640	The Spanish governor overthrown at Lisbon and the Duke of Braganza ascends the throne as João IV. The Portuguese expelled from Japan
1648	Dutch expelled from Angola
1655–63	Loss of Ceylon and Malabar to Dutch
1656–83	Afonso VI
1662	Catherine of Braganza sails to England to marry Charles II; Tangiers and Bombay ceded to England as part of dowry
1663	Portugal defeats Spanish forces at the battle of Ameixial (May)
1664	Portuguese defeat Spanish besieging Castelo Rodrigo
1665	Spanish defeated at Montes Claros (June)
1668	Afonso's brother, Pedro, marries his former sister-in-law and becomes prince regent
1680	Colony of Sacramento on the Río de la Plata founded
1683–1706	Pedro II
1690s	Alluvial gold found in Minas Gerais
1699	The first shipment of gold from Brazil arrives in Lisbon
1703	The Methuen trade treaties signed with Britain
1703–13	Portugal sides with Britain during the War of the Spanish Succession
1704	The Archduke Charles reaches Lisbon (March). Spain declares war on Portugal (April). Berwick advances into Portugal, but retires that July
1705	The widowed Catherine of Braganza is regent for several months. The Portuguese take Valencia de Alcântara and Albuquerque (May)
1706–50	João V
1709	Portuguese defeated near Arronches (May)

1712	Suspension of arms in Portugal (November)
1715	Portugal concludes peace with Spain (February)
1717	Construction of Mafra commenced
1720	Royal Academy of History founded in Lisbon
1729	Diamonds discovered in Bahia, Brazil
1734	Gold discovered in Mato Grosso, Brazil
1749	The Águas Livres aqueduct at Lisbon completed
1750–77	José; Pombal in office
1751	The Indians of Brazil emancipated
1755	The Great Lisbon Earthquake (1 November)
1758	Assassination of José thwarted
1759	The Jesuits expelled from Portugal and her overseas territories
1761	Slavery abolished in mainland Portugal
1763	The capital of Brazil transferred from Salvador to Rio de Janeiro
1777–1816	Maria I. Pombal dismissed from office (1777)
1792	Regency of the future João VI (1816–26), whose mother's insanity causes him to govern in her name after 1791, from 1799 acting as prince-regent
1797	The battle of Cape St Vincent (14 February)
1801	'The War of the Oranges', in which Spain invades Portugal, and forces her to cede Olivença
1805	The Battle of Trafalgar (21 October)
1807	Portugal invaded by the French under Junot; the royal family embark for Brazil. Lisbon under enemy occupation from 30 November
1808	Start of the Peninsular War. The occupying French are defeated by Wellesley (later Wellington) at Roliça (17 August), and Vimeiro (21 August), and repatriated after the Convention of Cintra
1809	Sir John Moore killed at Corunna (16 January)
	Soult driven from Oporto (12 May)
	The battle of Talavera (28 July)
1810	Masséna's advance into Portugal checked at the battle of Buçaco (12 September), and obstructed by the Lines of Torres Vedras. Allied army formed
1811	The French retreat to the Spanish frontier. The battles of Fuentes de Oñoro (3–5 May), and Albuera (16 May)

1812	Ciudad Rodrigo (19 January) and Badajoz (6 April) taken by Wellington. The battle of Salamanca (22 July)
1813	The French finally thrust out of Portugal in mid-May. The battle of Vitoria (21 June)
1814	Final Allied victory at Toulouse
1822	Brazil independent. Portuguese Constitution proclaimed
1826	Pedro IV abdicates, leaving the kingdom to his daughter, Maria
1828–34	The War of the Two Brothers. Miguel, appointed regent, and who proclaimed himself king, eventually forced to capitulate at Evoramonte
1834–53	Maria II, 'da Glória'
1834	The religious orders expelled from Portugal
1853–61	Pedro V
1858	Pedro marries Stéphanie of Hohenzollern-Sigmaringen, who dies of diphtheria two months after reaching Portugal
1861–89	Luís
1890	British demand evacuation of territories between Angola and Mozambique
1895	Mozambique occupied
1889–1908	Carlos (assassinated 1 February)
1905	Angola occupied
1908–10	Manuel II, 'the Unfortunate', who abdicated
1910	The Republic proclaimed (5 October)
1916	Portugal enters First World War on side of Allies
1926	Military dictatorship of General Gomes da Costa
1928	António de Oliveira Salazar Minister of Finance
1932–68	Salazar 'Prime Minister'
1974	Revolution (25 April)
1986	Mário Soares first civilian Head of State for 60 years. Portugal enters the European (Economic) Community.

COMPARATIVE HISTORICAL CHRONOLOGY

Readers may wish to located events in Portuguese history within the framework of contemporary events elsewhere. The brief selection of events below is likely to be familiar chiefly to readers in the West; limitations of space preclude any comprehensive global setting.

c.3000–c.1400	Minoan civilization in Crete
c.1400–c.1200	Mycenean civilization in Greece
753 BC	Foundation of Rome
509	Rome a republic
336–323	Alexander the Great king of Macedon
264–241	First Punic War
218	Hannibal crosses the Alps
146	Destruction of Carthage
58–51	Gallic wars
44	Assassination of Caesar
AD 14	Tiberius emperor
53	Nero emperor
79	Destruction of Pompeii
117	Death of Trajan
337	Death of Constantine I
410	Rome sacked by Visigoths
527	Justinian emperor
c.570	Birth of Mohammed
718	The 'battle' of Covadonga, initiating the reconquest of Iberian Peninsula
732	Muslim invasion of France checked at Poitiers by Charles Martel
748	Kyoto becomes capital of Japan
791	Oviedo established as a Christian capital
800–14	Charlemagne emperor
910	Monastery of Cluny founded
914	León established as Christian capital
928	Al-Andalus proclaimed a caliphate by Abd al-Rahman III
1031	The caliphate disintegrates into *taifas*
1066	William the Conqueror invades England: the Battle of Hastings

1085	Toledo recaptured by Alfonso VI of Castile
1094	The Cid seizes Valencia
1099	Jerusalem captured by the Crusaders
1114	St Bernard founds Clairvaux
1118	Templars founded. Saragossa captured by Alfonso I of Aragon
1146	Almohad invasion from North Africa
1158–66	Military orders of Calatrava, Santiago and Alcântara founded
1190	Start of the Third Crusade
1201	Start of the Fourth Crusade
1206	Oxford University founded
1208	Commencement of the Albigensian Crusade
1212	Christian victory of Las Navas de Tolosa
1214	The battle of Bouvines
1215	Magna Carta signed
1233	The Teutonic Knights founded
1239	Jerusalem lost to the Christians
1270	Eighth Crusade; death of St Louis at Tunis
1282	Peter III of Aragon conquers Sicily
1311	The Templars abolished
1337	Commencement of the Hundred Years War, carried on until 1453
1346	The battle of Crécy
1368–1644	Ming dynasty in China
1415	The battle of Agincourt
1443	Kingdom of Naples conquered by Alfonso V of Aragon
1453	The Turks take Constantinople
1455–85	The Wars of the Roses
1469	Marriage of Isabel of Castile and Fernando of Aragon
1492	The Spanish capture Granada; the re-discovery of 'America' by Columbus; Jews expulsed from Castile and Aragon
1513	Balbao discovered Pacific ocean
1516	Charles V, the first Habsburg to rule Spain
1519–21	Hernán Cortes conquers Aztec kingdom of Mexico
1520	Luther excommunicated. Field of the Cloth of Gold (meeting between Francis I and Henry VIII)
1525	The battle of Pavia

1527	Sack of Rome by Imperial troops
1529	The Turks overrun the Balkans as far as Vienna
1533	Fernando Pizarro captures the Inca capital of Cuzco in Peru
1533–84	Reign of Ivan the Terrible
1535–8	Suppression of the monasteries in England
1539	Society of Jesus founded by St Ignacio de Loyola and St Francis Xavier
1544–63	Council of Trent
1545	Silver discovered at Potosi
1554	Philip I marries Mary Tudor
1558–1603	Reign of Elizabeth I
1565	Spain occupies the Philippines
1571	Turkish fleet vanquished at Lepanto
1572	Massacre of St Bartholomew
1579	The 'United Provinces' proclaim their independence, recognized by Spain in 1609
1588	The Spanish Armada destroyed
1598	The Edict of Nantes, protecting Protestants
1618–48	The Thirty Years War
1620	The 'Pilgrim Fathers' sail to America
1632	Death of Gustavas Adolfus
1640–1852	Foreigners expelled from Japan under the Tokugawa shogunate (1603–1867)
1643	Spanish defeated at Rocroi
1643–1715	Reign of Louis XIV
1644–1912	Manchu or Ch'ing dynasty in China
1640	The Catalans revolt against Castile
1642–52	The English Civil War
1648	The Peace of Westphalia: Holland independent
1651	Cromwell protector
1655	England captures Jamaica from Spain
1659	The Peace of the Pyrenees
1660	The Restoration in England
1666	Great Fire of London
1683	Vienna besieged by the Turks
1685	Revocation of the Edict of Nantes
1702–13	War of the Spanish Succession, ended by Treaty of Utrecht
1704	The battle of Blenheim; Gibraltar captured by British

1740	War of the Austrian Succession
1740–86	Reign of Frederick the Great
1756–63	The Seven Years War
1768	Captain Cook sails for Tahiti
1775	America at war with England
1776	Declaration of American Independence
1787	English colony established at Botany Bay
1789	Commencement of the French Revolution
1798	Bonaparte in Egypt; Nelson destroys French fleet at Aboukir
1799	Napoleon First Consul, and in 1804, emperor
1807	Abolition of slave trade in Britain; and in 1834 in its colonies
1812	Spanish liberal Constitution of Cadiz
1815	Congress of Vienna; the battle of Waterloo
1827	Turkish fleet destroyed at Navarino
1833–9	First Carlist War in Spain
1854–6	Crimean War
1861–5	American Civil War
1870–1	Franco-Prussian War
1872–6	Second Carlist War
1898	Spanish-American War. Spain loses her remaining empire
1901	Death of Queen Victoria
1904–5	Russo-Japanese War
1914–18	First World War
1917	The Russian Revolution
1936–9	Spanish Civil War
1939–45	Second World War
1958	European Economic Community becomes effective
1963	President Kennedy assassinated.
1989	Communism collapses in Soviet Union and subsequently in Eastern Europe

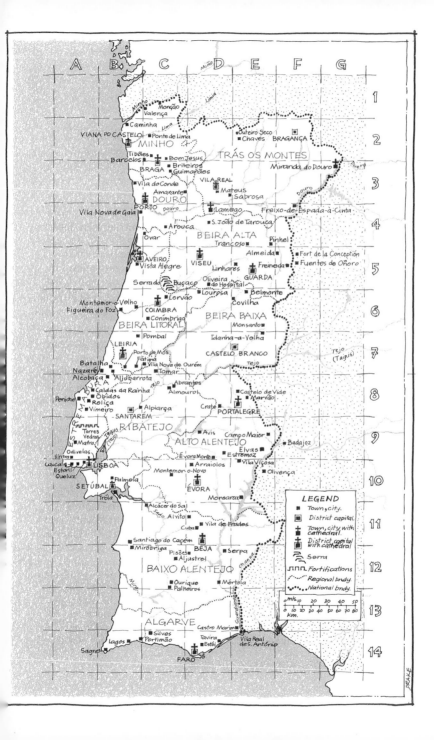

Historical gazetteer

Map 15: *Portugal – a historical gazetteer*

The map on the preceding page is designed to accompany the historical gazetteer which follows. Against each place-name in the gazetteer will be found co-ordinates [A5, E10 etc] which indicate the square on the map where the place can be found.

Abrantes [C8], built on a strategic site commanding the Tagus, repulsed an Almohad attack in 1179; some two hundred years later it was the headquarters of João de Avis before the battle of Aljubarrota (q.v.). British troops wintered here in 1704, during a pause in the War of the Spanish Succession. In 1807 it was occupied by General Junot while leading French troops into Portugal prior to the outbreak of the Peninsular War, for which facile exploit he was dubbed Duc d'Abrantes by Napoleon. Wellington (although he was not so-named until after that bloody battle), concentrated his forces here in 1809 before marching on Talavera in Spain and it remained an important base of the Anglo-Portuguese forces, even passing into proverb: *'Quartel General em Abrantes; tudo como dantes'* (Headquarters at Abrantes; everything as before).

The town itself is of comparatively slight interest, although the castle keep commands a wide view, while Santa Maria do Castelo, now a museum, contains also the tombs of the Almeida family.

Alcácer do Sal (B11], Roman Salacia, and once a strong Moorish fortress, was able to resist capture by Afonso Henriques, wounded here after having taken Lisbon in 1147. It was not until 1217 that it was eventually taken by the Christians, after a long siege in which a contingent of Crusaders, anchored off the estuary *en route* to the Holy Land, had participated.

The restored castle (containing a *pousada*) encloses Romanesque Santa Maria. Nearby are relics of the convent of Aracoeli, Renaissance Santo António, and the former church of Espírito Santo, in which Dom Manuel I married his second wife, Maria of Castile, in 1500; it has a Manueline window and archaeological collections.

Alcobaça [B8], is justly famous for its magnificent although mutilated Cistercian abbey, of which Lady Holland remarked in 1805 that it was 'far the best and least disgusting' convent she had ever seen. Behind a baroque façade stands the massive church, with its impressively long nave, founded by Afonso Henriques *c.*1153 after capturing Santarém (q.v.), and completed in 1223. It was visited by William Beckford in 1793, but his evocative description of the excursion to it and Batalha was not published until 1835. Although savagely pillaged by the French in 1810, the delicately carved tomb of Dom Pedro I, facing the equally beautiful tomb of his mistress, Inês de Castro, survived desecration as did those of Dom Afonso II and Dom Afonso III and their respective wives. Notable are the chapter-house, monks' hall and dormitory, the magnificent tiled kitchen with its immense chimney (referred to by Beckford as the 'most distinguished temple of gluttony in all Europe'), the vaulted refectory, and the Sala dos Reis, displaying idealized royal statues.

Aljubarrota [B7] gives its name to the crucial battle of August 1385, which in fact took place near Batalha (q.v.), at which João, Master of Avis, together with the Constable Nun'Álvares Pereira and a contingent of English archers, virtually destroyed the Castilian army of Juan I, invading the country to claim the crown by force after the death of Dom Fernando, his father-in-law. Among those killed were a high proportion of the landed aristocracy of Portugal who had opposed Dom João's succession.

Aljustrel [C12], pre-Roman Vispasca, has copper-mines known as early as the second millennium, but they were only exploited actively by the Romans, whose shafts descended to 120m. The extent of the slag heap gives some idea of the mines' importance; there is a mining museum.

Almeida [F5] While it fell twice in the 14th century during Spanish incursions across the frontier, and was forced to surrender to them in 1762, its Vaubanesque fortifications with their bomb-proof casemates were to make it one of the most powerfully defended strongholds in Portugal. It was a base of operations against Spain in 1704, and in the latter half of the century was frequently governed by British officers in the Portuguese service. After a period of dilapidation its bastions were again put in a state of defence, but in spite of a spirited delaying action by General Crawfurd's Light Division in July 1810, the French under Masséna were able to invade the place. Colonel Cox, the commandant, was forced to capitulate shortly after the bombardment commenced, for a chance shot caused the explosion of the central magazine, reducing the castle and cathedral to a pile of rubble, and killing outright 500 of the garrison.

There is still much to see: the town's fortifications alone make it worth visiting and the main gate dated 1796 is remarkable; they alone make it worthwhile visiting. While here, those interested in such matters are strongly recommended to make the expedition across the border to see the impressive hill-top **fort 'de la Concepción'**, 10km due east as the crow flies, which was blown up by Craufurd to make it untenable by the French. It stands above the road on approaching Aldea del Obispo, a drive of c.30km from Almeida, and may be reached by crossing into Spain at Vilar Formoso and immediately turning north. Also in this area are Fuentes de Oñoro and Freneida (q.v.).

Almourol [C8] The castle, its keep surrounded by a rampart and nine other towers, standing on its picturesque island site in the Tagus, was rebuilt by the Templars in 1171 on the foundations of an earlier fortress. It was referred to in Francisco de Morães's *Crónica do Palmeirim de Inglaterra*, which was translated by Southey in 1807, correcting Anthony Munday's Elizabethan version of the romance.

Alpiarça [B8], north-east of Santarém (q.v.) contains the former home, now a museum, of José Relvas (1858–1929), the politician and collector, who proclaimed the Republic in 1910. At nearby **Moron** are earthworks identified as the military base of Decimus Junius Brutus in *c.*138 BC, before he marched his troops north to the Lima; see also Ponte de Lima.

Alvito [D11] retains a curious half-Moorish, late 15th-century castle (recently converted to house a *pousada*), displaying moulded brick horse-shoe arches typical of the district; the church at a higher level in the small town contains good mid-17th-century *azulejos*.

Amarante [C3], a straggling old town on the Tâmega, the deep valley of which is here crossed by a handsome obelisk-embellished bridge of 1790, was the site of fighting in the late spring of 1809, when Beresford's Corps came to the support of Silveira's Portuguese, which caused the French under Loison to jettison their wheeled transport and artillery and retreat north-west.

The conventual church, with two Renaissance cloisters, is dedicated to São Gonçalo, the local saint and a vigorous fellow by all accounts, who in the mid-13th century is said to have reconstructed the earlier, Romanesque, bridge with his own hands, being beatified for his labours in 1561. Although this particular erection collapsed in 1763, his tomb, reputed to retain potent properties, continued to be visited by husband-hunters past their first youth, who had merely to rub their bare flesh against it to be granted a spouse within a year; and to make doubly sure, at the biannual festivals in his honour, phallic-shaped cakes called *testículos de São Gonçalo* were baked and nibbled, which still have a ready sale. The cylindrical church of São Domingos contains a fine organ-case and rococo *talha*; while further up the hill stands São Pedro, with a notable sacristy.

Arouca [C4], remotely sited among convoluted wooded hills between Oporto and Viseu, contains the Cistercian convent of Santa Maria, rebuilt after a fire in the early 18th century. It is associated with Mafalda, daughter of Sancho I, who retired here after her marriage in 1215 (aged twenty-one, to the twelve-year-old Enrique I of Castile) had been annulled. In 1734, not to be outshone by her sisters at Lorvão (q.v.), her remains were placed in a silver casket displayed in the church, in which the choir-stalls are remark-able, but the stone statues of female saints have not been improved by coats of whitewash. A later inmate was Clara Warre, visited here by Lord Beresford and her brother, General Sir William Warre, during a lull in the Peninsular War.

Arraiolos [D10], with its ruined castle, was long reputed for its blue and red embroidered carpets. When Beckford acquired some 'of strange grotesque patterns and glaring colours' in 1787, the manufactory employed about 300 people. The Quinta dos Lóios, formerly a convent, attractively sited in a neighbouring valley, contains notable *azulejos* in its church.

Aveiro [B5], predictably referred to by those who must describe any water-logged town as 'the Venice of' wherever it may be, lies on the edge of salitrose mud-flats adjoining its *ria*. Until 1575, when a storm cast a sand-bar across the mouth of the Vouga, the place was a prosperous fishing-port. In 1808 General Hill transported his troops across the lagoon in its flat-bottomed *moliceiros*, or seaweed-harvesting vessels, by which amphibious operation he outflanked the French retreating on Oporto (q.v.).

The former Convento de Jesus is now a museum, and contains the portrait, attributed to Nuno Gonçalves, of Dom Afonso V's daughter, Santa Joana, who spent the last fourteen years of her life here, dying in 1489. Her hagiographer admired her capacity to suffer the lice bred in her chemise. Her tomb, a confection of marble marquetry, dates from 1711, eighteen years after her beatification. More attractive is the chinoiserie panelling of the upper choir and the *azulejos* in the refectory.

Among other buildings, the octagonal chapel of Senhor das Barrocas, with sculpture by Claude de Laprade, is of more interest than São Domingo, described formerly as 'a squalid and tawdry room', which when raised to cathedral rank was monstrously modernised.

Avis [D9] was granted in 1220 to the Spanish military order of Calatrava, referred to in Portugal as the Knights of Évora, who built the castle. They became known as the Knights of Avis and later as the Order of São Bento. Dom João I, the son of Dom Pedro I and Teresa Lourenço, was Grand Master of the Order before acceding to the throne in 1385 and founding the new royal dynasty of Avis.

Three imposing towers remain of the fortress, while of the monastery of São Bento, last transformed in 1711, the church retains a good baroque retable, and 16th-century sacristy.

Barcelos [C2], halfway between Braga and the coast, is an attractive and ancient town astride the lamprey-laden Cávado. The last count of Barcelos having been killed at Aljubarrota (q.v.), Dom Afonso, a natural son of João I, received the county on his marriage to Brites, daughter of Nun'Álvares Pereira (see Vila do Conde), and built a palace to guard the bridgehead. (Beatriz, another of Dom João's bastards, was married off by Philippa of

Lancaster to Thomas Fitzalan, Earl of Arundel, in 1405.) In the ruins is a museum, while the adjacent Igreja Matriz preserves fragments of an earlier church. Nearby is the twin-towered Solar dos Pinheiros. Beyond the Torre Nova are gardens embellished by baroque statuary and fountains, and the site of the Thursday market, and also the unusual octagonal church of Bom Jesus, with its granite cupola. Nossa Senhora do Terço contains good *azulejos*, ceiling panels, and a gilded pulpit featuring a crowned double-headed Habsburg eagle, which survived as a decorative element even after the Spanish domination of Portugal.

Batalha [B7] The construction of this great 'battle-abbey' dates from 1388, in consequence of a vow made by Dom João I prior to the battle of Aljubarrota (q.v.), fought in the vicinity. Outstanding features are: the Capela do Fundador, with its octagonal lantern and elaborate star-vault, below which stands the double tomb of Dom João and Philippa of Lancaster (adjacent are those of Henry 'the Navigator' and their other sons); the convoluted tracery of the Claustro Real, off which open the chapter-house and a lavabo; and the extraordinary Capelas Imperfeitas, an unfinished octagon of exuberantly decorated chapels, their upper stories truncated, which lie beyond the east end of the nave, and are entered through a separate portal, an exotic masterpiece of lace-like tracery in stone. See also Alcobaça.

Beja [D11] Roman Pax Julia, now the capital of the Lower Alentejo, is dominated by its lofty castle keep, near which is the Santo Amaro, preserving Visigothic columns. A former inmate of the mid-15th-century convent of Nossa Senhora da Conceição, now a museum, was Mariana Alcoforado, the assumed author of *Letters from a Portuguese Nun*. The 13th-century convent of São Francisco has been converted to house a *pousada*.

At **Pisões**, to the south-west, lie the extensive remains of a Roman villa.

Belmonte [E6], a village commanded by its granite castle, was once the centre of a Crypto-Jewish community. It was also the birthplace of Pedro Álvares Cabral, 'discoverer' of Brazil in 1500 (see also Santarém). Nearby are remains of a 'domus municipalis' (cf. Braganza), while off the road to Guarda stands the Torre Centum Cellas, a curious ruin of Roman origin, fortified in the medieval period.

Braga/Bom Jesus [C2] Substantial remains exist of Bracara Augusta, the main Roman station of northern Lusitania, which became the Suevic capital, and fell to Theodoric II in 456. With the conversion of the Visigoths to orthodox Catholicism, it grew in importance as a religious centre, although its primacy over other sees in the north-west of the Iberian peninsula was not confirmed until almost a century after its reconquest from the

Moors by Fernando I of Castile in 1040.

The south portal and west doors of the Romanesque cathedral have survived later reconstruction, while the Capela dos Reis contains the tomb of the founder, Count Henry of Burgundy and his wife, and of Archbishop Lourenço, wounded at Aljubarrota. The Capela da Glória is notable, as are the magnificent organs. The treasury contains material of interest, appallingly displayed. Also to be seen are the former Archiepiscopal palace and library; the Casa dos Biscainhos, now the museum; Santa Cruz, and the adjacent Palácio do Raio.

Some 5km east is the hill-top sanctuary of **Bom Jesus**, with its monumental double flight of steps, constructed after 1723, embellished with baroque chapels, fountains and statuary.

Braganza [F2], Celtic Brigantia, under the ancient high-lying capital of the Trás-os-Montes, long a provincial backwater, is widely known through providing the surname for Charles II's queen, Catherine. The dukedom was created in 1442 for a natural son of Dom João I, the 8th duke becoming Dom João IV in 1640. The upper, walled, town is commanded by a castle keep, and a church, adjacent to which is the over-restored 'domus municipalis', a rare survival of Romanesque civic architecture. Traditionally, Inês de Castro (see also Coimbra, and Alcobaça) was clandestinely married in São Vicente in 1354 to the future Dom Pedro I. The Museu do Abade de Baçal, in the former bishop's palace, contains archaeological and ethnographical collections of interest.

Briteiros, Citânia of [C3] One of the more accessible and impressive northern Celtiberian strongholds surviving, consisting of over 150 stone huts (some reconstructed) straddling a boulder-strewn hill surrounded by three defensive walls. The settlement, dating from *c.*300 BC, was probably abandoned by AD 300.

Buçaco [C5] The reafforested *serra* do Buçaco (anglicized as **Busaco**) was the 'damned long hill' north of Coimbra along which Wellington with his Anglo-Portuguese army had taken up an almost impregnable defensive position, and against which on 27 September 1810 Marshal Masséna repeatedly hurled his columns, ineffectively and with great loss. On the ridge stands a small military museum. Within the magnificent State Forest surrounding the former Carmelite convent rises a pseudo-Manueline confection built as a royal summer palace, now a luxurious hotel, to which General Spínola made a retreat in August 1974 during a crucial stage in his presidency.

Caldas da Rainha [A8] is an ancient spa which later flourished around a royal hospital, established in 1486. Its chapel, Nossa Senhora do Pópulo, has a curious Manueline cupola. It became a garrison town, from which a detachment of revolutionary troops marched prematurely on Lisbon on 16 March 1974, only to be turned back.

Caminha [B2], a former river-port near the mouth of the Minho, retains some of its fortifications, and several attractive old buildings. The late 15th-century Igreja Matriz, with a later tower, is the finest in the district, and preserves several features of interest.

Campo Maior [E9], of Roman origin, reconquered from the Moors in 1219, has a castle which was later much enlarged, and withstood minor attacks during the Peninsular War. In 1732 the citadel was destroyed when the magazine was struck by lightning, and 1,500 people were killed outright.

Cascais [A10], now a fashionable dormitory suburb of Lisbon, was sacked by the Duke of Alba in 1580 when imposing the Spanish claim to the Portuguese throne, and in May 1589 by Drake in a retaliatory expedition after the Armada's failure, but his attempt to take Lisbon was unsuccessful. Its chief monument is the baroque Nossa Senhora da Assunção, containing paintings by Josefa de Óbidos (see Óbidos).

Castelo Branco [E7], of ancient origin, was refounded by the Templars in the early 13th century. Its walls and castle were attacked by the Spaniards in 1704 and 1762, while Junot's forces sacked the place in 1807. São Miguel once served as a cathedral, while the former Bishop's palace, with its elaborate formal gardens embellished with baroque statuary and topiary, now accommodates the museum. Notable is the collection of *colchas* or embroidered bedspreads, for which the town has been reputed since the late 18th century.

Castelo de Vide [E8], an attractive old spa, preserving several old mansions and its medieval *Judiaria*. Seventeenth-century *azulejos* may be seen in Nossa Senhora da Alegria and São Tiago. The large castle successfully resisted a Spanish incursion in June 1704, but later capitulated in view of the Duke of Berwick's threat to put all to the sword and 'leave the women exposed to the brutality of the soldiers'. The Portuguese dumped their remaining gunpowder in a well, and the following year the castle was seriously damaged by an explosion.

Chaves [E2], Roman Aquae Flaviae, has keys (*chaves*) as its canting device, and it became an important fortress opposing Spanish Verín. It fell to the French early in 1809, but was recaptured, when some 1,200 troops were forced to surrender. The Tâmega is crossed by a Roman bridge, commanded by a castle, the imposing keep of which contains a small museum. The Misericórdia is also of interest, as is the octagonal nave of the Igreja da Madalena.

At **Outreiro Seco**, c.4km north, is a Romanesque church preserving features of interest.

Cintra *see* **Sintra**

Coimbra [C6], identified as Roman Æminium, took its name from neighbouring Conímbriga (q.v.), from which its Visigothic kings and bishops migrated after 486. It was re-conquered by Fernando I of Castile in 1064, and from 1139 until 1385 was the capital of Portugal, having supplanted Guimarães (q.v.). Its famous university was not definitively established here until 1537, at which date it also had an important school of sculptors. From 1567 Coimbra was one of the three seats of the Inquisition in Portugal. It was sacked by Masséna after the battle of Buçaco (q.v.). It was the birthplace of the poet Francisco Sá de Miranda, and in 1732 of Joaquim Machado de Castro, the sculptor, after whom its major museum is named.

Santa Cruz, in the lower town, founded in 1131 but rebuilt in the early 16th century, contains the tombs of Afonso Henriques and his son Dom Sancho I, reinterred here in 1520; the sacristy displays notable paintings. The adjacent Jardim da Manga is curious. In the walled upper town the Casa de Sub-Ripas was traditionally the scene of the murder of Maria Teles, who had married the eldest son of Inês de Castro (see Santa Clara, below). Nearby is the former Colégio Novo. The fortress-like Sé Velha (old cathedral), containing elaborate retables, is one of the finest Romanesque churches in Portugal. The old bishop's palace, flanked by São João de Almedina, on the site of a mosque, houses the important museum, below which is a Roman *cryptoporticus*. The adjacent Sé Nova was the Jesuit church until the suppression of that Order in 1759. Close by are late 18th-century university buildings designed by William Elsden, a British officer in the Portuguese service, beyond which are an aqueduct, botanical gardens and mid-18th-century seminary. Of the Old University, the main survivals are the buildings surrounding the Pátio das Escolas, among them the chapel, and the exuberantly decorated library.

At an upper level of the town are the Mosteiro de Celas, with a circular Manueline church and earlier cloister; and hill-top Santo António dos Olivais.

Across the Mondego lie Santa Clara-a-Velha, silted up by floods, in which Inês de Castro was first buried, before being translated to Alcobaça (q.v.). The mid-17th-century hill-top convent-church of Santa Clara contains the original tomb and silver shrine of St Isabel (died 1336; wife of Dom Dinis).

Conímbriga [C6] was a pre-Roman site (from c.800 BC), and important Roman station on the road from Lisbon via Tomar to Braga, until superseded in importance by Coimbra (q.v.) after its sack by the Suevi in 468. The collection of artefacts, now displayed in the site museum, was started in 1874, but it was only in 1912 that any serious excavation was carried out, which has continued more systematically since. The triangular walled site, between two gorges and fed by an aqueduct, consists of a large villa, several baths, a Flavian forum overlying one of the Augustan period, a temple, a buttressed *palaestra*, etc.

Covilhã [E6] has long been a textile centre, noted for its brown woollen blankets. In the late 17th century, weavers from Colchester were lured here to teach English techniques. It was a cavalry base during the Peninsular War, when dances, once described as 'barbarously brilliant balls', were got up to enliven the long winter evenings. Its monuments are few: relics of a castle and the Romanesque chapel of São Martinho.

Crato [D8] was from the mid-14th century the headquarters of a branch of the Hospitallers known as the Order of Crato, the last of whose Grand Priors was Dom António, a bastard son of the Infante Luis and Violante Gomes, who in 1580 was a rival to Philip II of Spain in his claim to the Portuguese throne. Slight remains survive of the once powerful castle, destroyed by Don Juan of Austria in 1662, and the Igreja Matriz retains some attractive features.

Cuba [D11] Mascarenhas Barreto has recently argued in *The Portuguese Columbus* that Salvador Fernandes Zarco, better known as Cristóbal Colón (or Columbus; 1448–1506), was a bastard of young Fernando, Duke of Viseu and Beja (1433–70; son of Dom Duarte), and whose mother was Isabel Gonçalves da Câmara, was born at either Cuba or neighbouring Vila Ruiva.

Elvas [E9], strategically sited on a height opposite Spanish Badajoz, was eventually recaptured from the Moors in 1230. Although long one of the strongest fortresses in Portugal, it gave way to the invading Spaniards in 1580, but successfully resisted retaliatory attacks after 1644, and was then strengthened by Vaubanesque defensive works, among them the outlying fort 'de Lippe', named after the English-born German count who reorganized the Portuguese army in the 1760s. It was an important British base during the Peninsular War, notably before the sieges of Badajoz in 1811 and 1812.

By the Lisbon road stands the imposingly buttressed Aqueduto da Amoreira, while the fortifications are entered at the Porta de Olivença. The more interesting of several churches is the early 16th-century cathedral, with an earlier tower, behind which is octagonal Nossa Senhora da Consolação. The hill-top Moorish castle has a later keep.

Estói/Milreu [D14] It was once thought that the 2nd–6th-century Roman villa here, largely excavated after 1877, was the site of the Roman town of Ossonoba (see Faro). Among the remains are 3rd-century baths, and a temple converted into a Paleo-Christian basilica.

Estoril [A10], a resort long popular with British valetudinarians – Aubrey FitzGerald Bell settled there in 1911 – later became the fashionable residence of miscellaneous monarchs and pretenders in exile, among them Carol of Rumania, Umberto of Savoy, and Juan de Borbon.

Estremoz [D9], a well-sited garrison town with a large central *praça*, is dominated by the lofty hill-top keep of its royal palace (now a *pousada*) in the upper town, rebuilt by Dom João V after an explosion in 1698. Isabel, the 'Rainha Santa', wife of Dom Dinis (see Santa Clara, Coimbra), died in the former palace in 1336. The Count of Ourém, while entertained here in 1380 when finalising secret negotiations between Richard II and Dom Fernando, contrived to make his not-so-saintly queen, Dona Leonor, pregnant.

Adjacent stands Santa Maria do Castelo, replacing a Gothic church on the site of a mosque, and the former Hospício de Caridade, housing a museum. In the lower town are the Tocha palace, and several convents, some in military occupation.

Évora [D10], Celtic Ebora, was awarded the title 'Liberalitas Julia' by Julius Caesar. An early bishop had attended the Council of Elvira in 300. On its reconquest by Geraldo Sem Pavor it became an important Christian bastion against the Moors, and is still picturesquely encircled by 14th-century walls. After the accession of the House of Avis in 1385, it was frequently a royal residence. Dom João II had his over-mighty brother-in-law, the Duke of Braganza, beheaded here in 1484. A Jesuit university was established in 1559, which survived for 200 years until suppressed by Pombal. Here in 1637 occurred the first serious revolt against the Spanish occupation of Portugal. The town was brutally sacked by the French in 1808, and a period of decline followed, its population falling to a mere 5,000. On 9 September 1973 the Roman temple was the rendezvous of those disillusioned junior army officers who were to bring about the bloodless revolution in the following April.

Several eminent architects were natives of Évora, among them Garcia de Resende, Diogo de Torralva and members of the Arruda family. So was Pedro Fernandes de Queirós, in 1563 a 'discoverer' of Australasia. The dramatist Gil Vicente died here *c.*1540.

The 2nd–3rd-century Roman temple stands within the upper enceinte, with partly Roman walls, adjacent to which are the former Monastery dos Lóios (now a *pousada*), with a Gothic and Renaissance cloister; São João Evangelista, containing Tentugal tombs, and the towered Melos or Cadaval palace. Nearby stands the former archiepiscopal library and palace, now the museum, displaying Roman sculptures, and a notable collection of paintings, including some by Frei Carlos, and by the Master of the retable of Évora cathedral. The granite cathedral, consecrated in 1204, and one of the finest in Portugal, may lie on the emplacement of a mosque. Remarkable are the cloister, treasury, and the central octagonal lantern of the Salmantine type. To the east, beyond a Moorish palace and the Torre de Sertório, stands the former university, with its courtyard, *sala dos actos* and refectory, and the adjacent church of Espírito Santo. South of the cathedral are the Misericórdia, with a baroque interior, a former Carmelite convent, and Nossa Senhora da Graça, embellished by huge stone rosettes. Further west stands Gothic São Francisco, with a macabre charnel-house, and relics of the Palácio de Dom Manuel, beyond which is cylindrically buttressed São Bás. In the central Plaça do Giraldo, partly arcaded, rises Santo Antão.

In the vicinity, beyond a stretch of the 16th-century aqueduct, is the Cartuxa, and Benedictine São Bento de Castrís, its cloister displaying Mudéjar influence; and to the north of Évora, the mid-15th-century convent of Nossa Senhora d'Espinheiro.

Evoramonte [D9] retains the restored castle of 1306, with cylindrical towers, and a later keep preserving Manueline piers and decoration. It was here in May 1834 that Dom Miguel signed the convention ending the futile Miguelite War, abandoning all further claim to the Portuguese throne.

Faro [D14] Little remains of Roman Ossonoba, the forum of which stood on the site of the present cathedral. It was taken from the Moors by Afonso III in 1249 and its large Jewish colony flourished. In 1596, when under Spanish rule, it was pillaged by the Earl of Essex, who parcelled up a library of indigestible theology and presented it to the Bodleian Library, Oxford, a generous gesture from a Cambridge man.

The walled enceinte contains the Renaissance cathedral, with its earlier tower, while nearby are the convent of Nossa Senhora da Assunção, now housing a museum (with a mosaic from Estói, q.v.), and São Francisco. Among other churches are São Pedro, and the Carmo.

Fátima [B7], described as 'the Lourdes of Portugal', is the focus of a massively commercialized mariolatrous cult promoted by the Catholic Church at the scene of apparitions claimed to have been witnessed by three ignorant peasant children in 1917, two of whom were then buried within the huge and oppressively ugly basilica, consecrated in 1953.

Figueira da Foz [B6] is an important fishing-port and resort at the mouth of the Mondego, at which Wellington, who briefly occupied the fort of Santa Catarina, disembarked his expeditionary force in August 1808 prior to marching south towards Roliça (q.v.). Its museum contains important archaeological artefacts.

Freineda [F5] lies a few kilometres south of Castelo Bom, on the road between the Spanish frontier at Vilar Formoso and Guarda (q.v. see also Almeida). The balconied granite house opposite the village church served as Wellington's spartan residence during two successive winters (1811–13), while his headquarters' staff were dispersed in neighbouring villages. Here too were kennelled his pack of hounds, with which he would hunt two or three times a week. (See also Fuentes de Oñoro.)

Freixo de Espada à Cinta [F4] may take its curious name – 'ash-tree of the girt sword' – from the gesture of Dom Dinis, who is said to have encircled a tree here with his sword-belt when founding the frontier fortress. It was the birthplace of Jorge Álvares, the navigator, and chronicler of Japan (in 1547), and of the poet Guerra Junqueiro (1850–1923). The Igreja Matriz, an imposing Manueline rebuilding of an earlier church, contains sixteen paintings ascribed to 'Grão Vasco'.

Fuentes de Oñoro [F5] The older, granite-walled, village lies to the south of the main road to Ciudad Rodrigo, a short distance beyond the frontier crossing of Vilar Formoso. It was here, early in May 1812, after their disastrous retreat from before the Lines of Torres Vedras (q.v.) and having received reinforcements, that the French under Masséna – intent on restoring his tarnished reputation, and not learning the lesson from Buçaco – turned on Wellington and repeated the error of making an impetuous frontal attack on the imperturbable Allied lines. Although the hard-fought two-day battle to which the village gave its name was described by Wellington as 'the most difficult one I was ever concerned in and against the greatest odds', the result was in little doubt. After severe hand-to-hand fighting in its alleys (from which the Allies were dislodged through sheer weight of numbers) the French were driven out, and an informal truce next day allowed the place to be cleared of dead and wounded. Masséna next concentrated his forces in an attack on Wellington's right flank, which was forced to pivot on Fuentes, facing south; but the French eventually gave up the struggle from sheer exhaustion and retired to lick their wounds, while Wellington, on one of the rare occasions during the whole war, ordered his troops to 'dig in'. In the vicinity are Fort Concepción (see Almeida) and Freneida (q.v.).

Guarda [E5], the highest and coldest town in Portugal, and long of strategic importance as commanding the upper valleys of the Mondego and the Zêzere, and facing Spain, was founded in 1197 by Dom Sancho I as a frontier guard against the Moors. Sir John Moore's army entered Spain from here in November 1808, and it became a base of Wellington's operations in 1811–12.

The town retains three gateways and stretches of defensive walls. Remains of a castle overlook the fortress-like cathedral, completed c.1540, and inspired by Batalha (q.v.), containing several Manueline features. The bishop's palace houses the regional museum; the Misericórdia displays a baroque façade; and the 18th-century São Vicente has contemporary *azulejos*.

Guimarães [C3] contends with Braga (q.v.) for the title of 'cradle of the Portuguese monarchy'. In 840 Alfonso II of León convened a council here and it became a centre of Suevic settlement. Henry of Burgundy made it his court in 1095, and his son Afonso Henriques may have been born here. An alliance with England was signed here in July 1372, prior to the Treaty of Windsor. It was the birthplace of Gil Vicente, the dramatist, in 1470.

The hill-top castle has been reconstructed, and the *Paço* of the Dukes of Braganza has been tastelessly over-restored. Also in the upper town are the Misericórdia and the convents do Carmo and de Santa Clara. Of more interest are Nossa Senhora da Oliveira, much rebuilt since founded in the 10th century, and with a Manueline tower. The Museu Alberto Sampaio is housed in conventual dependencies abutting a Romanesque cloister, and contains a triptych traditionally associated with the victory of Aljubarrota (q.v.). The Museu Martins Sarmento displays artefacts from the *citânias* of Briteiros (q.v.) and Sabroso among other important archaeological finds.

The former monastery of Santa Marinha da Costa, south of the town, rebuilt in the 18th century, and now a *pousada*, deserves visiting.

Idanha-a-Velha [E7] was the site of Roman Egitana and the seat of a bishopric from 596 until 1199, although it had been sacked by the Moors some time before the latter date. The present village takes up only part of the original walled enceinte. A medieval tower stands on the podium of a Roman temple, while Roman remains collected in the vicinity are preserved within a restored Paleo-Christian basilica. Both a ruined baptistry and bishop's palace may be seen, while a Roman bridge spans the little river Ponsul.

Lagos [B14], which succeeded Roman Lacobriga (the site of which may have been at adjacent Monte Molião), was not reconquered from the Moors until 1241. It was a headquarters for Henry the Navigator's exploratory expeditions (see Sagres), and later a port of assembly for Dom Sebastião's ill-fated Moroccan campaigns, shortly after which it became the capital of the Algarve, until 1755, when it was laid in ruins by the Lisbon earthquake. In 1759 Boscawen defeated a French squadron off the coast here.

Stretches of its mid-14th-century defensive walls survive, together with a later aqueduct. African slaves were formerly auctioned below the custom-house. Santa Maria has Manueline windows; Santo António displays rich *talha* and *albarrada azulejos*.

Lamego [D4], which may have been Roman Lamaecum, is an old episcopal city standing high above the south bank of the Douro. It was re-conquered in 1057. During the summer of 1811 a train of Wellington's heavy artillery was hauled up from the river here and then across country towards Almeida (q.v.). The cathedral, mainly Gothic, but partly Romanesque and with a partly Renaissance cloister, contains damaged frescoes by Nasoni. 'Grão Vascos' retable is preserved in the museum housed in the former bishop's palace, into which has been built the chapel of São João Evangelista. Several other churches and 17th–18th-century mansions stand in the vicinity, together with remains of a castle and vaulted cistern.

The town is dominated to the south by Nossa Senhora dos Remédios, approached by a long flight of steps with baroque embellishments similar to that at Bom Jesus, Braga (q.v.). In the vicinity are the Visigothic basilica of **São Pedro de Balsemão**, dating in part to the 7th century; **Ferreirim**, with panels by Cristóvão de Figueiredo in its church; and **São João de Tarouca**, part of the first Cistercian monastery in Portugal, with the tomb of Dom Pedro (died 1354), count of Barcelos, a bastard of Dom Dinis.

Leiria [B7] was long contested before its eventual reconquest. The first *Cortes* in Portugal at which the Commons were represented was assembled here by Dom Afonso III in 1254. It was later a residence of Dom Dinis, but only became an episcopal city in 1545. Leiria was the scene of Eça de Querós's novel *The Sin of Father Amaro* (1876). The 16th-century cathedral is a plain building; the 18th-century bishop's palace contains a museum. São Pedro, with a Romanesque portal, is passed on ascending to the castle, with its keep dominating the town, in which is the restored royal palace, retaining an imposing hall and loggia/*miradouro*.

Linhares [E5] Formerly Leniobriga, the hill-top village of ancient origin on the old road skirting the north flank of the Serra da Estrela, was once the seat of a Visigothic bishopric. It preserves numerous 15th-century houses, and is commanded by partly restored castle ruins displaying remarkable stonework.

Lisboa [A10], anglicized as **Lisbon**, the capital of Portugal, its conurbation with a population approaching 2 million, extends along the north bank of the broad estuary of the Tejo (or Tagus), spanned since 1966 by the Ponte 23 de Abril. In 1760 Joseph Baretti wrote that 'to range about such a wide scene as this metropolis and its neighbourhood, gives certainly much satisfaction to an inquisitive pair of eyes': it is as true today. Phoenician Olisipo was occupied by the Romans in 205 BC, after the Second Punic War, and under Julius Caesar it became the *municipium* of Felicitas Julia, and the most important city in Lusitania. In 409 it was occupied by the Alans, and then in succession by the Suevi and the Visigoths, until overrun by the Moors in 714. The Moors were not definitively ousted until 1147 after a siege by Afonso Henriques, aided by a contingent of Crusaders (see Oporto). Subsequently Gilbert of Hastings was consecrated its bishop.

Portuguese discoveries in the 16th century brought enormous wealth and incredible cargoes to the city, and it has been argued that had Philip II of Spain, when forcibly annexing Portugal in 1580, taken heed of his advisors and made Lisbon his capital rather than Madrid, the future history of the Peninsula might have been very different. His *armada* assembled here, and after its destruction, Drake and Norris made retaliatory but abortive attempts at sacking the city. Lisbon proclaimed its independence from Castilian domination in 1640. English merchants were given additional privileges after 1654, and established a 'Factory' here. In 1662 Catherine of Braganza set sail from Lisbon to become Queen of England, further cementing Anglo-Portuguese friendship. It experienced another period of opulence during the reign of Dom João V.

But on 1 November 1755 the city was devastated by an earthquake in which 5 per cent of its population perished. Rebuilding on a more regular plan was put in hand by the Marquês de Pombal, but it was not for several decades that Lisbon again flourished. In November 1807 the royal family set sail for Brazil in the face of French invasion, but Junot's occupation lasted less than nine months, his troops being defeated, and then repatriated by the Convention of Cintra (q.v., and also Vimeiro). The city remained the base of British operations throughout the Peninsular War, defended by the Lines of Torres Vedras (q.v.). It was frequently the scene of unrest during the Miguelite War and later in the 19th century. In 1910, two years after Dom Carlos had been assassinated there, the monarchy was overthrown and replaced by a republic. During the Second World War, as a neutral city strategically commanding sea lanes, it had the reputation, deservedly, of being 'a nest of spies'. In the 'Revolution' of 25 April 1974 the lead given by the capital was followed by the rest of the country, since when Lisbon has again prospered, although the Chiado was scarred by a fire in August 1988.

Among its many eminent natives have been Luís de Camões (Camoens; author of *The Luciads*), b. 1524; the Marquês de Pombal, b. 1699; and the poet Fernando Pessoa, b. 1888; Domenico Scarlatti lived there from 1721 to 1728 as music teacher to the Infanta María Bárbara de Braganza.

The uneven contour of Lisbon is one of its most characteristic features: George Borrow was not the first to notice this, remarking that 'the streets are in general precipitously steep'. In view of the widespread destruction caused by the earthquake in 1755, it is remarkable that any buildings survived. Among monuments and museums above and to the east of the 'Rossio' square and lower town or *Baixa*, laid out after that disaster, and dominated by the remains of the Castelo de São Jorge, are the battlemented *Sé* or cathedral; the collections of furniture, etc. of the Espírito Santo Foundation; and east of the upper part of the quaint Alfama district, São Vicente de Fora, later the pantheon of the House of Braganza; and Santa Engrácia, the national pantheon; and some distance beyond, the former convent of Madre de Deus, now a museum of *azulejos*.

At a lower level, near the spacious waterfront Praça do Comércio or 'Black Horse Square', are Nossa Senhora da Conceição Velha, and the diamond-bossed Casa dos Bicos. From west of this, the Chiado ascends to the Bairro Alto, with the Carmo, the Teatro São Carlos, Santa Catarina, and São Roque;

and further afield, the Basílica da Estrela, and nearby English Cemetery, in which lies Henry Fielding; and the impressive mid-18th-century Aqueduto das Águas Livres.

Further west, along the riverside, is the Museu de Arte Antiga, with its fine collections of furniture, sculptures, silver, glass and ceramics, Japanese 'namban' screens, etc., and paintings. Outstanding among those of the Portuguese School is Nuno Gonçalves's *Retable of the Infante*.

In **Belém**, beyond the impressive Ponte 25 de Avril, are the Museu dos Coches (a sumptuous collection of gilded coaches); the Hieronymite monastery of Santa Maria (dos Jerónimos), with its soaring columns, and cloister; the adjacent Naval Museum; the nearby Manueline Torre de Belém, lapped by the Tagus; and uphill, the early 19th-century Palácio da Ajuda.

North of the Avenida do Marquês de Pombal and the Parque Eduardo VII (with its hot-houses) are the admirable museums of the Calouste Gulbenkian Foundation; and some distance beyond, off the Campo Grande, the modern home of the Portuguese National Archives, still known as the Torre do Tombo; and the Museu da Cicade, graphically describing the history of Lisbon.

Lorvão [C6] is known for the 18th-century convent of Santa Maria, founded in the 12th century, and containing the magnificent silver tombs of two daughters of Dom Sancho I, who had been abbesses here (see Arouca). Among other remarkable features are the carved stalls.

Lourosa [D6] The village church of São Pedro, displaying broad horseshoe arches and *ajimece* windows, and with a 15th-century belfry, was probably built by Mozarabic workmen in 912, and is the only one of its kind surviving in Portugal. The typical Visigothic decoration in the porch, the baptismal stone and the confessional seat, are also of interest.

Mafra [A9] The village is dwarfed by its immense convent, its main façade being 220m long, terminated by two square pavilions likened by Beckford to 'pagodas'. Twin steeples frame the Italianate portico of the church, its crossing surmounted by a baroque dome. The building was erected in fulfilment of a vow made by Dom João V that he would found a convent on the birth of an heir to the throne; and its construction, regardless of the crippling expense, took place between 1717 and 1735. The well-proportioned church, hospital, the royal suite which it also accommodates, and the huge library are all notable, even if Byron, who visited the place in 1809, condemned the pile as an example of 'magnificence without elegance'.

Marvão [E8], a walled village straddling a rocky outcrop of the range known to the Romans as Herminius minor, has been fortified since remote antiquity. Its castle commands extensive views, with the Torre (1,991m) in the Serra da Estrela (the highest peak in Portugal) to the north-west.

Mértola [D12], founded in remote antiquity and known to the Romans as Myrtilis, was one of the four *municipia* of Lusitania. It was in Suevic hands until occupied by the Moors from 712 to 1236. Spectacularly sited above the Guadiana (the Roman Anas, and the Arabic Wadi-Anas), it is dominated by its castle, below which stands the battlemented and well-vaulted Igreja Matriz, a converted mosque retaining its *mihrab*. A tombstone from Mértola dated AD 525, now in Lisbon, displays the horseshoe 'Moorish' arch, confirming that it was used in the Peninsula long before the Moors' invasion in 711. Three small museums well display artefacts from the Roman, Palaeo-Christian and Moorish eras.

Miranda do Douro [G3], long an isolated frontier post overlooking the rapids of the Douro, was the seat of a bishop from 1545 until 1782, In May 1762 it was attacked by the Spaniards, when its castle blew up, killing some 400 people. In late May 1813 Wellington, having ridden from Salamanca, was slung across the gorge to inspect his Anglo-Portuguese army of 60,000 under General Graham, secretly assembled in the vicinity, which was to outflank the French near Zamora at the start of the brilliant offensive manoeuvre culminating only three weeks later in his victory at Vitoria, in the Basque provinces.

The walled town is dominated by its former cathedral, containing well-carved stalls and, among its more curious features, a naïve puppet-like figure of the infant Jesus sporting a bow-tie and wearing an opera-hat!

Monção [C1] was founded by Dom Afonso III and fortified in the 17th century to defend the south bank of the Minho. It was referred to as the 'Monson' at the turn of the 18th century by English factors who settled there to export its wines. Ruins of its castle survive, and the Romanesque church preserves the tomb of Deuladeu Martins, who held the Spanish at bay in 1368 by the expedient of throwing them loaves to show how well-supplied the defenders were. In 1658 it resisted a Spanish attack for four months before capitulating on advantageous terms.

Monsanto [E6], a curiously-sited village known for its numerous granite dwellings built into a boulder-strewn and castle-crowned hill, has relics of a Romanesque church, and a new *pousada*.

Monsaraz [E10] The fortified hill-top village, re-conquered by Geraldo Sem Pavor in 1167 and given to the Templars, later passed to the Order of Christ. In 1381 it was sacked by the unpaid English archers of Edmund of Cambridge.

Montemor-o-Novo [C10] retains a Moorish castle rebuilt in the late 13th century. A native of the town was Juan de Dios, or de Robles (St John of God, 1495–1550), of Jewish lineage, and the founder of the Order of

Charity, who devoted his life to the care of captives, foundlings and the sick.

Montemor-o-Velho [B6] was the birthplace of the navigator Diogo de Azambuja in *c.*1456, in *c.*1510 of the traveller and chronicler Fernão Mendes Pinto, and of Jorge de Montemayor, the poet and pastoral novelist, in 1519. Of ancient origin, the village was eventually reconquered in 1034 after being briefly captured in 1017. It is dominated by its castle, rebuilt in 1088, which once contained a royal palace. Within the enceinte stands Santa Maria da Alcáçova, displaying Manueline columns. Below lie Nossa Senhora dos Anjos, with Azambuja's tomb, and the Misericórdia.

Nazaré [B7] is an important fishing-village, the inhabitants of which are said to be of Phoenician descent, who unconcernedly carry on their work, disregarding the tourists who gape at their characteristic costume; tractors now haul their picturesque boats with their *meia-lua* (crescent-shaped prows) up the beach rather than teams of oxen, as formerly.

Óbidos [A8], an ancient, picturesquely walled town, was taken from the Moors by Afonso Henriques in 1140. The imposing castle (now a *pousada*) was built by Dom Dinis. Santa Maria displays *albarrada azulejos*, a tomb carved by Chanterene, and a painting by Josefa d'Ayala, born in Seville, but usually referred to as Josefa de Óbidos, having spent much of her life in a convent here, where she died in 1684. The museum contains a maquette of the Lines of Torres Vedras (q.v.) and miscellaneous collections. North of the town stands the unfinished mid-18th-century hexagonal church of Senhor da Pedra.

Odivelas [A9] Remains of the church, shattered in the Lisbon earthquake, survive from the convent in which Philippa of Lancaster died of the plague in 1415. It was later much frequented by the *freirático* (nun-loving) and philoprogenitive Dom João V, its inmates having provided him with three bastards, known as the 'Meninos de Palhavã': Dom José, later an Inquisitor-general, born to the Madre Paula Teresa da Silva; Dom Gaspar, later archbishop of Braga, the son of Madalena Máxima de Miranda; and Dom António, whose mother was a French nun.

Oliveira do Hospital [D5], as its name implies, formerly belonged to the Hospitallers. Its Igreja Matriz contains the tombs of the Ferreiros (a local family) and a carved equestrian knight similar to that displayed in the museum at Coimbra. Some Roman masonry is apparent in the area, while at neighbouring **Bobadela** stands a Roman arch.

Olivença [E10] lies *c.*25km south-west of Badajoz, from which it may be approached. Until occupied by the Spaniards in 1801 it was a fortified Portuguese frontier town, which was never returned to them despite provision to do so in the 1814 Treaty of Paris. Many of its churches – notably the Misericórdia and La Magdalena – among other buildings, display Maneuline features.

Oporto *see* Porto.

Ourém, Vila Nova de [C7] is dominated by an imposingly bastioned (but tastelessly restored) castle in which Dom Sancho II's queen was held captive by a band of barons in 1246, very likely with her connivance. The crypt of the Igreja Matriz has features similar to the synagogue at Tomar.

Ourique [C12] gives its name to a battle – probably no more than a raid into enemy-occupied territory – said to have taken place in its vicinity in July 1139, in which Afonso Henriques defeated no less than five Moorish 'kings', afterwards adopting as his coat of arms their five shields (*as cinco quinas*), each charged with the five wounds of Christ, to commemorate a vision of the Crucifixion he had the night before the engagement. This is now thought to have taken place at Chão de Ourique, near Santarém (q.v.). Nearby survives the rectangular walled enclosure of the Luso-Roman camp of **Castro dos Palheiros**.

Ovar [C4] was once of importance as a fishing-village, its short-skirted, big-boned, bare-footed fishwives or *'varinas* finding a living by carrying their catch in creels on their heads into the hinterland.

Palmela [B10] is commanded by a hill-top castle taken from the Moors, which in 1288 became the headquarters of the Portuguese Order of São Tiago (St James). One church – the other, on the site of a mosque, was destroyed in the 1755 earthquake – contains the tomb of Jorge de Lencastre (died 1551), a son of Dom João II and the last Grand Master of the Order. The fortress, providing a view described by the young and impressionable Robert Southey in 1796 as one of the most beautiful he had beheld, has been extensively restored to house a luxurious *pousada*.

Peniche [A8] is a fishing-port, with extensive canneries, on a rock-bound, flat-topped peninsula. Its strong defences, then in Spanish hands, were attacked without success in 1589 by both Drake and the Prior of Crato. In 1809 General D'Urban, perhaps with the recent drama of La Coruña in mind, suggested that it was perfect 'for the Embarkation of the British Army, should it ever be necessary to do so in the Face of the Enemy'. Under Salazar, its *Fortaleza* was used as a political prison by his repressive regime, from which the Communist leader Álvaro Cunhal escaped in 1960 by using the age-old device of tying sheets together. Its main monuments are São Pedro, Nossa Senhora da Conceição, and the Misericórdia, with painted ceiling panels.

Pinhel [E4], a bishopric until 1882, is commanded by an early 14th-century castle. Santa Maria, the Misericórdia, and the Igreja Matriz retain features of interest, while the Paço do Concelho contains archaeological collections. The former bishop's palace housed the headquarters' staff of Generals Graham and Picton at various times during the Peninsular War.

Pombal [B7], a market-town with a castle founded *c.*1174 by Gualdim Pais, is principally known as having given a title to the *'Gran Marquês'*, Sebastião José de Carvalho e Melo (1699–1782). In 1777 this dynamic if dictatorial statesman – the name Pombal, 'dovecote' in English, belied him – retired here in disgrace on the accession of the reactionary and priest-ridden Dona Maria I. His remains were first buried in Nossa Senhora do Cardal. The place was sacked by the retreating French in 1811.

Ponte de Lima [C2], picturesquely situated on the south bank of the river Lima, was known to the Romans as Forum Limicorum. On reaching the river, Decimus Junius Brutus had difficulty in persuading his troops to cross. Having already trudged across Iberia, they had assumed it must be Lethe, the River of Oblivion, its beauty having the effect of the lotus in making travellers forget their home and country; and only after he had waded into the stream, standard in hand, did they follow. As Lemici it was the birth-place in 394 of the Suevic annalist Hydatius. English archers played a vital part in Dom João I's capture of the place in 1385. Although few of its churches and mansions are outstanding, the town with its riverside *alameda* and market, established since 1125 near the ancient bridge (of which five Roman arches survive) is a place of some charm, 'pleasant to walk about in', in the words of Sacheverell Sitwell, and has numerous characteristic baroque residences in its vicinity.

Portalegre [E8], capital of the Alto Alentejo, and an episcopal city since 1545, was besieged in 1299 by Dom Dinis during the dynastic feuds of that period, and was attacked by the Spanish in 1704, but its history is unexceptional. The walled enceinte is dominated by its twin-pinnacled but otherwise plain cathedral, with massive pilasters and architectural retables. A museum is adjacent, while in the lower town the convent of Nossa Senhora da Conceição (or São Bernardo) contains a fine bishop's tomb (*c.* 1540) and *azulejos* of 1739.

Portimão [B14] It was here in July 1189 that a force of crusaders, including some English, led by Dom Sancho I, landed to besiege Silves (q.v.). Little of interest survived the earthquake of 1755, since when it has thrived as a fishing-port, although its recent growth has been unattractive.

Porto/Vila Nova de Gaia [C3/B4] *O porto*, the port, and thus anglicized as **Oporto**, is the second city of Portugal, and with its sprawling suburbs has a population approaching 1 million. The first settlement, referred to as Portucale as early as 456, grew up around the Pena Ventosa, rising above the rugged north bank of the Douro, here crossed by ferry to the site of the Roman *castro* of Cale, probably a strengthened Lusitanian fort ('Portugal' took its name from Portucale). In the 6th century a church was built on the commanding height. The town was recaptured definitively by the Christians in 982, and in 1147 a fleet of Crusaders landed here before sailing south to assist Afonso Henriques in capturing Lisbon. In 1387 Dom João I and Philippa of Lancaster were married in the cathedral, and their fourth son, Henry, 'the Navigator', was born here in 1394. Porto became progressively associated with the English, although their interest in exporting the wine of the upper Douro valley, known as 'Port', did not mature for another 300 years.

The Lisbon earthquake of 1755 did not affect Oporto physically, and most of the several mansions built to embellish the city by Nicolau Nasoni, who died here in 1773, have survived. The French under Soult occupied the place in March 1809, but on 12 May, taken by surprise by Wellington's sudden attack with troops that had been surreptitiously ferried across from the south bank, they were forced to flee precipitously.

In 1832–3 the city, its defences partly manned by a motley 'International Brigade' (largely Glaswegians and Cockneys), was besieged by Miguelite forces for some eighteen months, who eventually retreated, after blowing up and setting fire to the lodges or *armazéns* in transpontine **Vila Nova de Gaia**, when some 27,000 pipes of wine flowed into the Douro, turning its swirling waters a muddy red. During the later 19th century Porto flourished, becoming a stronghold of Liberalism, and the base of opposition to several reactionary regimes. In 1878 the first Republican deputy was elected here. It is now the hub of the largest industrial and commercial complex in the country, providing some 60 per cent of the national revenue.

Among those born in Oporto were the artist Francisco Vieira, in 1765; and Almeida Garrett, the poet and novelist, in 1799.

'To walk about this city is, I assure you, rather a violent exercise, not one street in it being on a level excepting that where the most part of the English inhabit', wrote 'Arthur Costigan' two centuries ago, and little has changed in this regard as far as the maze of lanes in the older, formerly walled, enceinte is concerned, where recent and continuing restorations have not destroyed its character. Among its more notable buildings – east of the avenue approaching the Ponte de Dom Luís I, a vertiginous bridge erected by Eiffel in 1886 – is Santa Clara, with remarkable carved and gilded woodwork. To the west rises the granite cathedral, reconstructed in the 12th century, with its twin towers framing a rose-window, but ineptly 'modernised' in the 18th, when a north porch and staircase were added by Nasoni, probably responsible also for the design of the silver altarpiece, and organ-cases.

Adjacent is the former bishop's palace, its façade by Nasoni, providing a plunging view of the older nucleus and across to the port-wine lodges at **Vila Nova de Gaia**, which should also be visited later. Steps descend past São Lourenço or Dos Grilos, a Jesuit church of 1577, to the Rua do Infante Dom Henrique (formerly the Rua Nova dos Inglezes, as painted by J.J. Forrester in 1834), flanked by the imposing *Feitoria Inglesa* or Factory House of the British Association, designed by Consul Whitehead, completed in 1790, and since then the main stamping-ground of the British establishment in Porto, so long influential in the wine trade.

Nearby is the rebuilt 'House of Henry the Navigator', traditionally his birthplace and, at a lower level, the quayside Praça da Ribeira. Further west rises the late 14th-century São Francisco, with a profusely carved and gilded interior in the baroque style. Adjacent are the *Bolsa* or Stock Exchange, with its pseudo-Moorish ballroom, and the Port Wine Institute. West of the latter stands the mid-16th-century São João Novo, opposite which is Nasoni's Palácio de São João Novo, still housing the Museum of Ethnography and History. Not far away is the Misericórdia, in which is displayed 'The Fountain of Mercy', an anonymous Flemish masterpiece of 1520, in which Dom Manuel and his queen, its founders, are depicted.

Conspicuous at a higher level, outside the formerly walled enceinte, rises the Torre dos Clérigos, Nasoni's belfry of 1763, dwarfing the oval church, behind which are the main university building, twin Carmelite churches and, further west, the colonnaded façade of John Carr of York's huge Hospital de Santo António, started in 1770 but never completed. Beyond is the former palace 'das Carrancas', now the Soares dos Reis museum, with good collections of paintings, furniture, glass, ceramics and silver, some showing strong English influence.

Also in this area are the Quinta da Macieirinha, with a Romantic museum, and to the north, the *Cemitério Inglês* (since 1785; before which Protestants were buried at low tide on the banks of the Douro), and some distance beyond, 12th-century São Martinho da Cedofeita, much rebuilt, founded on the site of the Suevic king Theodomir's conversion from Arianism to Orthodoxy in the mid-16th century.

Porto de Mós [B7] is commanded by its 13th-century castle, built on a Roman site. It preserves a richly decorated balcony similar to that at Leiria (q.v.). It was here, in August 1385, that the Portuguese army heard mass before the crucial battle of Aljubarrota (q.v.), fought not far to the north-west.

Queluz [A10] The rococo palace, the entrance courtyard of which was designed in emulation but in miniature of the Cour du Marbre at Versailles, was built for the Infante Dom Pedro in 1747–52 and – after the experience of the 1755 earthquake – single-storey extensions were added. Several salons are charmingly decorated. Beckford, who attended a hushed fête held in its formal gardens, embellished with topiary and *azulejo*-lined canals, recalled the sensation of horror at hearing the agonising wails of Dona Maria I, who thus exhibited her incipient madness.

Roliça [A8], a village within a horseshoe of low hills, gave its name to the first engagement of the Peninsular War in which the future Duke of Wellington saw action, on 17 August 1808, after having landed his troops near Figueira da Foz (q.v.). French troops, under Delaborde, were obliged to retire to avoid being outflanked by the two wings of the British expeditionary force advancing south from Óbidos (q.v.) towards the mouth of the Maceira river, where reinforcements were to land. Their defensive position being carried by a subsequent frontal attack, the French retreated southeast. The more serious battle of Vimeiro (q.v.) took place four days later.

Sagres [B14], now a small windswept resort and fishing-port, retains a house claiming to have been occupied by Prince Henry the Navigator, but this, known as the Vila do Infante – 'remote from the tumult of people and propitious for the contemplation of study' – was more certainly nearer Cape St Vincent, further west, which was sacked by Drake and further damaged in 1755. It was here that Henry founded an influential school of navigation, set up an observatory, and died in 1460, after which the place decayed, the centre of maritime studies moving to Lisbon.

On Cape St Vincent itself, the barren south-western extremity of Europe, is a ruined 16th-century monastery and lighthouse, far below which heaves the Atlantic. The Roman Promontorium Sacrum takes its present name from the legend that in the 8th century the relics of the martyred St Vincent were brought here, from which, guided by a pair of ravens, they were miraculously translated to Lisbon in 1173. Off the rockbound headland several naval battles took place: in 1693, when Rooke defeated Tourville; in 1780, when Rodney attacked a Spanish fleet, another of which was scattered by Jervis and Nelson in 1797; and in 1833, when a small Miguelite squadron was routed by Sir Charles Napier.

Santarém [B8], on a commanding height above the Tagus, was Roman Scallabis, dignified by Julius Caesar with the title 'Praesidium Julium'. It derives its name from Santa Iria, a nun of Tomar (q.v.), martyred in 653, whose body was washed ashore here. As Shantariya it was a Moorish stronghold from 715 until finally recaptured in 1147 by Afonso Henriques, who founded Alcobaça (q.v.) in gratitude. Being near Almeirim, a favourite royal summer residence, it was frequently the seat of the *Cortes* in the 14th–15th centuries. Dom Dinis died here in 1325; and in 1557 the murderers of Inês de Castro were executed here. The place was sacked by Masséna when retreating from before the Lines of Torres Vedras (q.v.); in 1833 it was the last stronghold of the reactionary Miguelites.

Its finest church is that of Graça, with its rose-window and the tombstone of Pedro Álvares Cabral (died c.1526; see Belmonte), discoverer of Brazil. São João de Alporão, now a lapidary museum, contains the over-restored tomb – preserving a tooth only – of Duarte de Meneses (died 1464), a governor of Alcácer-Quibir. The Seminary of 1676, and church of Marvila, also have features of interest.

Santiago de Caçém/Miórbriga [B11/12] is a pleasantly situated little town on a hill slope dominated by a ruined Moorish castle rebuilt by the Templars. On a neighbouring height are the extensive remains of Roman Miróbriga Celticum, partly excavated, built on the site of an *oppidum* in occupation since the 8th or 9th century BC.

Serpa [D12], thus also known to the Romans, was not finally reconquered from the Moors until c. 1232 and not resettled – due to the territory being disputed by the Castilians – until 1297. It was reoccupied by the Spaniards in 1707–8. Within stretches of wall are a ruined castle, a huge *nora* or Moorish chain-pump and aqueduct, Gothic Santa Maria, and the convent of Santo António.

Setúbal/Tróia [B10], an important commercial and fishing-port, with nearby shipyards, was long famous for the export of salt extracted from the adjacent flats of the Rio Sado. It takes its name from the Roman *oppidum* of Caetobriga, probably of Phoenician foundation, the site of which was once assumed to be at **Tróia**, on the far bank of the estuary, overwhelmed by a tidal wave in the 5th century, where fish-salting tanks have been excavated. The present town, which suffered severely in the earthquake of 1755, was founded in the 12th century, and it was here that Dom João II married Leonor de Lencastre in 1471. It was then familiarly known to English sailors as 'Saint Ubes'. Among its defences was the Castelo de São Filipe (now a *pousada*), erected by Philip II of Spain to cow the locals and protect the place from English attack. Among its natives were the poet Bocage, a 'pale, limber, odd-looking young man', whose compositions 'thrilled and agitated' Beckford; and the opera-singer Luisa Todi, after whom the main avenue is named. Its chief monument is the Igreja de Jesus, begun in 1494 by Diogo Boitac, with its spiralling cable-like columns and rope-like ribs, which became characteristic of the Manueline style. Notable in the adjacent museum are paintings by the 16th-century 'Master of Setúbal'.

Silves [C14], as Shalb or Xelb, was the former capital of the Moorish kingdom of Algarve, possessing a port and shipyards, and according to Idrisi, of fine appearance and with well-furnished bazaars. It became the centre of Ibn Qasi's revolt against the Almoravids in the mid-12th century. In 1189 it was sacked by Dom Sancho I after a three-month siege (see Portimão), but was not definitively reconquered for another sixty years. A decline set in with the silting up of the river, and it suffered in the 1755 earthquake, being described a century later as 'one of the most desolate and deserted places in Portugal'. The walled enceinte is dominated by its dark red sandstone cathedral, probably built on the site of a mosque, but not improved by post-1755 restorations. What remains of the Moorish castle, with vaulted cisterns and a parapet walk, provides views of neighbouring orchards and orange-groves.

Sintra, previously spelt Cintra [A9], the attractions of which have often been praised in poetry and prose, lies on the northern slope of its bosky *serra*, where, some time before 1415, Dom João I set about enlarging a former royal residence to palatial proportions, of which two oasthouse-like chimneys are the most conspicuous features; and it was here that he decided on the Ceuta expedition of 1415. In 1578 Dom Sebastião held his last audience here before setting out on his disastrous African expedition. Dom Afonso VI spent his last impotent years mewed up here, where he died in 1683. Among the main salons of the palace are the Sala dos Brasões, its *artesonado* dome blazoned with coats of arms; the Sala das Pêgas, its compartmented ceiling embellished by painted magpies, each bearing the device 'Por Bem', said to satirize the chattering gossips of the court after Dom João I had been surprised surreptitiously embracing a lady-in-waiting; and the Sala dos Cisnes, decorated with gold-collared swans.

Roy Campbell, the South African poet, lived at Sintra during the 1950s, and is buried in the San Pedro Cemetery.

Among the several sights of interest in the vicinity is the palace of Seteais (seven sighs), now a luxurious hotel, long supposed to be the scene of the signature of the so-called 'Convention of Cintra', which in fact took place in Lisbon, by which Junot's forces, defeated at Vimeiro (q.v.), were allowed to evacuate Portugal (with their spoil), being transported to France in British ships, rather than taken prisoner. Thus, since the publication of Byron's vitriolic lines in *Childe Harold*, Sintra has been associated with this disgrace to British military diplomacy. The Quinta de Monserrate with its exotic gardens, which once belonged to a rich merchant, Gerard de Vismes, who entertained William Hickey there in 1782, was described by Beckford, who rented it a dozen years later, as 'a beautiful Claude-like place, surrounded by the most enchanting country'; but in the 1850s it was orientalized by Sir Francis Cook, with more money than taste. The *serra* itself is dominated by a Manueline-Gothick pile known as the Palácio da Pena, an ungainly confection commissioned by Dona Maria II's consort, a cousin of Prince Albert, and built on the site of an Hieronymite monastery, the cloister and chapel of which have survived.

Tavira [D14] was once assumed to have been Roman Balsa, but this is now thought to be further west, near Luz. It was reconquered from the Moors in 1239, and raised to the rank of city in 1520, but later declined with the silting up of the port, dredged in 1932. Of interest within the walled enceinte are the Misericórdia and, adjacent to the castle ruins, Santa Maria do Castelo. An attractive feature is the unusual oriental-looking triple-gabled roofs of the 18th-century houses flanking the river Gilão, here spanned by a 17th-century bridge.

Tibães [C2] is dominated by the imposing and long-ruined monastery of São Martinho. Although of Romanesque origin, the present church, by Manuel Álvares, dating from the mid-17th century, contains contemporary choir-stalls, a mass of gilded woodcarving, and a baroque organ. Its four derelict cloisters are under restoration, as are its water-garden, described as charming by Lord Porchester in 1827, when the roses were in full bloom.

Not far away is the Visigothic chapel of **São Frutoso de Montélios**, built on a Greek Cross plan during the second half of the 7th century, although its dome and barrel-vaulted apsidal arms have been reconstructed. The exterior walls are embellished by Lombardic blind arcades terminating in alternate pointed and semicircular sections, and bands of marble.

Tomar [C7], a town of some charm on the Rio Nabão, is commanded by the former castle of the Knights Templar, known as the Convento de Cristo. Gualdim Pais, Grand Master of the Order, may have already founded the much rebuilt church of Santa Maria dos Olivais (in which he was buried) on lower but less defensible ground on the left bank of the river near the Roman site of Sellium, where remains of the villa of Nabancio have been excavated. From the medieval town, in which a 14th-century synagogue and the church of São João Baptista are of some interest, a road winds uphill past Nossa Senhora da Conceição to the huge Convento de Cristo.

The papal suppression of the Templars in 1314 was only nominally enforced in Portugal, and Dom Dinis replaced it five years later by founding the Order of Christ, its headquarters being established at Tomar in 1356. Prince Henry the Navigator was Grand Master from 1417 until his death. It passed into Dom Manuel's hands in 1492, and he set about extending the building. Its decline dates from the Spanish occupation of Portugal in 1580, when Philip II was proclaimed king here; while during the Peninsular War it was sacked repeatedly by Masséna's troops. Extensive restoration of the whole complex continues to be undertaken.

Outstanding features are the 'Charola', the original sixteen-sided Templar church with its central octagon; the Great Cloister, its design attributed to Diogo de Torralva, completed in 1587 by Filippo Terzi; and the sensational Manueline window of the west front of the church, an anonymous masterpiece of stone-carving, in which the Cross of the Order of Christ surmounts the royal arms and the armillary sphere of Dom Manuel, which are connected by a writhing mass of carved ropework, seaweed and coral-stems, etc. The colossal buckled Garter encircling one buttress may symbolize the English Order presented to the king by Henry VII. Also notable, apart from several other dependencies, is the Aqueduto dos Pegões, with its 180 ogival arches, bringing water to the convent.

Torres Vedras [A9], although formerly a royal residence, and the birthplace in 1436 of Eleonor of Portugal, who married the Emperor Frederick III, and died at Wiener Neustadt (in Austria), is better known for giving its name to the famous Lines constructed across the neck of the broad peninsula on which Lisbon stands. These comprise two main bands of hill-top redoubts and batteries – many of which are still extant – erected on Wellington's instructions during the year prior to the orderly retreat from Buçaco (q.v.) in October 1810. Manned by some 30,000 Anglo-Portuguese troops, they held Masséna's army at bay until early the following March, when sheer starvation forced the demoralised French to retreat precipitously towards Spain, losing virtually their entire baggage train. For the battle fought athwart the frontier two months later, see Fuentes de Oñoro.

Trancoso [E4], a small walled town, well-sited for defence on a hill-spur, and formerly of importance, was the venue in 1283 of the marriage of Dom Dinis and Isabel of Aragon. A Spanish army was routed here in 1385, where, two years later, John of Gaunt concluded negotiations for his daughter Catherine of Lancaster to marry the future Enrique III of Castile in return for a large indemnity in money and the surrender of his own claims to Portugal. In the 1580s a local cobbler, Gonçalo Anes, composed verses describing the return of Dom Sebastião, which propagated the messianic cult of Sebastianism. In 1810 General Picton briefly occupied a house here, while General Beresford was given the title of Conde de Trancoso after the battle of Buçaco (q.v.). Its Romanesque churches have been altered; the ruined castle of 1160 has been repeatedly rebuilt, but several characteristic old houses survive within the enceinte.

Valença do Minho [C1], now dominated by a modern viaduct spanning the river, also crossed by a bridge of 1885 constructed by Eiffel, retains a characteristic enceinte, entirely enclosed within 17th-century ramparts facing the Spanish frontier fortress and cathedral-town of Tuí. Until rebuilt in 1262, it was known as Contrasta, but apart from sustaining two minor sieges by the Decembrists in 1837 and a decade later, it has seen little action, and its walls are thus in a perfect state of preservation.

Viana do Castelo [B2], a well-sited fishing-port and resort on the north bank of the Lima, has traded in *bacalhau* (cod) for centuries, while from before 1580, when they were expelled by the Spanish, its English community had been exporting Minho wines. A British Factory established itself here in 1700, but partly due to the silting up of the harbour, integrated later with the one at Oporto. Several buildings of interest survive in the older town, among them the Misericórdia of 1598; the arcaded Town Hall; the

Igreja Matriz, with its Romanesque towers; the Barbosa Maciéis palace, housing a museum; classical São Domingos; and the Castelo de Santiago da Barra, guarding the mouth of the Lima. Above the town may be seen the Celtic *citânia* of Santa Luzia.

Vila do Conde [B3], a resort and fishing-port at the mouth of the Ave, defended by a 17th-century fort, and with a Manueline church in the lower town, is dominated by the huge convent of Santa Clara, begun in 1777, but first founded in 1318 by Afonso Sanches, a bastard of Dom Dinis, who together with his wife is buried in the adjacent church, as is Brites Pereira, daughter of Nun'Álvares and the wife of the first Duke of Braganza. Also notable is the ruined early 18th-century aqueduct. Within ten kilometres to the north-east are the impressive 12th-century churches of São Pedro at **Rates**, and São Cristovão at **Rio Mau**, both with remarkable capitals.

Vila de Frades/São Cucufate [D11] The Roman villa here is an imposing structure of brick-vaulted rooms preserving early mural decoration. It was later converted to monastic use, remaining so until the 16th century. In an idyllic setting, it continues to be excavated.

Vila Real [D3], now the largest town of the Trás-os-Montes, was granted royal rights by Dom Afonso III in 1271. In 1832 the reactionary Count of Amarante established the headquarters of an insurrectionary movement here prior to the *pronunciamento* at Vila Franca de Xira against the liberal government of the time. It was the birthplace of Diogo Cão, the first navigator to reach the mouth of the Congo, in 1482. **Sabrosa**, some twenty kilometres south-east, was the birthplace of Fernão de Magalhães (Magellan) in *c*.1480, one of whose fleet of five ships, commanded by Juan Sebastián de Elcano, a Basque, was the first to circumnavigate the globe (1519–22). Magellan himself had been killed in the Philippines. At **Mateus**, just east of Vila Real, is the baroque finialed mansion built by Nicolau Nasoni in 1743, which has gained publicity by being illustrated on a blended rosé wine label during recent decades.

Vila Real de Santo António [E14], which lies at the mouth of the Guadiana, was run up in 1774 by Pombal near the site of Santo António de Arenilha, possibly of Phoenician origin, but engulfed by the sea in *c*.1600. The new town was laid out on a grid plan at ruinous expense, for the ashlar used in its construction had been transported from Lisbon, after which stone quarries were 'discovered' in the neighbourhood.

Roman Baesuris, now **Castro Marim**, with a huge castle, the first head-quarters of the Order of Christ before its transfer to Tomar (q.v.), lies to the north.

Vila Viçosa [E10], dominated by its bastioned castle, which was the original *solar* or seat of the ducal family of Braganza, was briefly Edmund of Cambridge's headquarters in the Anglo-Portuguese campaign of 1382. The adjacent Conceição contains good *azulejos*. The Paço Ducal is mainly 17th century. It was here that the future Dom João IV received the first overtures from the nationalist party, which was to bring about his accession in 1640. Catherine of Braganza was born here two years earlier. Dom Carlos I passed his last night here before his assassination in Lisbon in 1908.

The palace and its stables (displaying carriages) contains the collections and archives of the family, including the important library accumulated by Dom Manuel II during his long exile at Twickenham. The square is also flanked by the Chagas convent (now a *pousada*), and Santo Agostinho, rebuilt in 1634 as a ducal pantheon.

In the neighbourhood took place the battle of Montes Claros (June 1665), in which the Count-Duke Frederick of Schomberg, with a British contingent, defeated the Spaniards under the Marquês de Caracena.

Vimeiro [A8] was the site of the battle of 21 August 1808 fought shortly after the engagement at Roliça (q.v.). Wellington's reinforcements had disembarked from their transports at the mouth of the Maceira, adjacent, and his small but disciplined army took up defensive positions in the neighbouring hills to await French forces marching from Lisbon. Superior firepower from their extended lines caused havoc in the massed French columns, which were driven back repeatedly, and suffered heavy casualties. General Kellermann proposed a truce shortly after, known as 'The Convention of Cintra' (see Sintra). Wellington was forced to agree to this by elderly superior officers, landing to supersede him after the battle had commenced. They preferred the Convention to risking another engagement.

Viseu [D5], capital of its district and an episcopal city of ancient origin, is traditionally associated with the last stand of Viriatus against the Romans in 139 BC, and the burial in 711 of Don Rodrigo, the 'Last of the Goths', in São Miguel do Fetal, but there is no historical foundation for either claim. Alfonso V was killed when besieging the place in 1028, and it was not reconquered for another thirty years. It was the birthplace of Dom Duarte (Dom João I's eldest son) in 1391, possibly of the artist Vasco Fernandes, better known as 'O Grão Vasco', in 1475, and in 1496 of João de Barros, the chronicler of Portuguese conquests in Asia.

On a walled rocky outcrop stands the late Gothic and Manueline cathedral, on the site of a former mosque, displaying a fine vault, ribbed with knotted cables, good *albarrada azulejos* in the cloister, and with a treasury. The lower Renaissance cloister preserves a Romanesque portal. Adjacent, in the former bishop's palace, is the museum, notable for its paintings by 'Grão Vasco' and those attributed to Gaspar Vaz. Opposite is the attractive twin-towered façade of the Misericórdia. Other churches of some interest are São Bento, the Carmo, and São Francisco.

Vista Alegre [B5] has china clay deposits exploited after 1824 by José Ferreira Pinto Basto. The fragile ware produced in his factory is said to have been formerly carried to Oporto and Lisbon on camel-back, these creatures providing the smoothest form of transport on rough Lusitanian roads. There is a museum of porcelain. Nearby, in Nossa Senhora da Penha, is a dramatic tomb sculptured by Claude de Laprade.

Brief Biographies

Afonso Henriques (1105?–85), 'the Founder' of what is now Portugal. His early life was devoted to establishing the countship of Portucalense's independence from León, by defeating his mother's Galician-influenced party at São Mamede (near Guimarães) in 1128. Its independence was confirmed formally by the papal legate in 1143. He then concentrated on the Reconquest of Moorish-held territory north of the Tagus, capturing Lisbon in 1147 and then pushing south into the Alentejo. His later years were spent consolidating his kingdom.

Albuquerque, Afonso de (1462?–1515), following in the wake of Vasco da Gama, became the first Portuguese viceroy of India, where he landed in 1503, capturing Goa in 1510. It remained the base of further conquest in Asia until his death.

St Anthony 'of Padua' (1195–1231), patron saint of Portugal and Lisbon, where he was born, spent most of his life as a Franciscan preacher and teacher in France and Italy. He was canonized the year after his death in Padua. He is popularly known as the 'finder of lost property'.

Beckford, William (1760–1844), known as 'England's wealthiest son', and the author of *Vathek*, visited Lisbon on several occasions in the last decades of the eighteenth century, resulting in his later *Recollections of an Excursion to the Monasteries of Alcobaça and Batalha* (1833; see Bibliography), which did much to put Portugal on the map among British connoisseurs. He had also lived in the vicinity of Sintra.

Beresford, William Carr (1768–1854), during and after the Peninsular War (in which he commanded at the battle of Albuera), was marshal of the Portuguese army, and was largely responsible for its complete reorganisation, but his apparent involvement in the suppression of a Liberal conspiracy in 1817 did not enhance his waning popularity. He was created Portuguese Count of Trancoso in 1810 and British Viscount in 1823.

Braganza, Catherine of (1638–1706), born and 'bred hugely retired', and virtually uneducated at Vila Viçosa, was the daughter of Dom João IV. In 1662 she sailed to England to marry Charles II, bringing as part of her dowry both Tangiers and Bombay, being compelled soon after to receive at the dissolute court his mistress Lady Castlemain. She remained in England after the king's death in 1685 until her return in 1692 to Lisbon. She later supported the Anglo-Portuguese Methuen Treaty and acted as Regent for her brother.

Cabral, Pedro Álvares (1467?–1520?), born in Belmonte, in 1500 commanded a fleet which followed in the wake of da Gama's pioneering sea voyage to India. Contrary winds and currents carried his ships to the coast of Brazil, the discovery of which he claimed for Portugal. He eventually landed at Calicut, and sailed back to Lisbon laden with exotic commodities from Asia.

Camões, Luís de (1525?–80), Portugal's national poet, the date of whose death (10 June) is annually commemorated as Portugal's national day ('The Day of Portugal, of Camões, and of the Portuguese communities'). A widely-read humanist scholar, he was also a man of action – a soldier and adventurer in the then newly-accessible Far East. His lyric poetry was once celebrated throughout Europe, but he is best known for his epic *Os Lusíadas* (*The Lusiads*) which, within a framework of incidents from Portuguese history and Vasco da Gama's opening of a sea-route to the Indies, raises moral issues arising from European excursions into Eastern civilizations. 'The first epic poem which in its grandeur and its universality speaks for the modern world' (C.M. Bowra).

Castro, Inês de (?–1355), the Galician mistress of the Infante Pedro, with whom she set up house in 1345 on the death of his wife Constanza. He later claimed to have married her in Braganza in 1354. A clique of noblemen, fearing possible Castilian intervention at the succession, extracted the tacit permission of Pedro's father, Dom Afonso IV, for her 'removal', and murdered her in cold blood at Coimbra. Her magnificent tomb at Alcobaça stands opposite that of her royal lover, while their romantic story has been frequently retold since in verse and prose in the literature of many countries.

Eça de Queirós, José Maria (1845–1900), a prolific and influential essayist and author of realistic novels portraying Portuguese society during the last decades of the 19th century. Many of them were written while he was consul in England and later at Paris, where he died.

Egas Moniz, António Caetano (1874–1955), trained at Coimbra, in 1911 he held the chair of Neurology at Lisbon, in 1949 receiving a Nobel Prize for his pioneering work in neuro-surgery. Between 1903 and 1919, when he headed the Portuguese delegation to the Versailles Peace Conference, he was also involved with politics, being a supporter of Sidónio Pais.

Forrester, Joseph James (1809–61) joined his uncle's firm of Port wine shippers in 1831. As author of influential books on Port, he became the doyen of the 'pure wine' school. He was also a pioneering photographer, a fine watercolourist, and cartographer, honoured with the Portuguese title of Baron for his survey of the Douro, in the rapids of which he was eventually drowned.

St Francis Xavier (1506–52), with his fellow Basque, St Ignatius of Loyola, was a founder-member of the Jesuits in 1539. In the following March St Francis went to Lisbon, at the invitation of Dom João III, to help evangelize Portugal's settlements in India and further East (eventually to Japan). In eleven extraordinary years this 'Apostle of the Indies' is said to have walked 100,000 miles and converted 300,000 souls. He died in San-chuan, on his way to convert China. His body was brought back for final burial in the cathedral in Goa. He was canonized in 1622.

Gama, Vasco da (1468?–1524), born at Sines, he was given command of the fleet which in July 1497 set out to discover the sea-route, via the Cape of Good Hope, to India, reaching Calicut the following May. He returned to Lisbon in 1499, and was honoured by Dom Manuel for his great achievement. He later made a second voyage, which led to the further expansion of the spice trade, and died in India after many years in the service of his country.

Garrett, Almeida (1799–1854), born in Oporto, was a prolific romantic poet, playwright and novelist, and also an influential Liberal politician (partly in exile). He was referred to by Aubrey Bell as having been a great civilizing and renovating force in the life and literature of his country.

Gulbenkian, Calouste Sarkis (1869–1955) was born in Skutari, Turkey, into an already wealthy Armenian family. His later education was in Britain, and he became a British citizen in 1902, living in London and Paris. His fortune was acquired by organizing companies for the exploitation of oil in the Middle East, and taking, as 'Mister-five-per-cent', a small royalty on all dealings. With the German occupation of Paris in 1940 he went to Lisbon and remained there until his death. By his will, a Foundation was set up, with its headquarters in Lisbon, to further work of a charitable, artistic, educational and scientific nature. Museums there display the outstanding collection of art and artefacts he had spent a lifetime accumulating.

Prince Henry the Navigator (1394–1460), the fifth child of Dom João I and Philippa of Lancaster, was born in Oporto. After taking part in the capture of Ceuta in 1415 and becoming Grand Master of the Order of Christ at Tomar in 1417, he remained in Portugal, largely in the vicinity of Cape St Vincent, where, after 1421, he sponsored cosmographical research and several early voyages of discovery. He was also known as the 'Infante de Sagres' (where he died).

Dom João I (1357–1433), an illegitimate son of Dom Pedro II , he was founder of the Avis dynasty. By winning the battle of Aljubarrota in 1385 (with the help of Nun'Álvares Pereira and an English contingent), he reinforced the independence of Portugal against the pretensions of Castile. In 1387 he married Philippa of Lancaster, and later built the battle-abbey of Alcobaça, in which they were buried.

Dom João III (1502–57), succeeded Dom Manuel in 1521, and it was during his reign that the overseas empire which he inherited further expanded, notably in Brazil. A patron of culture, he also introduced the Inquisition into Portugal in 1536 and, a decade later, reformed the university at Coimbra.

Dom João IV (1604–56), formerly the 8th Duke of Braganza. Although chiefly interested in music and the chase, he was chosen by the nationalist party to be their figurehead in the Revolution of December 1640, which restored Portuguese independence from Spanish domination. Supported by England, this first member of the Braganza dynasty was able to repel subsequent incursions, and in 1654 he reaffirmed the long-standing Anglo-Portuguese alliance. His daughter was Catherine of Braganza.

Dom João V (1689–1750) was proclaimed king in 1707, and his long reign coincided with further expansion and exploitation in Brazil. Its gold and diamonds enabled him to indulge in conspicuously extravagant building projects, among them the immense baroque palace-convent at Mafra. While his revenues were thus lavished on the church, his subjects continued to languish in poverty.

John of Gaunt, Duke of Lancaster (1340–99), fourth son of Edward III, having fought under the Black Prince at Najera (1367), later married Constance of Castile, and laid claim to the Castilian crown. In 1386 he led Anglo-Portuguese troops in Galicia to force the issue, but later resigned his pretensions in favour of his daughter Catherine's marriage to the future Enrique III of Castile in 1387, in which year Philippa, Lancaster's elder daughter, married Dom João I of Portugal.

General Junot (1771–1813), Duke of Abrantes, led the first French invasion of Portugal in October 1807, but his army was defeated by Wellesley's expeditionary force at both Roliça and Vimeiro in the following August. He fought under Masséna at Buçaco, but his advice, based on experience of the withering fire of British lines, was ignored. He left the Peninsula after the battle of Fuentes de Oñoro. He then served in Russia, and later committed suicide.

Magalhães, Fernão de (angliciszd as Ferdinand Magellan; 1480?–1521) was born at Sabrosa in the Trás-os-Montes. After a controversy with the Portuguese court he offered his service as a navigator to Spain. In 1519 he set sail from near Cadiz with a fleet of five ships on an exploratory voyage of circumnavigation. Magellan himself was killed in the Philippines, but one vessel, commanded by Juan Sebastián Elcano, a Basque, survived the epic journey, limping home in 1522.

Dom Manuel I (1469–1521), 'the Fortunate', ascended to the throne in 1495, at a significant moment in Portugal's expansion as a mercantile power. It was during the first decade of his reign that Vasco da Gama discovered the sea-route to the Indies and Pedro Álvares Cabral discovered Brazil. In 1496 Dom Manuel decreed that all Jews in Portugal, including all those entering from Spain in 1492, would be expelled if they did not accept Christian baptism. Those that remained, ostensibly converted, were later to cause a problem of integration. Under his aegis numerous buildings were erected in the 'Manueline' style, such as the enlargement of the Convent of Christ at Tomar, although later he concentrated his interest on constructing the Jeronomite monastery at Belém, his future mausoleum.

Marshal Masséna (1758–1817), Prince of Essling after the battle near Vienna in 1809, was sent to command Napoleon's 'Army of Portugal', which suffered severely at Buçaco in September 1810 and was then held at bay by the Lines of Torres Vedras. He was forced to retreat the following March, after a disastrous campaign in which he lost some 25,000 men, 9,000 mounts and his entire baggage train. He was recalled to France after the subsequent battle of Fuentes de Oñoro (May 1811), where despite reinforcements, he was unable to defeat the Allies. As Wellington was to admit: 'When Masséna was opposed to me, I never slept comfortably.' He was replaced by Marshal Marmont.

Mendes Pinto, Fernão (c.1510–83), author of the posthumously published *Peregrinação*, written on his return home after his travels in India and the Orient during two decades in the Portuguese service. Long considered to be extravagantly embroidered descriptions of his numerous adventures, shipwrecks, and captivities as soldier of fortune, trader, pirate, agent and ambassador, his picaresque autobiography is now thought to be reasonably close to the truth, and one of the most evocative works of 16th century prose.

Dom Miguel (1802–66), brought up in Brazil, sailed to Lisbon in 1822 as leader of the reactionary clerical and Traditionalist party, opposing the liberal Constitutionalists. He was later exiled, but in 1828 he returned and proclaimed himself Absolutist king, ignoring the decision of his elder brother (Dom Pedro IV, Emperor of Brazil), who had abdicated, that his daughter Maria da Glória should be the queen on reaching her majority. This precipitated the return of Pedro to Portugal and the start of the civil war 'of the Two Brothers' or Miguelite War (1831–4), in which Dom Miguel was eventually defeated and, at Evoramonte, again exiled.

Pessoa, Fernando (1888–1935), a prolific poet and prose-writer, known and admired in his life-time in Portuguese avant-garde circles, and since recognized much more widely, as for example 'one of the evident giants in modern literature' (George Steiner) and 'perhaps the greatest poet of the twentieth century' (Antonio Tabucchi). He has a place in the literature and consciousness of the Portuguese-speaking world second only to that of Camões.

Philippa of Lancaster (1359–1415), daughter of John of Gaunt, married Dom João I in Oporto in 1387. Among her sons was the future Dom Duarte (Edward, after her grandfather, Edward III) and Henrique (Henry, 'the Navigator'). She is said to have had a civilizing influence on the Portuguese court. Her tomb lies at Batalha, her effigy hand in hand with that of Dom João, founder of the battle-abbey.

Marquis of Pombal (1699–1782), after diplomatic experience in London and Vienna, became the dynamic chief minister to Dom José (1750–77) in 1750, and remained a virtual dictator until his dismissal by Dona Maria I in 1777. He galvanized the country into action and largely rebuilt Lisbon after the disastrous earthquake of 1755, did much to improve its economy, kept the nobility in its place, and in 1759 expelled the Jesuits from Portugal.

Salazar, António de Oliveira (1889–1970), a Catholic professor of economics at Coimbra, who was invited in 1928 to enter the government as Minister of Finance, a position which he used to propel himself into the position of Prime Minister in the 'New State', becoming virtual dictator under the presidency of General Óscar Carmona and later Américo Tomás. Though Salazar shared some common ground with Franco's regime in Spain, he was apprehensive of Spanish ambitions; in the Second World War he kept Portugal officially neutral (at Churchill's urging, who feared having to divert scarce resources there), and yet allowed the Allies to use the Azores. He effected some economic progress and, despite several attempts to oust him, was able to retain power – by enforcing censorship and being well-buttressed by the repressive police – until incapacitated in 1968.

Dom Sebastião (1554–78) came of age in 1568, and for the following decade was obsessed with the idea of forging an African empire. An opportunity presented itself when the succession of the sultanate of Fez was disputed and, raising a force of 18,000 men, he quixotically set sail from the Algarve, only to have his army decisively defeated at Alcácer-Quibir. He was killed in the mêlée. His body was never recovered, which left space for the heartening prospect of his return to rescue Portugal from the occupying Spaniards, and for the rise of numerous impostors. With the passing of time, 'Sebastianism' became a form of Portuguese messianism, intensifying especially when a sense of decline or desperation made a prophesied return to greatness a consolation.

Viriatus, the Lusitanian hero who later became a symbol of Portuguese resistance to foreign invaders (principally Spanish), having kept Roman legions at bay for two decades prior to his last stand and death in 139 BC, which traditionally took place at Viseu, in the Beira.

Duke of Wellington (1769–1852), born in Dublin as Arthur Wellesley, saw service in India before being sent to Portugal with an expeditionary force in 1808, where he defeated the occupying French at Roliça and Vimeiro that August. Returning to the Peninsula the following year, in May he ousted Soult from Oporto and, after the battle of Talavera that July received the title of Viscount Wellington. In September 1810, at Buçaco, he checked Masséna's advance towards Lisbon, and then at the barrier Lines of Torres Vedras. In the following spring Wellington dogged Masséna's retreat, inflicting further defeat on the French at Fuentes de Oñoro and Albuera. In July 1812 and June 1813 they were scattered at Salamanca and Vitoria respectively before being thrust back across the Pyrenees to Toulouse. Napoleonic armies were not finally crushed until Waterloo (1815). He was created Duke of Wellington in 1814, but his later political career was less successful than his military career.

Selective bibliography

The books listed below, with one or two exceptions, are in English. They were published, except where shown to the contrary, in the United Kingdom. The date of publication is that of the first edition; re-prints are not listed, except where a substantial revision has been involved. Works of fiction – poetry, plays, novels, etc. – have not been included. For the readers' convenience, the books have been listed in various familiar categories, but overlapping is inevitable. Many of the books are out-of-print and may therefore be hard to find, especially earlier descriptions and histories; the larger libraries should be able to provide copies.

Travel, Topography, and General Description:

Jorge de Alarção, *Roman Portugal* (1988; four thin volumes, with a comprehensive gazetteer).

James M. Anderson and M. Sheridan Lea, *Portugal: 1001 Sights; an Archaeological and Historical Guide* (1994); a useful outline.

Ana Margarida Arruda, *et al, Subterranean Lisbon* (Lisbon, 1994), a Museu Nacional de Arqueologia exhibition catalogue.

Ann Bridge (Lady O'Malley) and Susan Belloc Lowndes Marques, *The Selective Traveller in Portugal* (1949; revised 1967), which has been referred to as being 'thuriferous', is now somewhat dated, but remains entertaining and perceptive.

Rose Macaulay, *They Went to Portugal* (1946), and *They Went to Portugal Too* (1990), containing material not included in the former volume, are both essential and inimitable reading.

The *Naval Intelligence Division Geographical Handbook*, volume 2, *Portugal* (1942) contains much information, even if some is dated and quaint.

Ian Robertson, *Blue Guide: Portugal* (4th edition, 1996) describes the country and its monuments in historical perspective within the parameters imposed by the series. Additional background reading is found in his more personal *Portugal: a Traveller's Guide* (John Murray, 1992).

Sacheverell Sitwell, *Portugal and Madeira* (1954), urbane if uneven, but providing several insights.

Michael Teague, *In the Wake of the Portuguese Navigators. A Photographic Essay* (1988).

Among the numerous, if unequal, earlier descriptions of Portugal, are:

Anon. [J.-B.-F. Carrère], *A Picture of Lisbon taken on the spot* (1809), being a translation of his *Voyage au Portugal et particulièrement à Lisbonne* (Paris, 1798).

Marianne Baillie, *Lisbon in the years 1821, 1822, and 1823* (1825).

Joseph Baretti, *A Journey from London to Genoa* (1770; reprinted 1970, with an Introduction by Ian Robertson); earlier chapters only.

Huldane V. Beamish, *The Hills of Alentejo* (1958).

Beckford, *The Journal of William Beckford in Portugal and Spain 1787–1788*, edited by Boyd Alexander (1954); *Italy, with Sketches of Spain and Portugal* (1834); and *Recollections of an Excursion to the Monasteries of Alcobaça and Batalha* (1835; reprinted 1972, with an Introduction by Boyd Alexander); *The Travel Diaries of William Beckford of Fonthill*, two vols., edited by Guy Chapman (1928).

George Borrow, *The Bible in Spain* (1843), earlier chapters only, supplemented by *Letters to the British and Foreign Bible Society*, edited by T.H. Darlow (1911), and *George Borrow in Portugal*, by Ian Robertson (reprinted in The British Historical Society of Portugal's '21st Annual Report and Review'; Lisbon, 1995).

Jean François Bourgoing, *Travels of the Duke de Chatelet in Portugal* (1809).

William Bromley, *Travels through Portugal, Spain, etc.* (1702).

'Arthur Costigan' [Major James Ferrier], *Sketches of Society and Manners in Portugal* (1787).

Oswald Crawford, *Portugal, Old and New* (1880).

William Dalrymple, *Travels through Spain and Portugal in 1774* (1777).

General Dumouriez, *An Account of Portugal as it appeared in 1766* (1797).

William Henry Harrison, *Jennings' Landscape Annual, or, Tourist in Portugal* (1839), illustrated with steel engravings by James Holland.

Henry John George Herbert, Viscount Porchester, later third Earl Carnarvon, *Portugal and Gallicia* [sic] (1836).

Elizabeth, Lady Holland, *The Spanish Journal*, edited by the Earl of Ilchester (1910), also describes Portugal.

Terence Mason Hughes, *An Overland Journey to Lisbon at the close of 1846* (1847).

William Henry Giles Kingston, *Lusitanian Sketches* (1845).

William Morgan Kinsey, *Portugal illustrated* (1828), a pretentious account, and of comparatively slight value, but it contains numerous engraved plates, notably of costumes.

Henry Frederick Link, *Travels in Portugal* (1801).

Richard Muller, *Memoirs of the Right Hon. Lord Viscount Cherington* (1782).

James Murphy, *Travels in Portugal… in 1789 and 1790* (1795), and *A general view of the state of Portugal* (1798); he was the author of the equally dull, but influential, *Plans, elevations, etc… of Batalha* (1795).

John Mason Neale, *Hand-Book for Travellers in Portugal* (1855). Oswald Crawfurd referred to it as being 'not only the worst handbook in that eminent publisher's [John Murray] series – for that might still be high praise – but probably the very worst handbook that ever was printed'; nevertheless it is a curiosity of its period.

Dorothy Quillinan (*née* Wordsworth), *Journal of a few months' Residence in Portugal* (1847).

Robert Southey, *Letters from Spain and Portugal* (1797); and *Journal of a Residence in Portugal 1800–1801*, edited by Adolfo Cabral (1960).

Richard Twiss, *Travels through Spain and Portugal in 1772 and 1773* (1775).

History, Economics, Politics

Eric Alexson, *The Portuguese in South-east Africa 1600–1700* (Johannesburg, 1960).

Anon. [John Murray Browne], *An Historical View of the Revolutions in Portugal, since the close of the Peninsular War* (1827).

Silvio A. Bedini, *The Pope's Elephant* (1997), describing Manuels I's gifts to Pope Leo X.

Duncan T. Bentley, *Atlantic Islands: Madeira, the Azores and the Cape Verdes in Seventeenth Century Commerce and Navigation* (Chicago, 1972).

David Birmingham, *Frontline Nationalism in Angola and Mozambique* (1992).

Charles R. Boxer, (many of whose books, including most of the following, have been re-printed in the USA and UK; the date of first publication only is given). *Fidalgos in the Far East 1550–1770* (1948); *The Christian Century in Japan 1549–1650* (1951); *Salvador de Sá and the Struggle for Brazil and Angola 1602–1686* (1952); *The Great Ship from Amacon; Annals of Macao and the Old Japan Trade, 1549–1650* (1959); *Fort Jesus and the Portuguese in Mombasa, 1593–1729* (1963); *The Golden Age of Brazil 1695–1750* (1962); *Portuguese Society in the Tropics* (1966); *The Portuguese Seaborne Empire 1415–1825* (1969); *Mary and Misogyny* (1975); *Portuguese Merchants and Missionaries in Asia, 1602–1795* (1988).

Charles R. Boxer (editor and translator), *The Tragic History of the Sea, 1589–1622* – selections from *História Trágico-Marítíma* (1959); and *Further Selections, 1559–1565* (1959 and 1968).

Charles Boxer and J.C. Aldridge (editors), *Descriptive List of the State Papers of Portugal, 1661–1780 in the Public Record Office, London* (three vols., Lisbon, 1979–83).

Sarah Bradford, *Portugal* (1973).

Marcus Cheke, *Dictator of Portugal* (1938), a biography of Pombal; and *Carlota Joaquina, Queen of Portugal* (1947).

Ronald Chilcote, *Portuguese Africa* (Englewood Cliffs, 1967).

Robert Clancy and Alan Richardson, *So Came they South* – Portuguese 'discovery' of Australia (Sidney, 1993).

Gervase Clarence-Smith *The Third Portuguese Empire: a Study in Economic Imperialism 1825–1975* (1985).

John Colbatch, *An Account of the Court under Pedro II* (1700).

George Collingridge, *The First Discovery of Australia* (1836).

Maurice Collis, *The Grand Peregrination*, a biography of the sixteenth-century adventurer Mendes Pinto (1949).

Michael Cooper, *Rodrigues the Interpreter*, Jesuits in sixteenth-century Japan (New York, 1974).

David Corkhill, *The Portuguese Economy since 1974* (1993).

L.S. Davidson, *Catherine of Braganza* (1908).

Bailey W. Diffie, *Prelude to Empire: Portugal Overseas before Henry the Navigator* (Lincoln, Nebraska, 1960).

A.R. Disney, *The Twilight of the Pepper Empire. Portuguese Trade in Southwest India in the Early Seventeenth Century* (Cambridge, Mass., 1978).

António de Figueiredo, *Portugal: Fifty years of Dictatorship* (1976).

Harold E.S. Fisher, *The Portugal Trade. A study of Anglo-Portuguese commerce, 1700–1770* (1971).

Alan David Francis, *The Methuens and Portugal, 1691–1708* (1966); and *Portugal 1715–1808; Joanine, Pombaline and Rococo Portugal as seen by British diplomats and traders* (1985 – regrettably, published without an index).

Peter Fryer and Patricia McG. Pinheiro, *Oldest Ally: Portrait of Salazar's Portugal* (1961).

Tom Gallagher, *Portugal: a Twentieth Century Interpretation* (1983).

José Manuel Garcia, *Portugal and the Division of the World* (Lisbon, 1994).

Michael Glover, *Britannia sickens: Sir Arthur Wellesley and the Convention of Cintra* (1970).

Vitorino Magalhães Godinho, *Portugal and her Empire, 1648–88*, in the New Cambridge Modern History, vol V; and *Portugal and her Empire 1680–1720*, in vol VI (1961 and 1970).

Lawrence S. Graham and Douglas L. Wheeler, *In search of Modern Portugal: the Revolution and its Consequences* (Madison, 1983).

Max Justo Guedes and Gerald Lombardi (editors), *Portugal-Brazil: the Age of the Atlantic Discoveries* (Lisbon, 1990).

Richard Hammond, *Portugal and Africa 1815–1910* (Stanford, 1966).

Carl A. Hansen, *Economy and Society in Baroque Portugal, 1668–1703* (1981).

John Hemming, *Amazon Frontier. The Defeat of the Brazilian Indians* (1987).

Hans Janitschik, *Mário Soares* (1985).

Henry Kamen, *The War of Succession in Spain 1700–15*, chiefly concerned with economic issues (1969).

Hugh Kay, *Salazar and Modern Portugal* (1970).

Sir Benjamin Keene, *The Private Correspondence*, edited by Sir Richard Lodge (1933).

Thomas D. Kendrick, *The Lisbon Earthquake*, chiefly concerned with European reactions; will disappoint those expecting a full description of the disaster (1956).

Donald F. Lack, *Asia in the making of Europe*, vol 1, book 1 'The Century of Discovery' is essentially about the Portuguese (Chicago, 1965).

Charles David Ley, (editor and translator), *Portuguese Voyages, 1498–1663* (1947).

Harold V. Livermore, *A History of Portugal* (1947); the more compact *New History of Portugal* (1966); *Portugal: a Short History* (1973); and *The Origins of Spain and Portugal* (1971).

208   *Portugal: a companion history*

Fernão Lopes, *The English in Portugal 1367–87*, extracts from the Chronicles of Dom Fernando and Dom João, edited by Dereck W. Lomax and R.J. Oakley(1988).

A.H. de Oliveira Marques, *Daily Life in Portugal in the Late Middle Ages* (Madison, 1971); *History of Portugal*, 2 vols. (New York, 1972); and the more compact *History of Portugal* (Lisbon, 1991).

Kenneth Maxwell, *Conflicts and Conspiracies: Brazil and Portugal* (1973); *Pombal, Paradox of the Enlightenment* (1995); *The Making of Portuguese Democracy* (1995); and *The Portuguese* (forthcoming).

Kenneth G. McIntyre, *The Secret Discovery of Australia*, 'two hundred years before Captain Cook' (Sydney, 1977; revised 1982).

Thomas Pakenham, *The Scramble for Africa* (1991).

António Costa Pinto, *Salazar's Dictatorship and European Fascism* (New York, 1995).

Edgar Prestage, *The Portuguese Pioneers* (1933); and *Afonso de Albuquerque* (1929).

D.L. Raby, *Fascism and resistance in Portugal* (1988).

Richard A.H. Robinson, *Contemporary Portugal: a History* (1979).

Francis M. Rogers, *The Travels of the Infante Dom Pedro of Portugal* (Cambridge, Mass., 1961); *Atlantic Islanders of the Azores and Madeira* (Cambridge, Mass., 1979).

Cecil Roth, *A History of the Marranos* (1932; 4th edition, 1974), dated in part.

Peter Edward Russell, *The English Intervention in Spain and Portugal in the time of Edward III and Richard II* (1955).

A.J.R. Russell-Wood, *A World on the Move: the Portuguese in Africa, Asia and America, 1415–1808* (1992).

A.C. de C.M. Saunders, *A Social History of the Black Slaves and Freedmen in Portugal, 1441–1555* (1982).

L.M.E. Shaw, *Trade, Inquisition and the English Nation in Portugal 1650–1690* (1989); and *British Merchants in Portugal 1654–1810* (forthcoming).

Violet M. Shillington and Annie B.W. Chapman, *The commercial relations of England and Portugal* (1907).

Manuel Andrade e Sousa, *Catherine of Braganza* (Lisbon, 1994).

Sir Robert Southwell, *Letters* (1740).

Sanjay Subrahmanyam, *The Portugues Empire in Asia, 1500–1700* (1993); and *The Career and Legend of Vasco da Gama* (1997).

John Brande Trend, *Portugal* (1957).

John Ure, *Prince Henry the Navigator* (1977).

A.R. Walford, *The British Factory in Lisbon* (Lisbon, 1940).

Douglas L. Wheeler, *Republican Portugal: a political history, 1910–1925* (1978); and *A Historical Dictionary of Portugal* (New Jersey, 1993).

George Young, *Portugal, old and young: an historical study* (1917).

William Young, *Portugal in 1828* (1828).

Military

John Aitchison, *An Ensign in the Peninsular War: the Letters of John Aitchison,* edited by W.F.K. Thompson (1981).

Anthony Brett-James, *Life in Wellington's Army* (1972), a fascinating compilation.

Thomas Henry Browne, *The Napoleonic Journal of Captain Thomas Henry Browne,* edited by R.N. Buckley(1987).

George Lawson Chambers, *Bussaco* (1910).

William Granville Eliot, *A Treatise on the Defence of Portugal* (third edition, 1811).

Baron Nicolas Fagel, *Account of the Campaign in Portugal, 1705* (1708).

Alan David Francis, *The First Peninsular War, 1702–1713* (1975).

David Gates, *The Spanish Ulcer: a history of the Peninsular War* (1986).

Richard Glover, *Peninsular Preparation: the Reform of the British Army, 1795–1809* (1963).

Andrew Halliday, *The Present State of Portugal and of the Portuguese Army* (1812).

Donald D. Horward, *Napoleon and Iberia – The Twin Sieges of Ciudad Rodrigo and Almeida, 1810* (1984); *The Battle of Bussaco: Masséna versus Wellington* (1965).

J.A.C. Hugill, *No Peace without Spain,* also describing the War of the Spanish Succession (1991).

Lawrence James, *The Iron Duke,* an admirable description of Wellington as a military commander during the Peninsular War (1992).

John Thomas Jones, *Memoranda Relative to the Lines thrown up to cover Lisbon in 1810* (1829), included in his *Journal of the Sieges in Spain* (3rd edition, 1846).

Adam Neale, *Letters from Portugal and Spain* (1809).

Charles W.C. Oman, *Wellington's Army* (1913); and *History of the Peninsular War* (seven vols., 1902–30), the latter not easy to find complete, owing to the decimation of subscribers during 1914–18. Later volumes were published in much smaller editions. A reprint of the whole, but not including all the original cartography, is available.

Edgar Prestage, *Portugal and the War of the Spanish Succession* (1938).

Julian Rathbone, *Wellington's War* (1984), quoting from the Duke's dispatches.

August Ludolf Friedrich Schaumann, *On the Road with Wellington,* ed. by Anthony M. Ludovici; particularly racy narrative (1924).

Stephen G.P. Ward, *Wellington's Headquarters* (1957).

Jac Weller, *Wellington in the Peninsula,* a military history (1962).

Peter Young and J.P. Lawford, *Wellington's Masterpiece,* the background to the Salamanca campaign (1973).

In addition to the earlier works listed above, and apart from the general histories of Southey, and Napier (including the latter's very readable *Englsih*

Battles and Sieges in the Peninsula), and Wellington's own *Dispatches*, there were numerous contemporary narratives of the Peninsular War – most of which describe events in Portugal or near its frontier. Not including the reminiscences of those who reached the theatre of operations late in the war, one may list the following authors: Blakeney, Bragge, D'Urban, Frazer, Grattan, Harris, Hennell, Kinkaid, Larpent, Leach, Ormsby, Sherer, Simmons, Stothert, Surtees, Tomkinson, Warre, and Wheeler; but there were many more, almost all of whom have something of interest to say. Several have been reprinted in recent years.

The following are of some value for their illustrations:

Anon. [A.P.D.'G.'], *Sketches of Portuguese Life, Manners, Costume, and Character* (1826).

William Bradford, *Sketches of the Country, Character and Costume in Portugal and Spain* (1809).

George Thomas Landmann, *Historical, Military, and Picturesque Observations in Portugal* (1818).

Henry L'Evêque, *Portuguese Costumes* (1812–14); and *Campaigns of the British Army in Portugal* (1813).

Thomas Staunton St Clair, *A Series of Views… taken during the Peninsular War* (1815).

George Vivian, *Scenery of Portugal & Spain* (1839).

Little has been written in English since the 1830s concerning the 'War of the Two Brothers', or Miguelite War. Of interest are:

James Edward Alexander, *Sketches in Portugal during the Civil War of 1834* (1835).

Lovell Badcock, *Rough Leaves from a Journal kept in Spain and Portugal* (1835).

William Bollaert, *The War of the Succession in Portugal and Spain* (1870).

W. Nugent Glascock, *Naval Sketch Book* (1834).

Charles P. Hawkes and Marion Smithes (editors), *Siege Lady: the Adventures of Mrs Dorothy Procter of Entre Quintas* (1938).

G. Lloyd Hodge, *Narrative of an Expedition to Portugal* (1833).

Thomas Knight, *The British Battalion at Oporto* (1834).

Charles Napier, *Account of the War of Succession in Portugal* (1836).

Hugh Owen, *The Civil War in Portugal, and the Siege of Oporto* (1835).

Charles Shaw, *Personal Memoirs and Correspondence*, two vols. (1837).

Art and Architecture

Associação dos Arquitectos Portugueses, *Arquitectura Popular em Portugal* (Lisbon, 1980; contains several hundred photographs and some English text).

Carlos de Azevedo, *Baroque organ-cases of Portugal* (Amsterdam, 1972); and, with Chester E.V. Brummel, *The Churches of Portugal* (New York, 1985).

Alice Berkeley and Susan Lowndes, *English Art in Portugal* (Lisbon, 1994), a brief but attractively produced introduction to the subject.

Walter Crum Watson, *Portuguese Architecture* (1908), taking the subject to the end of the eighteenth century.

Delaforce, Angela (commissioner), *A Aliança Revisitada* (Lisbon, 1994), a Gulbenkian exhibition catalogue illustrating the artistic, scientific and intellectual relations between the United Kingdom and Portugal over the centuries.

José-Augusto França *et al* (editors), *Arte Portuguésa* (Madrid, 1986); volume XXX in the 'Summa Artis' series.

Júlio Gil, *The Finest Castles of Portugal* (Lisbon, 1986).

George Kubler and Martin Soria, *Art and Architecture of Spain and Portugal, etc., 1500–1800* (1959); and Kubler's *Portuguese Plain Architecture, 1521–1706* (Middletown, Connecticut, 1972), to be used with caution.

James Lees-Milne, *Baroque in Spain and Portugal* (1960).

J.A. Levenson (editor), *The Age of Baroque in Portugal* (Washington, 1993), a National Gallery of Art exhibition catalogue.

Sacheverell Sitwell, *Southern Baroque Re-visited* (1967).

Robert Chester Smith, *A Talha em Portugal* (Lisbon, 1962), a study of gilded wood-carving; *The Arts of Portugal, 1500–1800* (1968), a remarkable survey; and *Nicolau Nasoni, 1691–1773* (Lisbon, 1973).

José Cornélio da Silva and Gerald Luckhurst, *Sintra: a Landscape with Villas* (Lisbon, 1989).

Anne de Stoop, *Stately Homes in the Vicinity of Lisbon* (1989), *Palais et manoirs, le Minho* vol. 1 (Paris, 1995), and *Living in Portugal* (1995), for their photographs.

Other Subjects

H. Warner Allen, *The Wines of Portugal* (1963).

Jean Anderson, *The Food of Portugal* (1986). Recipes in the context of travels in Portugal.

Mascarenhas Barreto, *The Portuguese Columbus: Secret Agent of King John II* (1992).

Aubrey F. Bell, *Portuguese Literature* (1922; reprinted 1970, with an updated bibliography).

Patrick Bowe, *Gardens of Portugal* (1989).

Sarah Bradford, *The Englishman's Wine* (1969), revised under the title *The Story of Port* (1978).

Manuel Carlos de Brito, *Opera in Portugal in the Eighteenth Century* (1989).

Helder Carita and Homem Cardosa, *Portuguese Gardens* (1991).

Gerald Cobb, *Oporto Older and Newer* (1966).

John Delaforce, *The Factory House at Oporto* (1979; revised edition 1990); and *Joseph James Forrester, Baron of Portugal, 1809–1861* (1992).

Joseph James Forrester, *A Word or Two on Port Wine* (1844); and *The Oliveira Prize-Essay on Portugal* (1853).

Alan David Francis, *The Wine Trade* (1972).

Rodney Gallop, *Portugal: a Book of Folk-ways* (1936).

Trevor Housby, *The Hand of God: Whaling in the Azores* (1971).

Malcolm Jack, *William Beckford: and English Fidalgo* (1997); and edited, with an Introduction by, *Vathek and Other Stories: A William Beckford Reader*, also including non-fictional material (1993).

Alex Liddell, *Port Wine Quintas of the Douro* (1992).

Harold V. Livermore and William J. Entwistle (editors), *Portugal and Brazil: an Introduction* (1953), with essays covering a variety of topics.

D.J. Mabberley and P.J. Placito, *Algarve Plants and Landscapes: Passing Tradition and Ecological Change* (1993).

Vitória Mesquita, *et al.*, *Frederick William Flower: a Pioneer of Portuguese Photography* (Lisbon, 1994), a Museu do Chiado exhibition catalogue.

Jan Read, *Wines of Portugal* (revised edition 1987).

George Robertson, *Port* (1978).

Charles Sellars, *Oporto Old and New* (1899).

P.T.H. Unwin, *Portugal* (1987), an annotated bibliography.

Alan Villiers, *The Voyage of the Schooner Argos* (1951), Portuguese North Atlantic fishing.

An increasing number of attractively produced local guides, with an English text, are being published; a small random sample is listed below:

Museu Nacional de Arqueologia e Etnologia, *Portugal from its Origins through the Roman era* (Lisbon, 1989).

Silvana Bessone, *The National Coach Museum* (Lisbon, 1993).

Teresa de Almeida d'Eça, *Guide to the Biscainhos Museum, Braga* (Braga, 1990).

José Luís Porfírio, *Museum of Ancient Art* (Lisbon, 1994), a brief catalogue.

Cláudio Torres and Luís Alves da Silva, *Mértola: a museum town* (Mértola, 1989).

Portuguese Studies, edited by the Department of Portuguese, King's College, London, and published annually by the Modern Humanities Research Association, contains valuable articles, reviews, and bibliographies.

Several publications of The British Historical Society of Portugal (Rua Filipe Folque 2–4°, 1050 Lisbon) are of interest and value.

Glossary

Largely of architectural terms, which may be found useful:

Abóbada, a vault
Ajimece, a two-light window, divided by a slender column
Alameda, a tree-lined avenue or promenade
Almofados, rusticated masonry; or large raised panels in furniture
Artesonado, a coffered wooden ceiling
Auto-da-fé, an 'Act of Faith', or sentence of execution, usually by the burning of heretics, by the Inquisition
Azulejos, titles, usually of painted and glazed panels, depicting scenes, designs, or floral patterns (*albarrada*)
Bairro, a district or quarter of a town
Bilros, elaborately turned finials
Caciques, local political bosses
Cadeiral, choir-stalls
Câmara municipal, a Town Hall
Capela-mor, a chancel or sanctuary
Cartuxa, a charterhouse
Castro, a prehistoric, and usually hill-top, fortified settlement
Chafariz, a public fountain, often monumental
Citânia, a prehistoric hill-settlement
Claustro, a cloister
Coro, a choir, the *coro alto* or upper gallery often containing the stalls
Cortes, Parliament
Cruzeiro, the crossing of a church, or a cross
Dom, and *Dona*, king, and queen
Entalhador, woodcarver, see *talha*. The carver of images is an *imaginário*
Ermida or *eremitério*, a hermitage or chapel, often isolated
Espigueiros, equivalent to the *hórreos* of Galicia, and ubiquitous in the Minho, these granaries or store-houses are raised on mushroom-shaped pillars to obstruct the entrance of vermin
Forais, a charter
Igreja, a church; a parish church being an *igreja matriz*
Infante/a, a prince/princess
Janela, a window
Joanino, a late baroque style in fashion at the time of Dom João V
Judiaria, a ghetto
Junta, a council, usually political or military
Manuelino, the characteristic late Gothic style of architecture current during the reign of Dom Manuel I and later
Mármore, marble

Marrano, the former derogatory name for a Portuguese Jew, or Crypto-Jew, assumed to be converted only ostensibly to Catholicism

Miradouro, a balcony or belvedere

Misericórdia, an almshouse

Mosteiro, a monastery

Moçárabe, or Mozárab, a Christian subject to the Moors; a term extended to their architecture

Mudéjar, a Moslem subject to the Christians; and a term extended to their architecture and decoration

Muralha, wall

Muwallad or *Muladi*, a Christian converted to Islam

Nora, a water-wheel

Paço, a country house, or palace (usually *palácio*)

Pelourinho, a stone column, sometimes ornamented, and ubiquitous in the towns and villages of northern Portugal, but seen less south of the Tagus. These emblems of feudal or municipal jurisdiction also served as pillories or gibbets

Pombalino, the architectural style employed in the rebuilding of Lisbon after the earthquake of 1755, and named after the Marquês de Pombal

Pousada, one of a once partly state-subsidised network of hotels

Praça, a place or square

Pronunciamento, a *coup d'état*, usually of military inspiration

Quadro, or *pintura*, a painting

Quartel, barracks

Quartelões, bracketed pilasters

Quarto, a room

Quinta, a country estate, or the main residence on such

Rés do chão, the ground floor

Retábulo, reredos or high altar, often highly decorated

Retrato, a portrait

Sé, a cathedral

Século, century

Serra, a range of hills or mountains

Solar, a manor house, or the seat of an armigerous family

Taifa, a petty Moorish kingdom

Talha, carved work, usually of wood, and frequently *dourada* or gilded

Tecto, a ceiling

Torre de menagem, a castle keep

Tremido, parallel grooving in furniture

Zimbório, a cupola or dome

Index

The Index is confined essentially to the more important references to people and places occurring in the main text of this book (pp. 1–120). Such references are indexed in ordinary type. In addition, there are some index figures in bold type: these refer, as regards people, to subject paragraphs in the Brief Biographies (pp. 198–204) and, as regards places, to subject paragraphs in the Historical Gazetteer (pp. 168–197).